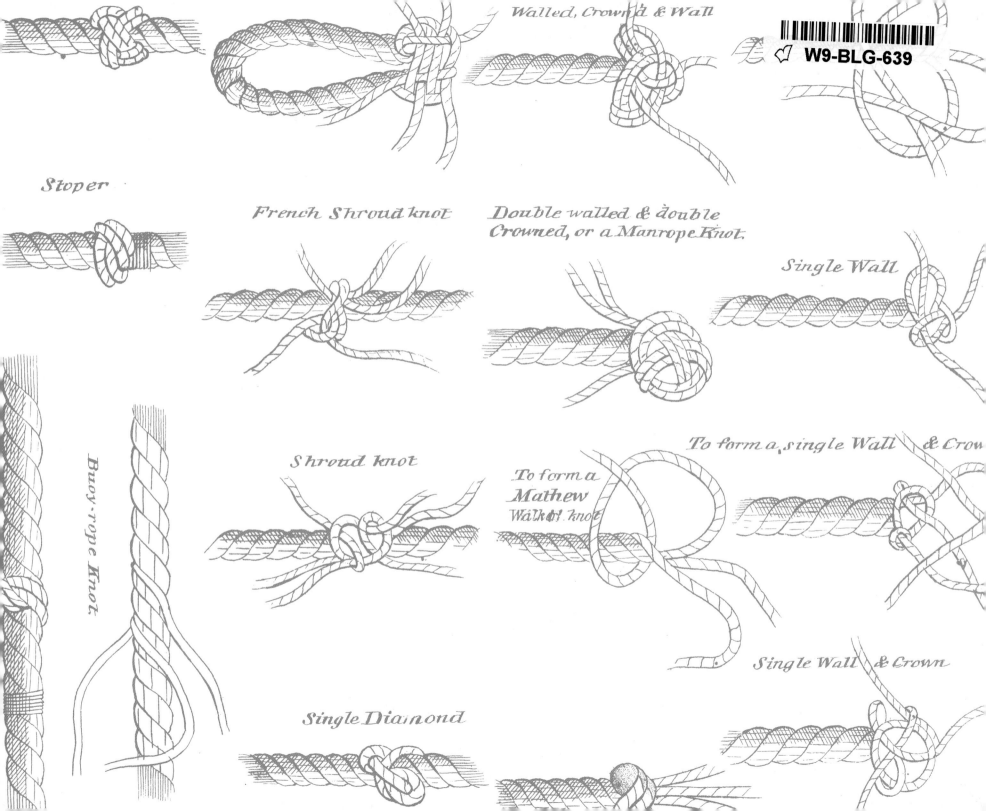

Walled, Crown'd & Wall

Stoper

French Shroud knot

Double walled & double
Crowned, or a Manrope Knot.

Single Wall

Buoy-rope Knot

Shroud knot

To form a
Mathew
Walker knot

To form a single Wall   & Crow

Single Wall   & Crown

Single Diamond

America's Naval Heritage

A Catalog of Early Imprints

From the Navy Department Library

America's Naval Heritage

A Catalog of Early Imprints
From the Navy Department Library

Thomas Truxtun Moebs

NAVAL HISTORICAL CENTER   DEPARTMENT OF THE NAVY   WASHINGTON 2000

SECRETARY OF THE NAVY'S SUBCOMMITTEE ON NAVAL HISTORY

Dr. David A. Rosenberg (Chair)

Commander Wesley A. Brown, CEC, USN (Ret.)

Dr. Frank G. Burke

Mr. J. Revell Carr

Vice Admiral Robert F. Dunn, USN (Ret.)

Vice Admiral George W. Emery, USN (Ret.)

Dr. Jose-Marie Griffiths

Dr. R. Robinson Harris

Dr. Beverly Schreiber Jacoby

Mr. David E. Kendall

The Honorable G.V. Montgomery

Dr. James R. Reckner

Dr. William N. Still, Jr.

Admiral William O. Studeman, USN (Ret.)

Ms. Virginia S. Wood

Cover
Berth-deck cooks in USS Tennessee, entry 123.

Endpapers
Plate no. 3 in William Brady, The Naval Apprentice's Kedge Anchor; or Young Sailor's Assistant *(New York: Frye & Shaw, 1841).*

Title page
Navy Department Library bookplate designed and executed in 1906 by Adolph C. Ruebsam of the Navy Hydrographic Office. Frigate Constitution, *depicted within a hippopus shell found in deep-ocean waters, symbolizes the United States Navy's victorious exploits on the high seas.*

Book design by DiAnn G. Baum
The U.S. Government Printing Office

∞ *The paper used in this publication meets the requirements for permanence established by the American National Standard for Information Sciences "Permanence of Paper for Printed Library Materials" (ANSI Z 39.48–1984).*

For sale by
The U.S. Government Printing Office, Superintendent of Documents, Mail Stop: SSOP, Washington, DC 20402–9328
ISBN 0–16–050565–8

Library of Congress Cataloging-in-Publication Data

Moebs, Thomas Truxtun
    America's naval heritage : a catalog of early imprints from the Navy Department Library / Thomas Truxtun Moebs.
        p.   cm.
    Includes bibliographical references and index.
    ISBN 0-945274-44-0
    1. United States—History, Naval—To 1900—Bibliography—Catalogs. 2. Unites States. Navy—History—Bibliography—Catalogs. 3. United States. Navy Dept. Library—Catalogs. I United States. Navy Dept. Library. II. Title.

Z1249.N3 M64 2000
[E182]
16.359'00973—dc21

00-055006

Contents

Sailors unload boat howitzers for escort duty in Japan with Commodore Matthew C. Perry, U.S. special envoy and commander in chief of naval forces in the East Indian seas. This view appears on the front endpapers to John A. Dahlgren's Boat Armament of the U.S. Navy, *1856 edition. Catalog entry 321 describes the earlier 1852 edition of this work.*

Illustrations

ABBREVIATIONS

DAB *Dictionary of American Biography*

DAH *Dictionary of American History*

DANFS *Dictionary of American Naval Fighting Ships*

NUC *The National Union Catalog*

OCLC Online Computer Library Center, Inc.

USNI United States Naval Institute

NUC and OCLC holdings are subject to change; individual institutions have not been contacted for verification.

Catalogue of the

Library of the

Navy Department

1824

Earliest recorded catalog of the Navy Department Library, 1824

Foreword

Near the center of the Washington Navy Yard, nestled in the Dudley Knox building complex, known as the Naval Historical Center, is a 19th-century vault. Within that vault rest the rare books and manuscripts of the Navy Department Library. Cared for and managed by Librarian Jean Hort and her faithful staff, hundreds of printed works of American and foreign origin await discovery.

As might be expected, among the books and documents are a number of rare early imprints related to the founding of the American Navy. Author Thomas Truxtun Moebs, named for his famous ancestor, Captain Thomas Truxtun, U.S. Navy, and himself a prodigious sailor who has crossed the Atlantic Ocean more than once in his sloop, has captured over three hundred titles in this masterfully created catalog. Its pages yield the early treasures in the collection, such as Truxtun's *Remarks, Instructions, and Examples Relating to the Latitude & Longitude,* the first published work of an American naval officer describing the professional duties of his shipmates, and the first to print a likeness of a 44-gun frigate. Congress authorized construction of three of these frigates in 1794, the very year Truxtun's work was published.

The collection contains the exceedingly rare first printed American signal book, *Instructions, Signals, and Explanations, Ordered for the United States Fleet,* published by Truxtun in 1797—apparently the author's copy with his signature, manuscript notes, and several pages illustrated with hand-colored signals. A manuscript entry in Truxtun's hand states that it was with him in the frigate *Constellation* on April 3, 1797, five months before she was launched in Baltimore!

Tom Moebs' thorough cataloging has identified a number of uncommon documents, including the 1798 *Plan for Establishing a General Marine Society* that also contains "Remarks on the Establishment of the Navy of the United States, and of the Plan for Recording and Registering the Seamen Thereof"; Thomas Paine's 1801 *Compact Maritime* that harbors a treatise . . . *for the Protection of Neutral Commerce, and Securing the Liberty of the Seas;* and ordinary seaman John Rea's 1802 remarkable dissertation, *A Letter to William Bainbridge, Esqr., Formerly Commander of the United States Ship George Washington: Relative to Some Transactions, On Board Said Ship,* alleging Bainbridge's mistreatment of the crew in the frigate *George Washington* during her infamous 1800 Mediterranean voyage transporting tribute to the Dey of Algiers.

The collection of early governmental rules, regulations, and instructions for the Navy features the first separately printed regulations approved by Congress, *Naval Regulations Issued by the Command of the President of the United States of America, January 25, 1802,* signed in manuscript by Secretary of the Navy Robert Smith; a unique manuscript of hand-colored flags with associated instructions relative to the Gulf navy titled *A Code of Signals, by David Porter, Commanding Officer,* *New Orleans Stations, Adopted There by Authority of the Navy Department in 1809;* and the rare *Regulations for the Navy of the Confederate States,* first printed in Richmond, Virginia, in 1862.

To these treasures add the first treatise on military medicine published by American naval surgeon Edward Cutbush, the 1808 *Observations of the Means of Preserving the Health of Soldiers and Sailors; and on the Duties of the Medical Department of the Army and Navy;* a previously unrecorded, firsthand account of the Mexican War action, the *Siege and Bombardment of Vera Cruz, and Surrender of That City . . . 29th March, 1847,* whose author, J.M.G., participated in that battle as a crewmember in the frigate *Potomac;* and Boatswain William Brady's *The Naval Apprentice's Kedge Anchor; or Young Sailor's Assistant,* the scarce 1841 first edition of a ubiquitous manual for American naval apprentices reprinted in no less than eighteen editions over the next half century.

The catalog represents a milestone for the Naval Historical Center as it presents to the public exciting samples heretofore unrecorded in any similar bibliography. From unique manuscript cruise journals of the early sailing navy to original blueprints for the first successful U.S. submarine design, from the original rules and regulations adopted for the Naval Academy at Annapolis to the 1895 laws regulating the first naval reserve, the rare books and manuscripts of the Navy Department Library present an eclectic mix of titles on the United States Navy.

George W. Emery
Vice Admiral
U.S. Navy (Retired)

N

North American Review ✓ up to 1821 . . . 8 vols. 8vo

Niles' Weekly Register ✓ *1 wanting* . . . 8vo

Nautical Tracts ✓ 1 . 8vo

National Register ✓ 5 . 8vo

Narrative of Robert Adams wrecked on coast Africa ✓ 1 . 8vo

Naval Chronicle U. S by C. W. Goldsborough 1 . 8vo

Naval Chronicle of England

Naval History of the U. S by Thomas Clark 2 .

Narrative of James Riley wrecked on N coast Africa 1 . 8vo

Naval Register 1824 8vo

Narrative of a Journey to Shores of Polar Sea by *Capt.* Joh Franklin 1 . 8vo

Naval & Military Magazine of G. Britain — 4 nos. 8vo

New Annual Register up to 1823 ~~twenty~~ 44 vol 8vo

Newman's Spanish Dictionary vol. 2 2vo

New York American from 1821 to 1824 2 vol. 8vo

Sample page from the earliest recorded catalog of the Navy Department Library, 1824

Preface

In celebrating its 200th anniversary in the year 2000, the Navy Department Library embarked on a project to highlight its unique role in preserving the nation's naval heritage. Established in 1800 with a small collection of books that served the Secretary of the Navy, the library holds the most comprehensive collection of U.S. Navy literature. For the past two hundred years, it has collected the books, documents, journals, and manuscripts that record the Navy's achievements in combat, international diplomacy, exploration, technological development, medicine, education, and social reform. This literature described in the catalog chronicles the more significant events, customs and traditions, organizations, and personalities in naval history, providing insight into the origins and development of Navy doctrine.

Author Thomas Truxtun Moebs, a graduate of the United States Military Academy and an expert in early military literature, has established his reputation as a rare book cataloger. His two highly acclaimed published works, *Black Sailors–Black Soldiers–Black Ink* and *Confederate States Navy Research Guide,* contain extensive source materials, subject bibliographies, and chronologies. Assisted by Navy Department Library staff, he selected the early imprints from cataloged holdings and a collection of uncataloged pamphlets and journals in the library's Rare Book Room.

Selecting, compiling, reviewing, and editing catalog entries required the commitment, dedication, and hard work of experts in early naval literature, a small library staff, and a conscientious editor. Special thanks go to in-house editor Barbara Auman, who coordinated the many processes required to bring a project like this to fruition. Grateful appreciation extends to Tonya Simpson and Davis Elliott, who provided important data entry and prepared the online version of the catalog; David Brown and Young Park, who guided the cataloging efforts that enable the public to access these historic materials online; and Glenn Helm, who researched the library's history and reviewed the style and format of catalog entries. Although new to the library and this project, Ora Branch helped in a variety of last-minute miscellaneous details. Much appreciation goes to Sandra Doyle, the Naval Historical Center's senior editor, whose close attention to detail helped ensure the accuracy and integrity of the catalog. We are also grateful for the insightful reviews and comments of Dr. Michael Crawford, head of the Early History Branch, and to retired Vice Admiral George W. Emery, author of *Historical Manuscripts in the Navy Department Library,* whose knowledge of the library's collections added scope and vision to this publication.

The publishing of *America's Naval Heritage* was made possible by the Department of Defense Legacy Program that identifies special military, natural, and cultural resources. For its part, the library's project sought to broaden access to historical materials, to encourage naval research and scholarship, and to identify, evaluate, and preserve important military heritage assets. Publishing this catalog not only celebrates the Navy Department Library's 200th year of continuous service but also gives all Americans and the international community of scholars a look into the rare and valuable literature that records the earliest traditions and history of the U.S. Navy.

Jean Hort
Director
Navy Department Library

State, War, and Navy Building, c.1920

Introduction

Origin

The Navy Department Library traces its roots as far back as 1794 when the Naval Bureau was part of the War Department in Philadelphia, the federal capital. In 1798, an act of Congress brought departmental status to the Navy and authorized the Secretary of the Navy to take possession of all the records, books, and documents relevant to naval matters that were then deposited in the office of the Secretary of War. After the library was forced to leave its War Department office, it found temporary refuge in a tavern in Trenton, New Jersey. When Washington became the permanent seat of government in 1800, and the Department of the Navy moved there, wagons-loads of naval books and records were hauled to the federal city, while library furnishings arrived in Georgetown by schooner.

The formal founding of the Navy Department Library dates to early spring 1800, just after the move to Washington. The documentation is a 31 March letter from President John Adams to Secretary of the Navy Benjamin Stoddert, asking the Secretary to establish a library for the Navy and

> to employ some of his clerks in preparing a catalog of books for his office. It ought to consist of all the best writings in Dutch, Spanish, French, and especially in English, upon the theory and practice of naval architecture, navigation, gunnery, hydraulics, hydrostatics, and all branches of mathematics subservient to the profession of the sea. The lives of all the admirals, English, French, Dutch, or any other nation, who have distinguished themselves by the boldness and success of their navigation, or their gallantry and skill in naval combats.

Early Years

In 1801 the library moved into the War Office building near the White House between G and H Streets (now the southern end of the State Department Building). During this period the Navy demonstrated its commitment to retaining important books and documents, as witnessed during the 1814 burning of Washington when the department commandeered wagons to rush the collection to safety north of the federal city. Having escaped the fate of other government libraries and agencies whose materials were destroyed or burned, the library's collection returned to Washington after the War of 1812 and occupied part of the two-story reconstructed building known as the Navy Department Building at 17th Street between F and G Streets N.W.

A feature article on the Navy Department Library appeared in the 26 February 1911 *New York Herald* under the headline "The Navy's Century Old Hall of Fame." Charles Stewart, library head at the time, provided insight into the evolution of the library and its collections. During the early years, according to Stewart, "there was no curatorial office within the Navy, so the library's collection included such items as John Paul Jones' sword, a fragment of the Penn Treaty Tree, and a block of wood from the chestnut tree that supposedly shaded Longfellow's village smithy."

In 1815 the department established the Office of the Commissioners of the Navy, comprising three experienced post-captains to assist the Secretary in the management of "matters connected with the naval establishment of the United States." Not to be outdone by the Secretary's Navy Department Library, the commissioners initiated their own collection efforts. An 1823 document, *Letter from the Secretary of the Navy Transmitting a List of Newspapers and Periodical Works, with a Catalogue of Books Purchased for the Use of the Navy Department, for the Last Six Years; and a Similar List and Catalogue for the Office of the Commissioners of the Navy,* provides a list of books and newspapers "purchased at the public expense" for both offices. When the commissioners' office was abolished in 1842, its library was distributed to the various bureaus according to the nature of their duties. Many of these volumes later became part of the Navy Department Library.

The library's 1824 catalog indicates the collection totaled 1,349 volumes. The 1829 catalog appears to reflect a decline in the number of volumes but includes titles of the portraits, engravings, and charts that were then part of the collection. Some of these original items remain, but historical accounts report the transfer of portraits, engravings, and charts to the Library of Congress. Catalogs and other library-related information for the next fifty years are difficult to document, but manuscript catalogs are again in evidence in 1882 and reflect many of the titles in the 1824 and 1829 catalogs. In 1891 a printed catalog was published.

State, War, and Navy Building (Old Executive Office Building)

In 1879 the Navy's library moved to its most prestigious location, the State, War, and Navy Building, later renamed the Old Executive Office Building and now the Eisenhower Building at 17th Street and Pennsylvania Avenue. At the time of construction, representatives of several leading European naval powers reported the work under way to their respective governments, leading several countries to send marble and other materials for the room's decoration in recognition of the services of Union naval officers. The library was housed in what later became known as the Indian Treaty Room, a richly decorated space with marble wall panels, 800-pound bronze lamps, gold-leaf ornamentation, and a frescoed ceiling studded with gold stars. In this elegant setting, the library not only provided research services for the Navy and other secretariats but also became a congenial meeting place for local leaders and foreign dignitaries.

Public Act No. 21 of 7 August 1882 officially established the library as a departmental institution. The act directed each Cabinet member to ascertain and report at the next session of Congress "the conditions of the several libraries in his department, number of volumes in each and plan for consolidation of the same so that there should be but one library in each department." Noted international lawyer and U.S. Naval Academy professor James Russell Soley accepted assignment as officer in charge of the newly consolidated departmental library under the Office of Naval Intelligence in the Bureau of Navigation. Soley began his tenure by gathering rare books, naval prints, and photographs scattered throughout the Navy bureau system, subscribing to professional and scientific periodicals, and classifying and cataloging diverse materials. More than anyone since President John Adams, he was responsible for envisioning and crafting the Navy Department Library.

In 1884, Navy Captain John Grimes Walker, Chief of the Bureau of Navigation, received funding for a project begun three years earlier to collect records of Union and Confederate naval operations for eventual publication. Even though Congress approved separate appropriations for the clerical staffs of the library and the war records project, Professor Soley supervised both activities operating under the title of "Office of Library and Naval War Records." These offices were transferred from the Bureau of Navigation and placed under the Secretary of the Navy's office in 1889 when Navy Lieutenant Commander F.M. Wise succeeded Soley as librarian and officer in charge of war records. Even after his appointment that year as Assistant Secretary of the Navy, Soley continued his interest in the library and gave it his enthusiastic support.

In 1893, Navy Captain Richard Rush, who successfully published the first five volumes of the *Official Records of the Union and Confederate Navies*, succeeded Wise. A new organizational structure combining a library, a record-keeping branch, and a mission to publish naval history formed the basis of the present-day Naval Historical Center in the Washington Navy Yard.

Appropriations for compiling and publishing war records and for the Navy Department Library remained separate until 1915 when Congress combined and changed the title of the joint office to "Office of Naval Records and Library." Between 1917 and 1921, the Office of Naval Records and Library underwent two major organizational changes: first, the restoration of the library to the Office of Naval Intelligence from the jurisdiction of the Secretary's office (Navy Order 1 of July 1919); and second, the revival of its earlier historical functions, which by the 1920s had almost eased to exist.

During World War I, senior naval officers and their staffs, U.S. government and allied officials, news correspondents, and others depended heavily on the library for information on treaties, international law, and subjects related to the war. Frequent moves, including three during World War I, and the lack of professionally trained librarians were symptoms of insufficient space and inadequate staffing that persisted throughout the library's history. Even the Secretary of the Navy in his 1920 Annual Report acknowledged the need for professional library management:

> The Navy Library, which contains more than 50,000 volumes and many rare manuscripts, could be made of much greater value if a competent librarian were secured. The law at present provides for a chief clerk, and for years the work was conducted under the direction of that official, but the position has remained long vacant, owing to the small compensation offered, $2,000, and the impossibility of securing, at that salary, a competent and experienced man.... Organized under a competent librarian, the library would be able to furnish officials of the department and others engaged in naval work or research, complete references on any subject desired. These references should extend to books in other libraries on technical or naval matters. There is increasing demand from many sources for information of this character, and the Naval Library should be able to furnish it, and could easily do so if an experienced man who possesses a knowledge of naval history and affairs as well as of library methods is secured....

Snow's "Historical Sketch of the Navy Department Library and War Records" (1926), based on personal recollections of those who served in the library, documents the visits of many government leaders and foreign dignitaries. It recalls that Theodore Roosevelt, Jr., as Assistant Secretary of the Navy during 1897, took an active interest in library matters. And as President, he continued to look after the library. For example, on one occasion he telephoned the librarian from the White House informing him "shades were drawn unevenly," and on another he noted that "growing plants should not be placed in the Library windows."

Main Navy Building

The Navy moved the majority of its offices to the Main Navy Building on 18th and B Streets N.W. in 1918. However, it was not until suitable space was provided in 1923 that the library was relocated. This move significantly enhanced the library's reference and research value to the Navy for it was once again in close proximity to a large number of Navy users. Retired Navy and Marine Corps officers continued to hold the position of superintendent of the library until 1931 when, as an economy measure, the position was combined with the Officer in Charge of Naval Records and Library. Commodore Dudley W. Knox, a gifted historian who served as that officer from 1921 to 1946, strengthened and reinforced the Navy's commitment to its historic heritage and traditions.

A 1931 *Washington Star* article highlighting governmental libraries described the Navy Department Library as being a large, well-arranged library with more than 77,572 volumes, records, and documents related to naval science, biography, and history. As World War II approached and the Navy expanded, space was once again a premium. The library was reduced in size, and its holdings transferred to the Navy Annex in Arlington, Virginia, the National Archives, and the Library of Congress. Only a small reference collection, with Constance Lathrop as librarian, remained at the Main Navy Building.

In the postwar years the library slowly recovered from its wartime scattering. In 1949 the Office of Naval Records and Library combined with Office of Naval History to form the Naval Records and History Division under the Office of the Chief of Naval Operations. This organizational designation was simplified in 1952 to the Naval History Division. The division including the library remained in the Main Navy Building where it had been consolidated just after the war.

Building 44, Washington Navy Yard

tory to form the Naval Records and History Division under the Office of the Chief of Naval Operations. This organizational designation was simplified in 1952 to the Naval History Division. The division including the library remained in the Main Navy Building where it had been consolidated just after the war.

Washington Navy Yard

Originally intended as a temporary World War I structure, the Main Navy Building was torn down in 1970, and numerous Navy organizations and offices were relocated. Joining the Navy Museum and the Operational Archives, the Navy Department Library moved to Building 220 in the Washington Navy Yard during the summer of 1970. An organizational change in 1971 established the history-related activities, including the Navy Department Library, as a field activity under the Chief of Naval Operations. Today's Naval Historical Center is the result of that change. The library and most of the center's activities came together in 1982, when they moved to their present location across from Leutze Park. This historic building complex was named to honor Commodore Dudley Knox.

Challenges and Opportunities

After Navy offices relocated and the library moved to the Washington Navy Yard, traditional patrons were once again separated from the library. But by the late 1980s and early 1990s, new technologies overcame these obstacles to providing service. The library began using a CD-ROM catalog in 1992, and by 1997 was providing worldwide access through the Internet. Having taken these first steps, the library continues to use technology to improve public access to its collections. As the 21st century begins, more than 90,000 patrons visit the library yearly from offices and homes around the globe.

Preservation grants have allowed the library to focus on conservation, cataloging, and public access to special materials. These grants have ensured the conservation of several hundred rare documents and manuscripts, brought thousands of rare volumes under bibliographic control, and provided technology to enhance public access to its collections. The Navy Department Library has met many challenges throughout its 200-year history. In the century ahead, with the ongoing support of the Navy, it will continue to find creative and innovative ways to balance the implementation of technology with stewardship of the nation's naval literary heritage.

SOURCES: J.W. McElroy, "Office of Naval Records and Library, 1882–1946." (Washington, D.C., 1946); "The Navy's Century Old Hall of Fame," *The New York Herald* part 2 (26 February 1911): 9–10; *The Old Executive Office Building: Victorian Masterpiece* (Washington, D.C.: Executive Office of the President, Office of Administration, 1984); Paul O. Paullin, *The Paullin's History of Naval Administration, 1775–1911* (Annapolis Md.: Naval Institute, 1968); Harry R. Skallerup, *Books Afloat & Ashore* (Hamden, Conn.: Archon Books, 1974); Isabel Smith and Elliot Snow, "Historical Sketch of the Navy Department Library and War Records" (Washington, D.C., 1926); and U.S. Navy, Office of Naval Intelligence, "Scope, Facilities and Size of the Library of the U.S. Navy Department, in the Office of Naval Records and Library," *U.S. Naval Administrative History of World War II*, vol. 26-D, Navy Dept. Library Rare Book Room (Washington D.C., n.d.).

Navy Department Library Reading Room (Indian Treaty Room) in the State, War, and Navy Building, 1915

A Catalog of Early Imprints

FROM THE NAVY DEPARTMENT LIBRARY

Professor James R. Soley organized and directed the Navy Department Library from 1881 until 1889, when he became Assistant Secretary of the Navy.

NUMBERS.	SIGNAL PENDANTS.	SIGNIFICATION OF DAY SIGNALS.
4 . 8		When in diſtreſs.
4 . 9		In want of artificers.
5 . 0		For boats to tow.
5 . 1		Stay by and aſſiſt a diſabled ſhip, returning expeditiouſly when the damage is repaired, and particular ſhip's pendant afterwards.

Compaſs Signals.

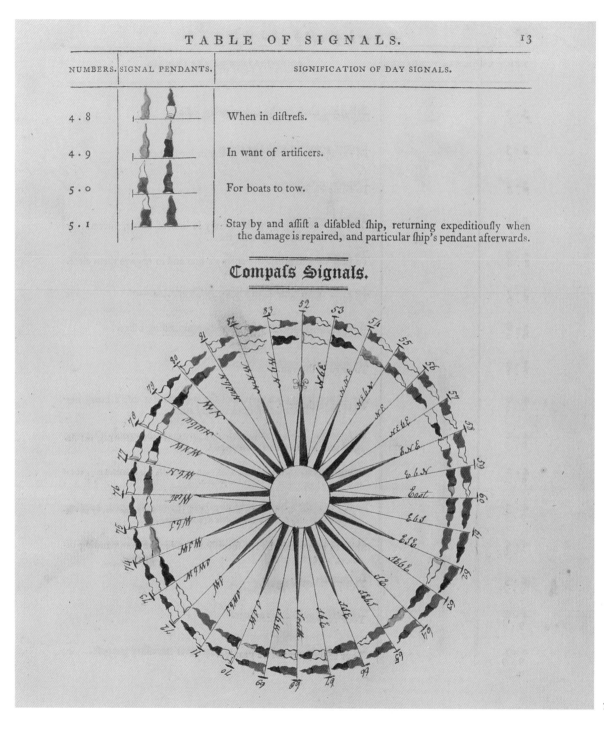

Truxtun's Table of Signals

{1785}

Pioneer American Observations on Naval Warfare

1. Anonymous.

Cursory Observations, Relative to the Mounting of Cannon in a New Way, and to Naval Warfare. *New-York: Printed by E. Oswald, for Elizabeth Holt, 1785. 2 l, [5]–23 p., 20 cm.*

The unknown author deals with a system for mounting cannon so that they may be employed in coastal defense of the New York harbor area. The author also discusses naval warfare, outlining a system of mounting cannon on warships to provide tactical advantage. This piece is certainly one of the earliest American printed works on naval warfare available in the period just after the peace treaty ending the American Revolution and the formation of the United States under the Constitution of 1787. Given the author's comment on his prior contact with Congress regarding naval warfare, his observations may well have been read by those involved in shaping the legislation founding the Navy in 1794 and guiding it thereafter. In his prefatory "To the Public," the author notes that the "ideas he has thrown out, will probably occasion some alteration in the established system of naval war; and may deserve some attention on that account." He discusses an improved mode of employing cannon: "Plain and clear as this reasoning is, when we apply the conclusion to naval warfare, it holds out such great and unexpected advantages. . . . If, as we have just now been led to believe, 10 guns in this way, are equal, at long shot, to 40 guns in the old way. . . let the smaller vessel be provided to fire 4 stern chases. Let her, on falling in with a ship of the line, feign to run away, and endeavour to steer such a course in her pretended flight, that the enemy can bring only his bow chases to bear upon her. . . [t]o illustrate still further the superiority of a vessel carrying guns mounted in the proposed way. . . . The preceding observations will explain to the gentlemen who were in Congress some years ago, why

I then took so much pains to call the attention of that honorable body to naval affairs." Some hint of the authorship is provided by the title page imprint link with Elizabeth Holt. In his *Printing in the Americas*, Oswald states: "Elizabeth Holt was a daughter of John Hunter, of Williamsburg, Virginia, where she was born in 1727. Col. Eleazar Oswald, who was a relative, was associated with her in business in New York until 1787." Eleazar Oswald (1755–1795) is the supposed author of a 1795 tract (**Evans,** #29256) on international relations, specifically, the treaty with Great Britain. This early work on naval warfare, given his military connection and strategic view, may have been from his pen.

Evans, #18979. **Oswald** (1), 186. **Sabin,** #18012. **National Union Catalog (NUC)** (Columbia University, John Carter Brown Library, Library Company of Philadelphia, Library of Congress, New York Public Library). **Online Computer Library Center (OCLC)** (Navy Department Library).

{1787–1788}

The Constitutional Convention Debates a Navy

2. Elliot, Jonathan (compiler).

The Debates, Resolutions, and Other Proceedings, in Convention, on the Adoption of the Federal Constitution: As Recommended by the General Convention at Philadelphia, on the 17th of September, 1787: With the Yeas and Nays on the Decision of the Main Question. Collected and Revised, from Contemporary Publications, by Jonathan Elliot . . . *Washington: Printed by and for the editor, 1827–1830. 4 vols. [8], 358; [8], 33–487; [8], 17–322; [8], 272, 404 p., 21 cm.*

"The controversies over ratification of the Constitution (which include naval argument, of course) have been collected by . . . Jonathan Elliot."—**Smelser.**

Howes, E98. **Sabin,** #22232. **Shaw and Shoemaker,** #28775. **Smelser,** 216. **NUC** (23). **OCLC** (86).

{1794}

First Detailing of Officer Duties on a Man-of-War

3. Truxtun, Thomas (1755–1822).

Remarks, Instructions, and Examples Relating to the Latitude & Longitude: Also, the Variation of the Compass, &c., &c., &c.: To Which Is Annexed, a General Chart of the Globe, Where the Route Made by the Author, in Different Ships under His Command, to the Cape of Good Hope, Batavia, Canton in China, the Different Parts of India, Europe, and the Cape De Verde Islands, Are Marked, for the Purpose of Shewing the Best Tract of Sea to Meet the Most Favourable Winds, and Avoid Those Perplexing Calms Which Too Often Attend Asiatic Voyages: Together with a Short, But General Account of Variable Winds, Trade-winds, Monsoons, Hurricanes, Tornadoes, Tuffoons, Calms, Currents, and Particular Weather Met in Those Voyages, &c., &c., &c. By Thomas Truxtun. *Philadelhpia [sic]: Printed by T. Dobson, at the Stone-House, No. 41 South Second-Street, 1794. 8, 74, 31, xxiii p., map (folding), plate (folding), 31 cm.*

"Few American books of the eighteenth century excelled in interest and usefulness the work of Commodore Thomas Truxtun. . . . All in all, the book is a contribution to the art of navigation, seamanship, shipbuilding, and naval customs reflecting credit upon the merchant and naval establishments of a young country struggling against odds for a place among the nations. It could not have failed to increase respect for that country among the mariners of the world."—**Wroth.** John Ewing (1732–1802), president of the University of Pennsylvania and an astronomer, wrote that Truxtun "had justly acquired the character of the first navigator that has ever sailed from the ports of the United States." Truxtun's book "includes examples of all then known methods of obtaining latitude and longitude at sea, with remarks and instructions on lunar observations. There are also tables of variations of the compass obtained in the years 1786–90 and 1792, in many localities, North and South Latitudes, East and West Longitudes."—**Robison.** Truxtun's' *Remarks* is notable not only for its navigational merits but also for being the first work by an American naval officer to detail duties in a man-of-war. Page xxiii contains "an essay on the general duties of officers of ships of war. . . . Truxtun was probably then the most informed officer in the navy."—**Skallerup.** The foldout plate is of the masting of an American frigate and is the first American print of that type. This work by Truxtun is rare, the copies located by the **NUC** being in general held by institutions with long collecting histories. The Navy Department Library has three copies. One, belonging to William Talbot Truxtun (1824–1887), carries on the front flyleaf an original sketch of an American frigate over the signature, "W. Talbot Truxtun U.S.N." The grandson of Thomas Truxtun, he saw considerable naval service, attaining the rank of commodore. His life is chronicled in the *Dictionary of American Biography.*

DAB (10), 21–23. **Ferguson,** 103–8. **Evans,** #27823. **Howes** (not recorded). **Robison,** 543. **Sabin,** #97281. **Skallerup,** 115. **Wroth,** 38. **NUC** (24). **OCLC** (8).

Truxtun's signal flags, 1797

First United States Navy Signals Book
Author's Copy with Important Manuscript Notes

4. Truxtun, Thomas (1755–1822).

Instructions, Signals, and Explanations, Ordered for the United States Fleet. By Thomas Truxtun. *1797. 38 p. (pp. 7–26 with hand-colored signals), illus., 29 cm.*

"[W]ritten primarily for the conduct of a squadron of eight frigates and two sloops."—**Robison.** This, the first United States Navy signals book, is a work of great rarity. The copy in the Navy Department Library belonged to the author, Commodore Thomas Truxtun. During the Revolutionary War, Truxtun, in the privateer *St. James*, 20 guns, had "brought back the most valuable cargo entered at Philadelphia during the Revolution, and Washington at a dinner in Truxtun's honor, declared his services worth a regiment."—**DAB.** The *Dictionary of American Biography* further notes that in "June 1794 he was made a captain in the new American navy" and that during the Quasi-War with France (1798–1801), "in popular regard he became unquestionably the hero of the war. . . . His fighting spirit and rigid discipline . . . set excellent standards for the young navy." The Navy Department Library copy is truly remarkable. On page 38, there appears, as the last printed line, the statement: "Given from under my hand on board the United States ship." Truxtun has completed that printed line with the manuscript entry "*Constellation* this 3d day of April 1797." He has then added his signature. It is possible that this copy of the first United States Navy signals book is the one that Truxtun had on board USS *Constellation* during preparation for launch and later gave to his wife before he departed for the West Indies, where he fought

and won the major naval engagements of the Quasi-War with France (French frigates *L'Insurgente* on February 9, 1799, and *La Vengeance* on February 2, 1800). The foregoing statement is based on manuscript entries made by Truxtun on the verso of the title page, where he has also penned, and signed with his initials, a patriotic poem:

> America's prosperity first from Commerce arose.
> To Commerce still her wealth she owes.
> Protect then Injured Commerce.
> And let each experienced Columbian Speedily impart
> His Naval Skill to perfect Naval Art.

There follows at the bottom of the title page, also signed with Truxtun's initials, "The rights of America we'll maintain and then return to you, Sweet girl again." In analyzing the poem, **Robison** takes a different tack, suggesting that it "seems to have been issued by Truxtun to one of his officers, or possibly signed by him, previous to submitting it to the Secretary of War, there being as yet no navy department." In suggesting those possibilities, the poem and "Sweet girl" inscription seem to have been dropped from consideration.

DAB (10), 21–22. **Evans** (not recorded). **Ferguson,** 127, 128. **Howes** (not recorded). **Robison,** 546–48. **Sabin** (not recorded). **Shipton and Mooney** (not recorded). **NUC** (Navy Department). **OCLC** (Navy Department Library).

[1797]

Final Pre-Launch Report on First United States Frigate

5. United States, War Department, Secretary.

Letter from the Secretary at War, to the Chairman of the Committee on Naval Equipment, Inclosing Sundry Statements Relative to the Subject: Accompanying a Report of the Committee Appointed on the 16th Ultimo, to Enquire into the State of the Naval Equipment: 25th January, 1797, Committed to a Committee of the Whole House, on Monday Next. Published by Order of the House of Representatives. *[Philadelphia: 1797]. [2], [3]–11 p., table (folding), 19.5 cm.*

Pages 4–5 are devoted to a "Statement of the progress made in building each of the first three frigates for the new United States Navy, the *Constitution*, *Constellation*, and *United States*." The remainder of the report deals with materials for construction, officers and crew and their annual pay, and names of officers appointed to command. This is a historic document, constituting the final congressional report on the first United States frigate prior to its launching. On May 10, 1797, the frigate *United States* was launched at Philadelphia; on September 7, 1797, the frigate *Constellation* was launched at Baltimore; on October 21, 1797, the frigate *Constitution* was launched at Boston.

Cooney, 18. **Clements,** 13. **Evans,** #33094. **Sweetman,** 17. **NUC** (not recorded). **OCLC** (Library of Congress, Navy Department Library).

Materials remaining on hand in the NAVY YARDS at *New-York*, *Norfolk*, and *Portsmouth* (N. H.) which have been provided, and deposited there for the Frigates, whose building has been suspended by an act of Congress.

NAMES OF PLACES WHERE DEPOSITED.	No. of pieces of live oak timber provided for the frames.	No. of feet of white oak timber in logs.	No. of feet of white oak timber of various descriptions.	No. of feet of white oak plank, for the bottom, cieling and topsides.	No. of feet of white oak plank for other uses.	No. of feet of carlings and ledges.	No. of feet of Georgia pine plank for decks.	No. of feet of yellow pine plank for various uses.	No. of pounds of copper for sheathing, &c.	Weight of iron kentledge for ballast.	Weight of 24 pound shot.	Number of anchors.	Number of pounds of iron.	Masts and spars of various sizes.	No. of white oak knees.	No. of pieces of bunting for colours.	Cabouse, with a complete set of cooking utensils, &c.
New-York	314	105,864	24,444	159,292	42,371	18,130	85,930	35,679	55,379	Tons 140	Pounds 57,561	2	3,562	17			1
Norfolk	402	48,052	57,948	17,877	Timbers 8,064		28,977	53,831					33,524 and 120 bars	All provided but not delivered.			1
Portsmouth	541	Maple 34,800	34,560	105,989	21,719	Feet 6,765	38,250					1 large anchor of C. qr. lb. 44 2 14	9,339	One complete set.	200	99 pieces	1

N. B. Considerable quantities of live oak timber, and other materials, have been selected out of the above Navy Yards, for the use of the Frigates under construction.

Navy yard shipbuilding materials

{1798}

Plan for Recording and Registering Navy Seamen

6. Fenno, John (publisher).

Plan for Establishing a General Marine Society Throughout the United States, and Systems of Regulations Therein; Written at Sea, in the Year 1794: Now Printed for the Benefit of that Institution, by the Author... *Philadelphia: Printed by John Fenno, 1798. 32 p., 22 cm.*

Pages 24–27 are "Remarks on the Establishment of the Navy of the United States, and of the Plan for Recording and Registering the Seamen Thereof." The preface is signed "S.K."

Evans, #33944. **Howes** (not recorded). **Sabin,** #63268. **NUC** (14). **OCLC** (Boston Athenaeum, Harvard University Library, Johns Hopkins University, Navy Department Library, New York Historical Society Archives, New York State Library, University of Virginia Library).

{1801}

Thomas Paine on "The Liberty of the Seas"
"It is the flag, not its cannon, that is to be respected."

7. Paine, Thomas (1737-1809).

Compact Maritime, under the Following Heads: I. Dissertation on the Law of Nations. II. On the Jacobinism of the English at Sea. III. Compact Maritime for the Protection of Neutral Commerce, and Securing the Liberty of the Seas. IV. Observations on Some Passages in the Discourse of the Judge of the English Admiralty. By Thomas Paine. *City of Washington: Printed by Samuel Harrison Smith, 1801. [2], [3]-24 p., 21.5 cm.*

Paine begins with a "Dissertation on the Law of Nations, Respecting the Rights of Neutral Commerce and the Liberty of the Seas" (pages [3]–9). Pages 16–21 are "Compact Maritime, of an association of nations for the Protection of the rights and commerce of nations that shall be neutral in time of war." At the time of publication of this tract, the issue of British molestation of American vessels was looming larger. Here the famous 18th-century propagandist of the rights of man adds his thoughts, noting: "I come now to a subject that makes what may be called the order of the day, which is, the pretended right set up by England, as a belligerent nation, to visit neutral vessels at sea. This she pretends to derive from the law of nations... the belligerent ship has no business with the neutral ship but to be assured of its flag, which being assured of, it has no business with its papers or its cargo. The faith of the government, under the flag of which the neutral merchant sails, is to be taken for all other matters. It is the flag, and not its cannon, that is to be respected."

Howes (not recorded). **Sabin** (not recorded). **Shaw and Shoemaker,** #1087. **NUC** (Library of Congress, Navy Department Library, New York Public Library). **OCLC** (Cambridge University, Indiana Historical Society, Navy Department Library, University of Virginia Library).

{1802}

Early Argument for a Permanent Navy

8. [Bronson, Enos].

An Address to the People of the United States, on the Policy of Maintaining a Permanent Navy. By an American Citizen. *Philadelphia: Printed by James Humphreys for E. Bronson, 1802. iv, [5]-51 p., 22 cm.*

"Ascribed also to Albert Gallatin."—**Howes.** "The Observations contained in the following Address were written in the winter of ninety-eight... and are now submitted to the people of the United States... on the policy of maintaining a permanent Navy. Its enemies, fertile in ingenious argument, have not only opposed our present armament, in every stage of its progress, but have laboured to prove the comparative uselessness of the commerce and navigation which it was designed to protect.... I endeavour to expose its most striking delusions. Among those, the glowing pictures of the happiness of states exclusively agricultural merit... examination.... Placed at a distance from the warlike nations of Europe, and taught rather to fear than to solicit an enlargement of territory by conquest, the American Politician must guard against national apathy, by allowing the principles that promote activity in peace an unrestrained operation."—**American Citizen.**

Harbeck, 164. **Howes,** E803. **Sabin** (not recorded). **Shaw and Shoemaker,** #1720. **NUC** (American Philosophical Society, Brown University, Clements Library, Library of Congress, Pennsylvania Historical Society, University of Pennsylvania, Western Reserve Historical Society). **OCLC** (12).

Basic Source on Creation of the Navy

9. [Hamilton, Alexander] (1755-1804).

The Federalist, on the New Constitution. By Publius. Written in 1788. To Which Is Added, Pacificus, on the Proclamation of Neutrality. Written in 1793. Likewise, the Federal Constitution, with All the Amendments. *New-York: Printed and sold by George F. Hopkins, at Washington's Head, 1802. 2 vols. [8], 318; [5], 351 p., 22 cm.*

"Most famous and influential American political work."—**Howes.** Within its pages is an important debate on the creation of the United States Navy: "Hamilton carried the burden of the naval argument. He wrote four times on significant points (numbers III, XI, XXIV, XXXII), and Madison and Jay each wrote once (XL and IV, respectively). Usually they addressed themselves to different aspects of the question, but all three developed the argument that only by ratifying the new Constitution could the nation be assured of having a navy."—**Smelser.** This edition is the last one printed during the lifetime of Alexander Hamilton, soon to die in a duel with Aaron Burr. Hamilton produced this work in collaboration with John Jay and James Madison, and it first appeared in 1787.

Howes, H114. **Sabin,** #23981. **Shaw and Shoemaker,** #2218. **Smelser,** 18–19. **NUC** (23). **OCLC** (64).

Remarkable Allegations of Abuse of Sailors in the Infant Navy

10. Rea, John.

A Letter to William Bainbridge, Esqr., Formerly Commander of the United States Ship George Washington: Relative to Some Transactions, On Board Said Ship, during a Voyage to Algiers, Constantinople, &c. By John Rea, at That Time, an Ordinary Seaman On Board. *Philadelphia: Printed for the Author, 1802. [2], [3]–24 p., 17 cm.*

Rea unleashes an astounding indictment against Bainbridge for alleged mistreatment of the crew of USS *George Washington* during a voyage to carry tribute to the Dey of Algiers in 1800. What impact Rea's allegations had on naval leaders and Congress in their day must be wondered at as they came very early in the organization of the new United States Navy. It is known that a copy of Rea's letter was in the personal library of Thomas Jefferson. Rea writes: "You will certainly be much surprised at the liberty I am taking, in addressing you at all. I have seen the time, when it would, indeed, have been a dangerous liberty.... *You* was [*sic*] then invested with power, which in the hands of a man as destitute of reason and humanity, as you, was truly dreadful: and I divested of every privilege of a freeman—even the privilege of vindicating my own innocence.... [W]e are now on a level—on the main deck of America, where 'all men are equally free.' *You* are divested of your tyrannical power; and I am invested with the liberty of speaking, and writing . . . yes, to a *Captain of a Man-of-War.* I therefore come forward, fearless of your *swords,* your *shackles, or cat of ninetails* . . . a duty I owe my fellow-citizens . . . warning them against endangering their lives in the hands of so desperate a wretch as you are.... Does the Law authorise a Captain to punish a man in *three* different ways for the same crime? *Riding a spanker-boom* upwards of three hours, . . . put in *irons,* and then *flogged....* I have it in my power to relate things far more wonderful than these—for, from the time I discovered your tyrannical disposition, I made a point of recording all your great actions.... Who could believe that on board of an *American* Ship, carrying but one hundred men, exclusive of Officers, in a nine months' voyage, upwards of fifty men should have been put in *irons*—upwards of forty *flogged at the gang-way;* amongst whom, *three hundred and sixty-five lashes* were distributed—exclusive of innumerable *rope's-ending's, sword beatings,* &c. &c. &c. And all this, except in one solitary instance (for *theft*) for *eating, drinking, sleeping, missing of muster,* or some other trifling fault.... Would it be believed, was I to mention the case of J. Robinson, whom you put hands and feet in irons, for *intoxication,* and whose *scull* [*sic*] you afterwards, for a *little impertinent language, fractured with your sword,* bringing him to the deck—whom you then took out of irons, streaming with blood—seized up at the gang-way and gave *thirty* lashes with the cat on the bare back!" In ending, Rea tells Bainbridge that he was "hated, cursed and ridiculed . . . by every man from stem to stern of the Ship." This copy belonged to Admiral George Henry Preble and bears his signature on the title page.

Howes (not recorded). **Sabin** (not recorded). **Shaw and Shoemaker** (not recorded). **Sowerby,** #3281. **NUC** (Clements Library, Harvard University Library, Library Company of Philadelphia, Library of Congress). **OCLC** (Arkansas Technical University, Boston Athenaeum, Navy Department Library, Ouachita Baptist University).

[36]

9. Convoys are to fail like divifions, and proper fignals to be made at feparation.

—⁂—

The President of the United States of America, ordains and directs the commanders of squadrons, and all captains and other officers in the navy of the United States, to execute, and cause to be executed, the aforesaid regulations.

By command,

R. Smith

Secretary of the Navy.

Signature of Robert Smith, Secretary of the Navy, 1802

Signed by Secretary of the Navy
First Compiled and Separately Printed Navy Regulations

11. United States. Navy Department.

Naval Regulations Issued by Command of the President of the United States of America, January 25, 1802. *2 p. l., 36 p., 18 cm.*

On July 1, 1797, Congress approved regulations for the new United States Navy. Having had as their antecedent the 1775 Continental Navy regulations, the text of which may be found in the 1799 and 1800 U.S. Statutes, the compiled regulations of the new United States Navy were not issued in a separate printing until 1802. This copy of that milestone is signed in manuscript by Robert Smith, the serving Secretary of the Navy. Contents cover "Of the duties of a commander in chief, or commander of a squadron [;] Of the duties of a captain or commander, a lieutenant, a sailing-master, a surgeon, a chaplain, a boatswain and master sailmaker, a gunner, armorer, and gunsmith, a carpenter, a master-at-arms and corporal, a midshipman, a cook [;] Regulations to be observed respecting provisions, respecting slops, respecting the form and mode of keeping the log-book and journals, &c., respecting courts martial, and respecting convoys."

Cooney, 18. **Sabin,** #52083. **Shaw and Shoemaker,** #3374. **NUC** (Clements Library, Library of Congress). **OCLC** (Library of Congress, Navy Department Library, United States Naval Academy).

{1802}

First Uniform Regulations

12. United States. Navy Department.

The Uniform Dress of Captains and Certain Other Officers of the Navy of the United States. *[Washington, D.C.: Navy Department]*, 1802. 2 p., 27 cm.

"First," as it is used in the heading above, refers to printed regulations of two or more pages as opposed to a broadside (poster) printing. There is known to be a Philadelphia 1797 broadside issued by the U.S. War Department. Entitled *Uniform for the Navy of the United States*, that broadside bears the date of August 24, 1797 (see **Evans**, #33100). Issued in quarto format with caption title, this imprint is signed in print by R. Smith and dated August 27, 1802 at the Navy Department. It is organized under headings of Captains' Full Dress, Lieutenants' Full Dress, Midshipmen's Full Dress, Surgeons' Full Dress, Surgeons Mates' Full Dress, Sailing-Masters' Full Dress, and Pursers' Full Dress.

Shaw and Shoemaker (not recorded). **NUC** (University of Indiana). **OCLC** (Navy Department, United States Naval Academy).

{1805}

Nautical Bible for New Midshipmen

13. Duane, W. (publisher).

The Mariner's Dictionary, or American Seaman's Vocabulary of Technical Terms, and Sea Phrases, Used in the Construction, Equipment, Management, and Military Operations, of Ships and Vessels of All Descriptions. Improved from an English Work. Illustrated with Copper Plates, Descriptive of All Objects Appertaining to Seamanship. *Washington City: W. Duane, 1805. iv, 1 leaf, 256 p., 8 plates, 16 cm.*

"During the tenure of [Secretary of the Navy] Robert Smith an instructive little book, *The Mariner's Dictionary*, was also usually sent to new midshipmen. No other similar instructional book was provided gratis to young officers for years to come."—**Skallerup.** The English work cited in the title is that of J.J. Moore. It has erroneously been attributed to John Hamilton Moore.

Sabin, #44590. **Shaw and Shoemaker**, #8832. **Skallerup,** 111. **NUC** (13). **OCLC** (13).

{1808}

First Medical Book by an American Navy Doctor; Founder of First American Naval Hospital

14. Cutbush, Edward (1772-1843).

Observations on the Means of Preserving the Health of Soldiers and Sailors; and on the Duties of the Medical Department of the Army and Navy: With Remarks on Hospitals and Their Internal Arrangement. By Edward Cutbush. *Philadelphia: Printed for Thomas Dobson, at the Stone House, No. 41, South Second Street. Fry and Kammerer, printers, 1808. xvi, 336, 14 p., 2 plates, 3 folding tables, 31 cm.*

Cutbush, who entered naval service on June 24, 1799, established the first naval hospital in 1802. Located at Syracuse, Sicily, the hospital was intended for the care of Americans wounded from the wars against the Barbary pirates. Cutbush served until June 10, 1829.

Howes (not recorded). **Sabin** (not recorded). **Shaw and Shoemaker,** #14816. **USNI Almanac,** 190–91, 193–94. **NUC** (18). **OCLC** (32).

{1813}

{1813}

Predecessor of the *Navy Register*

15. Belcher, J. (publisher).

A Complete List of the American Navy; Showing the Name, Number of Guns, Commanders' Names, and Station of Each Vessel, with the Names of All Officers in Service, for October, 1813; and Steel's List of the Navy of Great Britain, for July, 1813. *Boston: Russell, Cutler, and Company and J. Belcher, 1813. 40, [37]–106 p., 17 cm.*

Belcher's list, dated September 30, 1813, from Boston, is a predecessor to the *Navy Register*. According to Belcher, "It is intended to publish, every three months, a corrected edition of these Lists, if the sale of the present promises encouragement to the undertaking. The deep and general interest which has been excited in the publick mind by the valorous achievements of our Naval heroes, induces a belief, that the permanent establishment of a complete 'List of the American Navy' must receive adequate patronage." Pages 4–8, "List of the American Navy," give the names of American warships together with their commanders, stations, and construction dates. Pages 9–13 list the vessels captured or destroyed by and lost by the Navy between 1812 and 1813. Pages 14–28 list American naval officers. There then follows a list of Navy yards, Marine Corps officers, Navy Department personnel, and miscellaneous information and corrections. Pages 41–100 are Steel's Royal Navy List.

Howes (not recorded). **Sabin,** #15059. **Shaw and Shoemaker,** #28198a. **NUC** (Boston Public Library, Harvard University Library, Library of Congress, Navy Department Library). **OCLC** (8).

{1814}

First Major Compilation of Naval Laws

16. United States. Navy Department.

Laws of the United States in Relation to the Naval Establishment, and the Marine Corps. Digested in Pursuance of a Resolution of the Senate, of the 18th of March, 1814. *[Washington]: 1814. Title leaf, contents leaf, [5]–144, i–ix p., 17 cm.*

This compilation is organized into Navy Department, Naval Armament, Marine Corps, Government of the Navy, Pensions, Navy Hospitals, and Resolutions of Congress. The **NUC** cites five printings of compiled naval laws. The recorded printings are 1814, 1826 in 165 pages, 1826 in 198 pages, 1841, and 1843.

Shaw and Shoemaker, #33243. **NUC** (College of William and Mary, Franklin D. Roosevelt Library at Hyde Park, Navy Department Library, New York Public Library). **OCLC** (15).

{1814}

The First Printing of Navy Register

17. United States. Navy Department.

Letter from the Secretary of the Navy, Transmitting a List of All the Commissioned Officers in the Navy of the United States, Showing Their Respective Rank, and Dates of the Commissions; Also, a List of All the Midshipmen, and the Dates of Their Warrants. February 21, 1814. Printed by Order of the Senate of the United States. *Washington City: Printed By Roger C. Weightman, 1814. 29 p., 18 cm.*

"In 1814, a listing of naval officers by rank and seniority, the *Navy Register* was authorized for yearly publication. Together with the annual report of the secretary of the navy it served to present the status of the service."—**Skallerup.** "The first volume of the official *Navy Register* was issued in 1814, and registers were printed annually from that year to 1861, inclusive, with the exception of the year 1816, when the printing of the *Navy Register* was for some reason omitted."—**Harbeck.**

Harbeck, 137. **Shaw and Shoemaker,** #33260. **Skallerup,** 111–12. **NUC** (Library of Congress, University of Virginia Library). **OCLC** (Navy Department Library, University of Pennsylvania, University of Virginia Library, Yale University).

Condition and Prospects of the Navy

18. Niles, John M[ilton] (1787-1856).

The Life of Oliver Hazard Perry. With an Appendix, Comprising Biographical Sketches of the Late General Pike, and Captain Lawrence, and a View of the Present Condition and Future Prospects of the Navy of the United States. By John M. Niles Esq. *Hartford: Published by William S. Marsh, R. Storrs . . . printer, 1820. xii, [13]–376 p., [2] leaves of plates (1 folded), illus., 19 cm.*

Pages 362–76 are caption-titled: "A View of the Present Naval Force of the United States; Its Increase, and Future Prospects."

DAB (7), 522–23. **Howes,** N157. **Sabin,** #55320. **Shoemaker,** #2554. **NUC** (16). **OCLC** (59).

September 10.th 1813.
"We have met the enemy, and they are ours."

Stipple engraved portrait of Oliver Hazard Perry

[1826]

Second Compilation of Naval Laws

19. United States. Navy Department. Secretary.

Laws of the United States in Relation to the Naval Establishment, and the Marine Corps. Collected and Arranged by Order of the Secretary of the Navy, from the Laws of the United States, to the End of the First Session of the Nineteenth Congress. *Washington: Printed by Davis & Force, 1826. xxiii, [13]–198 p., 18 cm.*

The **NUC** cites five printings of compiled naval laws. The recorded printings are 1814, 1826 (165 pages), 1826 (198 pages), 1841, and 1843.

Shoemaker and Cooper, #27157. **NUC** (Connecticut College, Georgetown University, Library of Congress, Navy Department Library, New York State Library). **OCLC** (15).

[1827]

Manning of a 24-Gun Warship

20. Gauntt, Charles.

Watch, Quarter and Station Bill, of the United States Ship Warren, of 24 Guns: Lawrence Kearny Esq'r, Commander; As Arranged at Syracuse, Sicily. By Charles Gauntt, First Lieutenant, May 14th, 1827. *[Philadelphia: Printed by Charles Stockton Gauntt, 1837]. [3], 4–74 p. including page of hand-colored signal flags and unnumbered p. 73A, 19 cm.*

A sterling little publication, it gives the name and rank of every member of USS *Warren* in 1827 within a diagram format that shows capacity and location where serving. The printing history of this piece is remarkable. The verso of the title page carries the following note descriptive of that history: "For a private purpose, in compliance with his father's wishes, and for his own amusement, this book was arranged and printed by Charles Stockton Gauntt, [self taught,] at 13½ years of age. Philadelphia, 1837." Page 73 carries boat signals, a series of hand-colored flags.

Sabin (not recorded). **NUC** (Navy Department Library, Yale University). **OCLC** (Navy Department Library).

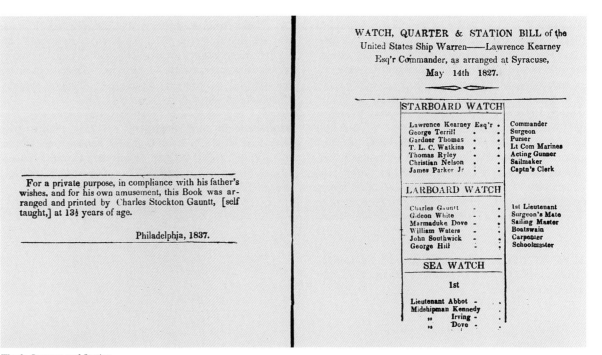

Watch, Quarter and Station Bill printed by 13½-year-old Charles Gauntt

{1838}

Lady Rebuts Newspaper Attack
Upon the Navy

21. Kenney, Lucy.

A Letter Addressed to Martin Van Buren, President of the United States, in Answer to the Late Attack upon the Navy by the Official Organ of the Government. *[Washington: 1838]. 6, 6 p., 21 cm.*

"Sir: I have read with astonishment and indignation the late libel and calumny of the Globe upon the character and standing of the navy, that noble arm of our national defence.... The 'whole' navy has been the object of this slander and abuse. Old and meritorious officers have been abused, insulted, and vilified, and the faults of the few have been made to attach to the many.... I shall now pass to the most exceptionable part of the libel, ... [t]he charge that the officers 'had adopted the maxims and principles of tinkers and cobblers.'" The second six pages of the pagination is "A Satire. Being a Rejoinder to a Reply by Mrs. E. Runnells to My Letter in Vindication of the Navy." There is another issue of this tract that paginates "8, 7 p." Only the Library of Congress copy is located by the **NUC**. The second piece by Kenney is a reply to Eliza B. Runnells who had replied to Kenney's *Letter Addressed to Martin Van Buren with a Reply to a Letter Addressed to Mr. Van Buren, President of the United States, Purporting To Be Written by Miss Lucy Kenney, the Whig Missionary,* 1838 (see **Sabin,** #74141).

Sabin, #37451. **NUC** (Library of Congress, Navy Department Library). **OCLC** (Navy Department Library, University of South Carolina).

{1842}

Inquiry into Reorganization
of the Navy

22. By an Observer.

An Inquiry into the Necessity and General Principles of Reorganization in the United States Navy, with an Examination of the True Sources of Subordination. By an Observer. *Baltimore: Printed and Published by John Murphy, 146 Market Street, 1842. [2], [3]–46 p., original blank leaf, 21 cm.*

"We propose to show, that the spirit, if not the letter of our present naval organization, is utterly inconsistent with the spirit of our institutions, and with the character of our people.... We expect to arrive at the following conclusions: that the naval service is divided into two classes, an entirely irresponsible, commanding, and an equally unprotected, commanded, class.... We now proceed to examine the system of government, at present in operation over the United States navy."

Rinderknecht and Bruntjen, #42–2543. **Sabin** (not recorded). **NUC** (Library of Congress, Pennsylvania Historical Society). **OCLC** (Boston Athenaeum, Howard University, Library of Congress, Navy Department Library, Williams College).

{1850}

Seeking a Navy "Republican" in
Its Organization

23. Officers. Line and Staff.

Suggestions upon Naval Reform by a Few Sea Officers of Both the Line and Staff. *[1850]. 20 p., 22 cm.*

This tract concludes: "The essential reforms needed to render the Navy an economical and efficient military body, republican in its organization, is to graduate appointments to the service in proportion to vacancies occurring, and to avoid the absurdity of the junior corps being filled by old and inefficient men. To create a naval public opinion, and abolish a blind seniority rule, by the grades saying who of their number are most fit for advancement. The separation of staff corps from the line, giving each its appropriate honors and rewards. Short and active cruising."

Sabin, #93477. **NUC** (Duke University, Huntington Library, Newberry Library in Chicago). **OCLC** (Adelphi University, Navy Department Library, Princeton University, University of Delaware).

{1852}

Impact of Steam on Naval Force Deployment

24. Du Pont, Commander Samuel Francis (1803-1865).

Report on the National Defences, by Commander S.F. Du Pont. *Washington: Printed by Gideon & Co., 1852. 28 p., 22 cm.*

"In 1851 Du Pont made a valuable report to the secretary of war on the national defenses, in which he discussed the effect on them of the 'new element,' of steam. The report was highly commended by Sir Howard Douglas the British expert on naval gunnery."—**DAB.** Du Pont concludes his report with: "It would be ill suited, indeed, to the spirit of this nation to retain its naval forces in its own waters during a war, especially if that war was with a naval power. Steam, this new element in the affairs of the world, has very materially changed our position with reference to other nations.... These United States have hitherto been advancing the general cause of human liberty, by an active and progressive peace; but do not events abroad more and more indicate that we may, at no distant day, be forced, in our own defence, to aid this cause of freedom by an active war?" This copy belonged to Admiral George Henry Preble and bears his signature on the title page.

DAB (3), 529–33. **Sabin,** #21388. **NUC** (14). **OCLC** (19).

{1852}

First Navy Surgeon General
Reforming the "Naval Institutions of a Republic"

25. Wood, William Maxwell (1809-1880).

The Naval Institutions of a Republic: An Address Written for the Irving Literary Institute, of the City of Erie, Pa. By Wm. Maxwell Wood, M.D., Surgeon U.S. Navy. *Buffalo: George H. Derby and Co., 1852. viii, [9]–63 p., 18.5 cm.*

"Reform; naval reform is the general cry. Every rank and grade of the navy calls for it. Those who hold the position of command, say; there is no efficient discipline, and we have more trouble with officers than with men. Put two gentlemen of the highest grade in the navy on board ship—one to command the ship, and the other to command the squadron to which she belongs—and even though they both be men of good sense, and good feeling, the ill-defined position of each soon leads to discord and dissension; and, if the government is not burdened, and the service disgraced by a court martial, one is compelled to abandon the duty... and to return to his home.... To effect reform in the navy, the subject must be taken up by the people; if left to navy boards, it is too apt to be lost in the influence of preconceived opinions."—**Preface.** Wood apparently struck some concern, for the following year his tract was reprinted. Wood began his naval service on May 10, 1829, serving in the steamer *Poinsett* during the Seminole war in 1838–'41. He was "appointed fleet-surgeon of the Pacific squadron in 1843, and brought the first intelligence of... the Mexican war... to Commodore Sloat.... He was fleet surgeon of the East India squadron in 1856–'58 and present at the capture of the Barrier forts in Canton River, China.... On 1 July, 1869, he was appointed surgeon-general of the navy."—**Appleton.**

Appleton (6), 598. **Sabin** (not recorded). **NUC** (Cornell University, Huntington Library, Library Company of Philadelphia, Library of Congress). **OCLC** (8).

{1854}

"When the Storm Comes"
The Historic Debate over Military Readiness

26. Woodhull, Maxwell.

[Our Navy: What It Was, Now Is, and What It Should Be]. *Washington: H. Polkinhorn, Printer, [1854]. [1]–10 p., 25 cm.*

"Shall our Navy be called the Glory or the Shame of the Republic?... The nations of Europe are just on the eve of engaging in a general war... and boastfully announce that *they will act in concert also in such interference as they may deem it prudent to make in the affairs of the Western hemisphere!* They evidently have a design upon Cuba.... [A] bill for the creation of six steam frigates has been introduced in both houses of Congress... but Congressmen are too dilatory in voting the appropriations for these steam frigates, not dreaming, perhaps, that it will *take two years* at least to complete each one.... Put the nation, its Navy, and its defenses in a position consistent with its importance, its dignity, and its great interests. These are the truths. Read, reflect, and act, so that when the storm comes our government may be found 'Semper Paratus.' " The tract bears the Latin caption title, *Aluid est Ventilare, aluid Pugnare.*

Sabin, #105110. **NUC** (Harvard University Library, Library of Congress, New York Public Library). **OCLC** (Navy Department Library, Virginia Historical Society Library).

{1855}

First Published Naval Academy Graduation Address
Delivered by One of Navy's Greatest Scientists

27. Davis, Charles Henry (1807-1877).

Address to the Graduating Class of the United States Naval Academy. By Commander Charles Henry Davis . . . *Cambridge: Metcalf and company, 1855. 32 p., 23 cm.*

It was on June 10, 1854, that the "first formal graduation exercises were held at the Naval Academy."—**Cooney.** This graduation address is the earliest one located for Annapolis following 1854. The speech was delivered by Charles Henry Davis, who later attained the rank of rear admiral and was considered "one of the navy's greatest scientists in hydrographic studies and surveys from about 1842 to 1856 . . . [a] planner and organizer of naval strategy during early months of the Civil War."—**Cogar.** Davis notes the opportunities of a peace-time Navy: "If a state of war is the period which subjects the qualifications of officers to the severest test, yet a state of peace is by no means deficient in interest. The opportunities of doing good by protecting commerce, by assisting our countrymen abroad, and by relieving misfortune in various forms, are among the most cherished privileges of the Navy. In time of peace, Navies constitute the police of the high seas." Commander Louis M. Goldsborough presided over the first (10 June 1854) graduation of the United States Naval Academy, as such. Neither the **NUC** nor the **OCLC** records a printed graduation address by Goldsborough.

Cogar (1), 41–43. **Howes** (not recorded). **Cooney,** 71. **Sabin,** #18807. **NUC** (Library Company of Philadelphia, Library of Congress, New York Public Library). **OCLC** (Arkansas Technical University Library, Harvard University Library, Library of Congress, Navy Department Library, State Historical Society of Wisconsin Library, SUNY at Stony Brook, United States Naval Academy Library).

{1864}

Should the Marine Corps Be Transferred to the Army?
Naval Officer Views in 1864

28. Harris, John (c.1795-1864).

Letters from Naval Officers in Reference to the United States Marine Corps. *Washington, D.C.: Franck Taylor, 1864. 14–39 p., printed front wrapper, 21.5 cm.*

Colonel John Harris, commandant of the Marine Corps, had in 1863 solicited letters from naval officers on the congressional resolution that the Marine Corps be transferred "to the army as an additional regiment." Here he has published the thoughts of Farragut, Du Pont, Shubrick, Lardner, Porter, Paulding, Breese, Dahlgren, Pearson, Radford, Wilkes, Turner, Palmer, Dornin, Pope, and other officers at the rank of admiral and commodore as well as the comments of a group of officers to the rank of lieutenant. "Harris oversaw the deployment of marines through the first three years of the Civil War, in which they continued their traditional distinguished service aboard the navy's fighting ships but saw little action ashore."—**Webster.**

Sabin, #40591. **Webster,** 166. **NUC** (not recorded). **OCLC** (8).

{1872}

Admiral Porter Argues for the Retention of the Grades of Admiral and Vice Admiral

29. Porter, David D[ixon] (1813-1891).

Letter from Admiral David D. Porter: On the Subject of Senate bill No. 848, Entitled "A Bill for the Reduction of the Number and Grades of Officers of the Navy, and for Other Purposes." *Washington, D.C.: 1872. 8 p., 22 cm.*

"After the Civil War, the U.S. Navy lagged behind while other navies were making steady progress with steam and iron. For this Admiral David D. Porter was partly responsible; he laid up the cruiser *Wampanoag*, the fastest vessel afloat, and tried to keep the Navy's scattered cruisers under sail as far as possible."—**DAH.** Whatever Porter's thoughts concerning sail versus steam, he felt strongly about retention of high rank in the Navy, arguing for retention of the grades of vice admiral and admiral. Porter's letter is here promulgated as Senate Miscellaneous Document No. 122 (42d Congress, 2d Session).

DAH (Concise), 998. **NUC** (not recorded). **OCLC** (Navy Department Library).

Timber Shed and Mould Loft,
New York Navy Yard, 1876

Photographs of the New York Navy Yard
USS *Vermont* at Dockside

30. Anonymous.

Photographs. U.S. Naval Centennial Exhibit. Navy Yard, New York. *[New York: 1876]. [1] p., 22 original photographs on original heavy board mounts. 38 x 48 cm.*

A wonderful piece of pictorial history from the New York Navy Yard, this collection is in the original binding that bears on the front board in gilt the entitlement as in the main entry above. The photographs are preceded by a single page of text that reads: "Hon. George M. Robeson, Secretary of the Navy. Rear-Admiral Thornton A. Jenkins, Representative of the Navy Department at the International Centennial Exhibition of 1876, at Fairmont Park, Philadelphia, Pa." The photographs depict the following from the New York Navy Yard as seen circa 1876: Commandant's House, Officer's House, Officer's House, Officer's House, Officer's Houses, Civil Engineer's Office, Lyceum, Receiving Store, Ship House "D," Ship House "E," Ship Carpenters Mill & Joiners Shop, Ordnance & Navigation Offices & Store, Chain Cable Store & Rigging Loft, Cooperage, Steam Engineering Receiving Store, Smithery, Plumbers Shop and Boiler Shop, Ordnance Machine Shop, Timber Shed and Mould Loft, Timber Shed, Timber Shed, and USS *Vermont*.

NUC (not recorded). **OCLC** (Navy Department Library).

{1876}

14 Photographs of the Navy Department Centennial Exhibition

31. [Centennial Photographic Company].

Photographic Views of the Naval Department of the United States International Centennial Exhibition of 1876. *[Philadelphia: Centennial Photographic Company, 1876]. 2 printed leaves on stiff board, 14 original photographs mounted on stiff board, 37 x 42 cm.*

This series of 14 original mounted photographs by Edward L. Wilson and W. Irving Adams consists of two exterior views and 12 interior views. The exterior views depict the transit of Venus instruments. The interior views depict display cases, a case of prints and photographs, ropewalk products, a uniform in a display case, flags, and artifacts from Siam. The **NUC** calls for just 13 photographic plates.

NUC (Library of Congress). **OCLC** (Navy Department Library).

The Centennial Exhibit, Philadelphia, 1876, featuring boilers, inclined steam engine, and portrait of Navy Admiral David G. Farragut

Centennial exhibit of Navy ordnance, Philadelphia, 1876

[1876]

6 Photographs of the Navy Department Centennial Exhibition

32. [Centennial Photographic Company].

Photographic Views of the Naval Department of the United States International Centennial Exhibition of 1876. *[Philadelphia: Centennial Photographic Company, 1876]. 2 printed leaves on stiff board, 6 original photographs mounted on stiff board, 61 x 72 cm.*

This series of six photographs is in larger format than the preceding series. The Navy Department copy is in its original binding. The folio photographic plates, by Edward L. Wilson and W. Irving Adams, consist of two exterior views and four interior views. Exterior views show the exhibition building before which are seen a double-turreted gun and various pieces of ordnance. Interior views present a masted warship built to a scale of approximately one-eighth; the masted warship with sails set and surrounded by ordnance and a torpedo; flags, gatling gun, and ordnance; and a propulsion plant.

NUC (Library of Congress). **OCLC** (Navy Department Library).

{1878}

Relation of Commerce and Naval Force Impetus for First Western Commercial Treaty with Korea

33. Shufeldt, Robert Wilson (1822–1895).

The Relation of the Navy to the Commerce of the United States: A Letter Written by Request of Hon. Leopold Morse, M.C., Member of Naval Committee, House of Representatives by R.W. Shufeldt, Commodore U.S.N., Washington. *Washington: J.L. Ginck, 1878. 10 p., 23 cm.*

Shufeldt had "advocated the use of the navy in extending American commerce ... and persuaded James Gillespie Blaine, then secretary of state, of the possibilities of a treaty with Korea ... [which] had not yet opened relations with any western power.... [He] was back in China in June 1881 as naval attaché and with full power to negotiate a treaty ... finally drawn up, [and] signed May 22, 1882.... Much more comprehensive than any previous American treaty with eastern nations, it established diplomatic relations, extraterritoriality, and privileges to Americans of trade and residence in open ports. The treaty was wholly the result of Shufeldt's initiative, pertinacity, and genuine diplomatic skill; it was the great achievement of his career."—**DAB.**

DAB (9), 139–40. **NUC** (Library of Congress, Navy Department Library, New York Public Library, Smithsonian Institution, State Historical Society of Wisconsin). **OCLC** (Johns Hopkins University, Library of Virginia, Navy Department Library, Smithsonian Institution).

{1881}

"New Navy" Vessels

34. Pitman, Pulsifer (compiler).

Compilation of Annual Naval Appropriation Laws from 1883 to 1903, Including Provisions for the Construction of All Vessels of the "New Navy." Compiled by Pitman Pulsifer, Clerk Committee on Naval Affairs, United States Senate. *Washington: Government Printing Office, 1904. 447 p., 24 cm.*

"In 1881, Secretary of the Navy Hunt began the movement for the 'New Navy' of steel ships. It resulted in the 'White Squadron' of the *Atlanta, Boston,* and *Chicago,* and the despatch boat *Dolphin.*"—**DAH.** This compilation of legislation and tables of vessel construction by Pitman is a basic source on the movement from the "Old Navy" to the "New Navy" and on the new ship construction involved in the transition.

DAH (Concise), 998. **NUC** (Harvard University Library, Library of Congress, New York Public Library, Naval Observatory). **OCLC** (Kent College of Law, Marine Corps Research Center, Navy Department Library, Texas Tech, U.S. Army Leavenworth).

{1895}

One of the Earliest Naval Reserve Conventions

35. Association of Naval Militias of the United States.

Record of the Convention of Officers of the Naval Militia Organizations of the United States: Held On Board the U.S.S Ship "New Hampshire," at New York, May 3d and 4th, 1895 *[New York?: The Association, 1895?]. 83 p., 23 cm.*

The earliest publication of this association in the **NUC** is dated 1896. The meeting documented by this tract is cited in introductory materials as "our first meeting." It is apparently the first meeting of this naval reserve association, perhaps, the first formal naval reserve convention. Contents include "The Development of a Naval Militia" by Commander Jacob W. Miller (pp. 13–22); "The Relation of the Naval Militia to the State" by Lieutenant E.V. Raynolds (pp. 23–29); "The Necessity of Engineer Divisions in the Naval Militia" (pp. 30–38); "What Is the Best Form of Organization for a Naval Militia Force?" (pp. 38–48); "Naval Militia Signaling" by Chief Quartermaster Frank B. Anderson (pp. 49–53); and "Report on the Type of Boat Best Suited to the Need of the Naval Militia" by Lieutenant William B. Duncan (pp. 65–67).

NUC (not recorded). **OCLC** (Navy Department Library).

{1895}

National Association of Civil War Naval Veterans

36. Simmons, William.

History of the National Association of Naval Veterans from the First to the Tenth Annual Convention Inclusive. By William Simmons. *Philadelphia: Dunlap Print. Co., 1895. 161 p., frontispiece, portraits, 22 cm.*

This is apparently the first national association of Civil War naval veterans. "As its title indicates, it treats of the origin and progress of the association during the first ten years of its existence.... The publication of the proceedings of each convention and appointments of each senior officer was at first complicated; this we found would require two volumes.... The proceedings are therefore prepared in a condensed form and only such matter used as will, we believe, prove generally interesting to all concerned. The portraits of all senior officers are included, except two."—**Preface.**

Harbeck, 8. **NUC** (Boston Public Library, Free Library of Philadelphia, Library of Congress, New York Public Library, Pennsylvania Historical Society, Princeton University, Western Reserve Historical Society). **OCLC** (18).

{1895}

First Compilation of Naval Reserve Laws

37. United States. Naval Militia.

Laws and Regulations, State and National Relating to the Naval Militia. *Washington: Government Printing Office, 1895. 52 p., tables, 23 cm.*

In a prefatory and printed letter of transmittal, Assistant Secretary of the Navy William McAdoo establishes the pioneer nature of this publication with his note that the "necessity for such publication has been felt for some time in this office, owing to the frequent inquiries which are made for the information which it contains." Section 1 prints the state laws and regulations; Section 2, the national laws and regulations. States included are California, Connecticut, Georgia, Illinois, Louisiana, Maryland, Massachusetts, Michigan, New Jersey, New York, North Carolina, Pennsylvania, Rhode Island, South Carolina, Vermont, and Virginia.

NUC (Navy Department Library). **OCLC** (Harvard University Library, Navy Department Library, United States Naval Academy Library, University of Minnesota Law Library).

{1897}

"We Ask for a Great Navy"

38. Roosevelt, Theodore (1858-1919).

"To Be Prepared for War Is the Most Effectual Means to Promote Peace." Address of Hon. Theodore Roosevelt, Assistant Secretary of the Navy before the Naval War College, Newport, R.I., Wednesday, June 2, 1897. *Washington: Navy Branch, Government Printing Office, 1897. [2], 3–24 p., 22.5 cm.*

Roosevelt concludes: "[W]e ask for a great navy, ... the possession of such a navy is the surest guarantee of peace." The body of his speech is divided into captioned sections that include "Battle Ships Safer Than Arbitration, Men Who Protest Against a Navy," "Our Chief Task to Build a Navy," "The Merrimacs of Foreign Nations Already Built," "Our Main Reliance a Navy, Monroe Doctrine Idle Without a Powerful Navy," and "A Navy Would Not Render Us Overbearing." As Assistant Secretary of the Navy, Roosevelt "advocated a strong military service for the United States and acted to achieve his aim, sometimes circumnavigating or assuming the authority of his superior."—**Webster.**

Webster, 358. **NUC** (Huntington Library, Library of Congress). **OCLC** (Navy Department Library).

[1899]

Early Argument for Naval Reserve

39. Britton, Edward E[arl] (1859-1921).

For a United States Volunteer Militia and a United States Naval Militia. *[Brooklyn, N.Y.]: E.E. Britton, [1899]. 63 p., 24 cm.*

"From the latter part of the nineteenth century, the cost of maintaining regular navies was rapidly rising. To provide a means of augmenting the regular establishment in time of war, major maritime powers established the policy of training civilian volunteers. Such a move began in the United States in the 1880s."—**Cogar.** On May 17, 1888, Massachusetts became "the first state to organize a naval militia."—**Sweetman. Cooney** calls this "the beginning of the modern U.S. Naval Reserve." Congressional support was provided on March 2, 1891, in the form of legislation under which the Secretary of the Navy could provide for arms and munitions. "Several states added naval branches to their existing militia forces and by 1894 twenty-five such branches had been created."—**Cogar.** On August 3, 1894, Congress followed with legislation providing for the loan of Navy vessels to naval militia units. During the Spanish-American War, the U.S. Auxiliary Navy Force was constituted. On February 16, 1914, Congress "gave the Navy Department the same powers and responsibilities for the state naval militia as the War Department had for the National Guard units."—**Cogar.**

Cogar (2), xviii. **Cooney,** 176. **Neeser** (2), 21. **Sweetman,** 98. **NUC** (New York Public Library). **OCLC** (Navy Department Library, New York State Library).

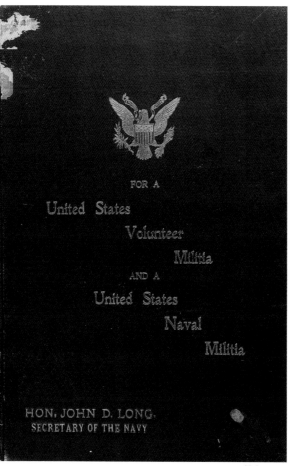

Title cover

[1900]

War Code for the "New Navy"

40. Stockton, Charles Herbert (1845-1924).

The Laws and Usages of War at Sea: A Naval War Code, Prepared by Captain Charles H. Stockton, United States Navy, President of the Naval War College, and Prescribed for the Use of the Navy. *Washington: Government Printing Office, 1900. 27 p., 19 cm.*

"This code of naval warfare was also issued as General order 551, 1900, of the Navy Dept."—**NUC.** Stockton "attained a proficiency in international law which led to his lecturing on that subject."—**DAB.** This war code was promulgated while Stockton was president of the Naval War College and approved by the President of the United States. Its sections are Hostilities (1), Belligerents (2), Belligerent and Neutral Vessels (3), Hospital Ships— the Shipwrecked, Sick, and Wounded (4), The Exercise of the Right of Search (5), Contraband of War (6), Blockade (7), The Sending In of Prizes (8), and Armistice, Truce, and Capitulations, and Violations of the Laws of War (9).

DAB (9), 41–42. **NUC** (Brown University, Duke University, Harvard University Library, New York Public Library, Philadelphia Bar Association, State Department Library, University of Michigan, University of Virginia Law Library). **OCLC** (11).

Early Analysis of Barbary Powers

41. [Morgan, John].

A Compleat History of the Piratical States of Barbary, viz. Algiers, Tunis, Tripoli and Morocco. Containing the Origin, Revolutions, and Present States of These Kingdoms, Their Forces, Revenues, Policy, and Commerce. Illustrated with a Plan of Algiers, and a Map of Barbary. By a Gentleman Who Resided There Many Years in a Public Character. *London: R. Griffiths, 1750. xiv, 368 p., map (folding), plan (folding), 21 cm.*

This early account of the Barbary states includes discussion of their military forces and policies. It is quite probable that the book was consulted by American leaders of the post-Revolutionary War period who confronted the Barbary problem.

NUC (Duke University, Harvard University Library, Library Company of Philadelphia, New York Public Library, Peabody Institute, University of Michigan, University of Pennsylvania, Victoria Public Library in Canada). **OCLC** (17).

Early Justification for Impressing American Seamen

42. Butler, Charles (1750-1832).

An Essay on the Legality of Impressing Seamen, by Charles Butler. *London: Printed for T. Cadell, 1778. xi, 138 p., 22 cm.*

Utilizing press gangs and boarding parties, Great Britain forcibly gained seamen to man its men-of-war. It was during the period 1790 to 1815 that the problem became significant for the United States. It is estimated that 10,000 American seamen were impressed into British service. Of that figure, probably only 10 percent were British citizens, deserters from the Royal Navy. "American protest against impressment dates from 1787 [and] . . . it came to assume first place in American diplomacy. . . . In 1812 Congress alleged impressment to be the principal cause of war. . . . Impressment of seamen has been, since 1815, nothing but an historical curiosity."—**DAH.**

DAH (Concise), 449–50. **Sabin** (not recorded). **NUC** (Boston Athenaeum, Harvard University Library, Library of Congress, Navy Department Library, New York Public Library, University of Indiana, University of South Carolina). **OCLC** (10).

[1794]

Origin of Rupture Between Algiers and United States

43. Carey, Mathew (1760-1839).

A Short Account of Algiers, and of Its Several Wars with Spain, France, England, Holland, Venice, and Other Powers of Europe, from the Usurpation of Barbarossa and the Invasion of the Emperor Charles V to the Present Time. With a Concise View of the Origin of the Rupture between Algiers and the United States. To Which Is Added, a Copious Appendix, Containing Letters from Captains Penrose, M'Shane, and Sundry Other American Captives, with a Description of the Treatment Those Prisoners Experienced. Second Edition, Improved. *Philadelphia: Printed for Mathew Carey, 1794. [2], [3]–50, [2-adv.] p., map (folding), 23 cm.*

Pages 33–50 deal with America and Algiers and American prisoners.

DAB (2), 489–91. **Evans,** #26733. **Sabin,** #80579. **NUC** (14). **OCLC** (13).

[1797]

1797 Account of American Captives of a Barbary Power

44. Stevens, James Wilson.

A Historical and Geographical Account of Algiers; Comprehending a Novel and Interesting Detail of Events Relative to the American Captives. By James Wilson Stevens. *Philadelphia: Printed by Hogan & M'Elroy, 1797. xi, [13]–304, [6] p., folding frontispiece, 17 cm.*

"In rendering an account of this famous regency who have so long signalised themselves by their villainy, . . . perspicuity instead of elegance and the complete development of TRUTH have been his [author's] primary objects. . . . The work . . . exhibits a more circumstantial detail of Algerine affairs of a recent date than was ever before published, and will we presume afford the American reader a tolerable idea of this famous piratical regency, to which the United States have lately had the mortification of becoming tributary. It comprehends, besides an ample account of the late American negociation, a variety of original observations upon the government, fortifications, customs and manners, punishments, religion, &c. of the Algerines; and for this original matter the public are under considerable obligations to Mr. ISAAC BROOKS, a gentleman of veracity and intelligence, who was one of the unfortunate number who were subjected to the miseries of unparalleled servitude. . . . [T]he author has recorded events which are recent in memory of all the captives."—**Preface.**

Evans, #32877. **Sabin,** #91534. **NUC** (16). **OCLC** (32).

[1798]

Humiliation and Impressment on USS *Baltimore*

45. Phillips, Isaac.

An Impartial Examination of the Case of Captain Isaac Phillips, Late of the Navy, and Commander of the United States Sloop of War Baltimore, in 1798. Compiled from Original Documents and Records, with the Proceedings upon His Application to Be Restored to His Rank in the United States Navy. *Baltimore: Printed by B. Edes, 1825. 119 p., 22 cm.*

On November 16, 1798, off Havana, Cuba, and under command of Captain Isaac Phillips, the U.S. war sloop *Baltimore* was stopped by a British squadron. Five American seamen were impressed from her into service in the Royal Navy. "Phillips was dismissed from the U.S. Navy in January 1799. The offense charged against him was that while in command of the *Baltimore* convoying a fleet of merchantmen, he allowed 55 [sic] members of his crew to be taken by Captain Loring in command of a British squadron."—**NUC.** The numbers in this episode are sometimes confusing. Fifty-five seamen from the American warship were taken by the British Captain Loring but only five were kept, the remaining 50 returned to *Baltimore.* Secretary of the Navy Stoddert's very cutting letter to Captain Phillips included in this tract, notes

'... it is impossible to find an excuse for some parts of your conduct; among these, it will be sufficient to mention your tame submission to the orders of the British lieutenant, on board your own ship. If you could not have resisted the assumption of your command on your own ship, by that officer, a point not to be admitted, surely, you might have contented yourself with passive submission; but you descended further, and actually obeyed his orders, to have all hands called, and to give him a list of their names. Under circumstances so degrading, it is improper that you should hold a commission in the Navy service."

Cooney, 19. **Howes** (not recorded). **Neeser** (2), 4. **Sabin,** #62493. **Shoemaker,** #21884. **NUC** (American Antiquarian Society, Library Company of Philadelphia, Library of Congress, Navy Department Library, New York Public Library, Pennsylvania Historical Society, University of Indiana, University of Tennessee at Knoxville, Yale University). **OCLC** (17).

{1803–1805}

"American Tars in Tripoli"
Prison Life of USS *Philadelphia* Captives

46. Ray, William (1771-1827).

Horrors of Slavery: or, The American Tars in Tripoli; Containing an Account of the Loss and Capture of the United States Frigate Philadelphia; Treatment and Sufferings of the Prisoners; Description of the Place; Manners, Customs, &c. of the Tripolitans; Public Transactions of the United States with That Regency, Including Gen. Eaton's Expedition; Interspersed with Interesting Remarks, Anecdotes, and Poetry, on Various Subjects; Written during Upwards of Nineteen Months' Imprisonment and Vassalage among the Turks. By William Ray. *Troy: Printed by Oliver Lyon, for the author, 1808. 298 p., illus, 17 cm.*

During October 1803, while commanding USS *Philadelphia* in operations against Tripoli, Captain Bainbridge and his crew were captured in Tripoli harbor after the inadvertent grounding of their warship. They remained imprisoned until 1805. The author was one of the imprisoned crew.

Harbeck, 14. **Howes** (not recorded). **Sabin,** #68034. **Shaw and Shoemaker,** #16035. **OCLC** (25).

{1804}

"The Most Daring Act of the Age"—
Lord Nelson

47. United States. Navy Department. Secretary.

Burning Frigate Philadelphia at Tripoli: Letter from the Secretary of the Navy, Transmitting, Pursuant to a Resolution of the House of Representatives, the Names of the Officers and Seamen On Board the Ketch Intrepid, in the Attack on the Frigate Philadelphia, in the year 1804, in the Harbor of Tripoli. *Washington: Printed by Gales & Seaton, 1826. 11 p., 22 cm.*

On February 16, 1804, Lieutenant Stephen Decatur with 80 volunteers clandestinely slipped into Tripoli harbor, where he destroyed the captured USS *Philadelphia*. Admiral Lord Nelson of England called this feat "the most daring act of the age." For his valor, Decatur was promoted at age 25 to the rank of captain, the youngest ever to hold that rank. Subsequently, during 1815, Decatur "successfully ended corsair raids from Algiers, Tunis, and Tripoli, ended U.S. payment of tribute to the Barbary states, and secured reparations for damages to U.S. shipping. At a dinner given in his honor shortly after his triumphal return to the United States, he proposed his famous toast: 'Our country! In her intercourse with foreign nations may she always be in the right; but our country, right or wrong.'"—**Webster.**

DAB (3), 187–89. **Harbeck,** 13 (variant). **Sweetman,** 21–22. **Webster,** 97–98. **Shoemaker and Cooper,** #26888. **NUC** (Navy Department Library). **OCLC** (Navy Department Library, Texas A&M University, United States Naval Academy).

Chesapeake and *Leopard* Affair
British Correspondence with Madison and Monroe

48. Great Britain. Parliament. House of Commons.

Papers Presented to the House of Commons, Relating to the Encounter between His Majesty's Ship Leopard, and the American Frigate Chesapeake. Ordered, by the House of Commons, to Be Printed, 17th February 1809. *London: 1809. 37 p., 34 cm.*

These papers, detailing the June 22, 1807 attack by HMS *Leopard*, 50 guns, on USS *Chesapeake*, 36 guns, were presented to the British Parliament in 1809. Commanded by James Barron, *Chesapeake* was sailing off Hampton Roads, Virginia, and was not cleared for action when she was defeated by *Leopard*. Four United States seamen were taken by the British and impressed into service in the Royal Navy. One was subsequently hanged as a deserter, one died while in British hands, and two were returned to the United States in 1812. Barron was court-martialed for this naval defeat, found guilty, and suspended without pay for five years. This episode raised a furor in the United States. Impressment of American seamen had come to "assume first place in American diplomacy. The climax occurred in 1807 when four men were removed from the frigate *Chesapeake*. In 1812 Congress alleged impressment to be the principal cause of war."—**DAH.** These papers consist of 21 letters and notes that passed between George Canning and G.H. Rose, officials of Great Britain, and James Madison and James Monroe of the United States, and are dated from July 25, 1807, to March 17, 1808.

Cooney, 28. **DAH (Concise),** 449. **Sweetman,** 25–26. **NUC** (Clements Library, Library of Congress, University of California at Berkeley, University of Indiana). **OCLC** (Cleveland Public Library, Navy Department Library, Northwestern University of Michigan, United States Military Academy Library, University of California).

Chesapeake and *Leopard* Affair

49. [Lowell, John] (1769-1840).

Peace without Dishonour—War without Hope. Being a Calm and Dispassionate Enquiry into the Question of the Chesapeake, and the Necessity and Expediency of War. By a Yankee Farmer. *Boston: Printed by Greenough and Stebbins, 1807. 43 p., 24 cm.*

Lowell "took an active part in the political controversies of the day, writing vigorous pamphlets and letters to the press generally supporting the Federalist point of view, and opposing the Embargo, Madison, the 'French alliance,' and the War of 1812."—**DAB.** Lowell notes here that "when therefore, a party of men, from sinister or from honest motives, misrepresent the conduct of a foreign nation, present an unnatural and distorted view of facts, appeal to the publick passions, attempt to silence all opposition, represent our ability to wage war in a most extravagant light, magnify our means of injuring our enemy . . . it is the most solemn duty which a citizen is ever called upon to exercise to correct such false statements."

DAB (6), 465–66. **Harbeck,** 14. **Howes** (not recorded). **Sabin,** #42455. **Shaw and Shoemaker,** #12947. **NUC** (22). **OCLC** (17).

Commodore Barron Is Critized for Harboring "Mutineers"

50. Osborn, J. (publisher).

The Voice of Truth, or, Thoughts on the Affair between the *Leopard and Chesapeake. In a Letter from a Gentleman at New-York to His Friend. New York: Printed for J. Osborn, 1807. 55 p., 21 cm.*

Now it appears to me, that, considering the men were mutineers, commodore Barron acted unwisely, if not illegally, in detaining them. The question respecting the men is no longer, whether they were or were not British subjects, but whether they were or were not mutineers. Mutiny is a crime of so high an order, that it signifies nothing who commits it, whether alien or citizen. An alien may escape from a ship, but an alien has no right to set fire to it, or create a mutiny in it to effect his escape. The navy of England has many foreigners. . . . American ships are swarmed with British seamen. . . . Commodore Barron little knows the duty of a seaman, or the laws of war, if he would suffer a British vessel to detain from him a British subject who had mutinied on board his vessel, and I hazard a conjecture, that no British captain would be guilty of sheltering such an offender."

Howes, V137. **Sabin,** #12491. **Shaw and Shoemaker,** #14143. **NUC** (10). **OCLC** (Boston Athenaeum, Cambridge University, Columbia University, Navy Department Library, United States Naval Academy, University of Connecticut, University of Notre Dame).

Marine Lieutenant's Death during the *Constitution* and *Guerriere* Engagement

51. [Raguet, Condy] (1784-1842).

A Masonic Oration on the Death of Brother William S. Bush, Lieutenant of Marines, Who Was Killed On Board the Frigate Constitution, during Her Engagement with the British Frigate Guerrier [*sic*], on the 19th of August, 1812, As Delivered on the 26th of November Following, Before the Officers of the R.W. Grand Lodge of Pennsylvania, the Officers and Members of Lodge No. 51, of Which the Deceased Was a Member. By the Junior Warden of Said Lodge. Published at the Request of the Brethren. *Philadelphia: Published by Bradford and Innskeep, James Maxwell, printer, November, 1812. 16 p., 22 cm.*

The "first important naval victory of the War of 1812 . . . took place 750 miles east of Boston. . . . [I]n thirty minutes of close action, the *Guerriere* had been totally dismasted. With a high sea running and the gunports rolling under water, Dacres could do nothing but surrender. The next day Hull was obliged to burn the *Guerriere* and return to Boston without his prize. The British lost twenty-three killed and fifty-six wounded, including Dacres; the American loss was only seven killed and seven wounded. The *Constitution* was nearly 50 percent superior in all features—such as size, sail area, weight of broadside, and accuracy of fire—but it was Hull's superior seamanship that made these factors count."—**DAH.**

DAH (Concise), 236. **Howes** (not recorded). **Sabin** (not recorded). **Shaw and Shoemaker,** #26557. **NUC** (9). **OCLC** (63).

{1812–1814}

A Surgeon's Account of Captivity during the War of 1812

52. [Babcock, Amos G.].

A Journal, of a Young Man of Massachusetts, Late a Surgeon On Board an American Privateer, Who Was Captured at Sea by the British . . . and Was Confined First, at Melville Island, Halifax, Then at Chatham, in England, and Last, at Dartmoor Prison. Interspersed with Observations, Anecdotes and Remarks, Tending to Illustrate the Moral and Political Characters of Three Nations. To Which Is Added, a Correct Engraving of Dartmoor Prison, Representing the Massacre of American Prisoners. Written by Himself. *Boston: printed by Rowe & Hooper, 1816. 240 p., frontispiece, 19 cm.*

"A valuable and moving tale of prison life."—**Fredriksen.** "A novel founded on fact."—**Allibone.** The author, captured while serving as surgeon on board the American privateer *Young Man* in January 1813, was Dr. Amos G. Babcock. His journal was edited by Benjamin Waterhouse. The massacre to which he refers occurred on April 6, 1815. Angered by continued imprisonment following conclusion of peace and by poor quality of prison food, the captives demonstrated. The prison commandant called out troops who fired upon the captives, killing seven and wounding sixty.

Allibone (3), 2599. **DAH (Concise),** 277. Fredriksen, #542. **Howes,** W155. Sabin, #102060. **Shaw and Shoemaker,** #39719. **NUC** (34). **OCLC** (29).

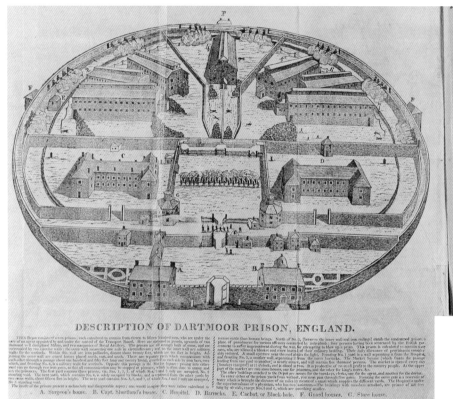

Dartmoor Prison (frontispiece and title page)

"We Have Met the Enemy and They Are Ours," drawn by J.R. Penniman (frontispiece)

1816 Battle Engravings

53. [Bowen, Abel] (1790-1850).

The Naval Monument, Containing Official and Other Accounts of All Battles Fought between the Navies of the United States and Great Britain during the Late War; and an Account of the War with Algiers, with Twenty-five Engravings. To Which Is Annexed a Naval Register of the United States. *Boston: A. Bowen, and sold by Cummings and Hilliard, 1816. [18], 316 [error for 320], p., [2], errata slip, 26 plates, 22 cm.*

The plates illustrating this work, are primarily woodblocks engraved by Abel Bowen after original drawings by M. Corne. Constituting an early iconography of American naval warfare, they include "Constitution's Escape from the British Squadron after a chase of sixty hours," "The Constitution Bearing Down for the Guerriere," "The Constitution in Close Action with the Guerriere," "The Wasp Boarding the Frolic," "The United States and Macedonian," "The Java Surrendering to the Constitution," "The Hornet Blockading the Bonne Citoyenne," "The Hornet Sinking the Peacock," "The Chesapeake & Shannon," "The Enterprize and Boxer," "First View of Com. Perry's Victory," "Plan of the First View of the Battle on Lake Erie," "Second View of Com. Perry's Victory," "Plan of the Second View of the Battle on Lake Erie," "Capture of the Essex," "The Peacock and the Epervier," "The Wasp and the Reindeer," "The Wasp and Avon," "Com. Macdonough's Victory on Lake Champlain Sept. 11th. 1814," "The President Engaging the Endymion, While Pursued by the British Squadron," "The Constitution Taking the Cyane and Levant," "The Hornet and Penguin," and "The Hornet's Escape from a British Seventy-Four."

Groce and Wallace, 70. **Harbeck,** 16. **Howes,** B658. **Neeser** (1), #7985. **Sabin,** #7045. **Shaw and Shoemaker,** #37062. **NUC** (21). **OCLC** (57).

Queen of the Ocean Unqueened
African Americans in Battle of Lake Erie

54. Cobbett, William (1763-1835).

The Pride of Britannia Humbled; or, The Queen of the Ocean Unqueen'd, "by the American Cock Boats"... Illustrated and Demonstrated by Four Letters Addressed to Lord Liverpool, on the Late American War. By Wm. Cobbett, Esq. Including a Number of His Other Most Important Letters, and Arguments, in Defence of the American Republic. To Which Is Added, a Glimpse of the American Victories, on Land, on the Lakes, and on the Ocean. With a Persuasive to Political Moderation... A New Edition. *Philadelphia: Published by William Reynolds, New York, Daniel Griffin [etc.], 1815. 215, [1] p., frontispiece, 19 cm.*

This work was written to "be presented to the American youth by their parents and guardians, for their serious investigation" in understanding the bravery of American arms and the superiority of American government over British government. In describing the Battle of Lake Erie, the following is an interesting extract: "The British were superior in the length and number of their guns, as well as in the number of men. The American fleet was manned with a motley set of beings, Europeans, Africans, Americans from every part of the United States. Full one fourth were blacks.... They were brave—and who could be otherwise under the command of Perry?" The frontispiece is an oval engraving within which appear the portraits of Bainbridge, Decatur, Perry, and Porter.

Howes, C523. **Rosenbach,** 139. **Sabin,** #14011. **Shaw and Shoemaker,** #34380. **NUC** (16). **OCLC** (96).

{1812–1814}

Pioneer Account of Privateer Operations
Illustrated with Fine Full-Page Lithographs

55. Coggeshall, George (1784-1861).

History of the American Privateers, and Letters-of-Marque, during Our War with England in the Years 1812, '13, and '14. Interspersed with Several Naval Battles between American and British Ships-of-War. *New York: The Author, 1856. [56], 438 p., 8 plates, 24 cm.*

"A collection of narratives of the irregular sea-fights of the War of 1812 . . . trustworthy and readable . . . most so when Capt. Coggeshall writes of the exploits of David Porter and the Leo, which he commanded. The work profits by its author's nautical knowledge. . . . For well-nigh half a century practically the only work on the exploits of American privateers."—**Larned.** The illustrations contained in this work are notable. Eight in number, they are tinted lithographs and consist of "Battle between the Constitution and the Guerriere, on the 19th of August 1812"; "Battle between the Schooner Saratoga, and the Brig. Rachel, on the 15th of Dec. 1812"; "Battle between the Schooner Atlas and two British Ships, on the 5th of August 1812"; "Battle between the Schooner Rossie, and the Ship Princess Amelia, on the 16th of Sept. 1812"; "Battle between the Schooner Dolphin, the British Ship Hebe and a Brig off Cape St. Vincent, on the 25th of Jan. 1813"; "Battle between the Schooner Decatur and the Schooner Dominica, on the 5th of August 1813"; "Schooner David Porter, Lying To in Bay of Biscay, Jan. 30th 1814"; and "Battle between the Brig Chasseur, and the Schooner St. Lawrence, off Havanna on the 26th of Feb. 1815."

Howes, C542. **Larned,** #1720. **Sabin,** #14194. **NUC** (31). **OCLC** (96).

War of 1812 sea battle, engraving

British Side of Naval Operations

56. James, William.

A Full and Correct Account of the Chief Naval Occurrences of the Late War between Great Britain and the United States of America; Preceded by a Cursory Examination of the American Accounts of Their Naval Actions Fought Previous to That Period: To Which Is Added an Appendix; with Plates. By William James. *London: Printed for T. Egerton, 1817. xv, 528, ccxvi, [16] p., [3] p. of plates, illus., 22 cm.*

In spite of an uncouth style and bitterly controversially and biased tone, James still remains the standard British authority on this subject; as a rule his statements have been unhesitatingly accepted and reiterated by later writers of his own nationality."—**Larned.**

Howes, J53. **Larned,** #1736. **Sabin,** #35717. **NUC** (29). **OCLC** (93).

Draw by Capt. Porter *Engraved by Ilderfieland*

Mouina,
Chief Warrior of the Taychs.

Nuku Hiva warrior,
engraving, drawn by
Captain David Porter

Pacific Ocean Commerce Raiding Expedition during the War of 1812
First United States Naval Vessel in Pacific

57. Porter, David (1780-1843).

Journal of a Cruise Made to the Pacific Ocean, by Captain David Porter, in the United States Frigate Essex, in the Years 1812, 1813, and 1814. Containing Descriptions of the Cape de Verde Islands, Coasts of Brazil, Patagonia, Chili, and Peru, and of the Gallapagos Islands . . . *Philadelphia: Bradford and Inskeep; [etc., etc.], 1815. 2 vols in one. vii, 263; 169 p., 14 maps and plates, 22 cm.*

"In July 1812 he [Porter] sailed from New York on a cruise during which he took nine prizes, including, on August 13, near Bermuda, the sloop of war *Alert*, 16 [guns], the first British naval vessel captured in the War of 1812. . . . [E]arly in 1813 rounded Cape Horn into the Pacific, making the *Essex* the first U.S. naval vessel to sail those waters. . . . During this voyage he took possession on November 19, 1813, of Nuku Hiva, one of the Marquesas Islands, renaming it Madison Island . . . He was forced to battle fierce Taipi (or Typee) natives to retain his base there."—**Webster.**

Howes, P484. **Harbeck,** 120. **Sabin,** #64218. **Shaw and Shoemaker,** #35674. **Webster,** 328. **NUC** (11). **OCLC** (33).

{1812–1814}

Prisoners of War Incarcerated at Dartmoor

58. United States. President.

Message from the President of the United States Transmitting a Report of the Secretary of State in Obedience to a Resolution of the House of Representatives, of the Twenty-eighth of February Last, of the Number of Impressed American Seamen Confined in Dartmoor Prison: The Number Surrendered, Given Up, or Taken On Board British Vessels Captured during the Late War: Together with Their Places of Residence. *Washington: Printed by William A. Davis, 1816. [6], 5–79 p., 36 cm.*

This is an essential source on American War of 1812 naval prisoners. Secretary of State James Monroe forwarded this report on April 27, 1816, noting: "The paper A, contains a list of such impressed seamen as were transferred from British ships of war to Dartmoor and other prisons in England. B, contains the names of those who were transferred in like manner to prisons in the West-Indies and Nova-Scotia. C, the names of those who were discharged in England from British ships of war since the peace." The document names 1,799 men, providing for each, "By what British man of war, or under what circumstances impressed and detained, Where first confined, Date of release, In what vessel returned to the United States, and Arrived."

Harbeck, 30. **Howes** (not recorded). **Shaw and Shoemaker,** #39553. **NUC** (Clements Library, Columbia University, Library of Congress, Navy Department Library, New York Public Library, Newberry Library). **OCLC** (Navy Department Library, New York Public Library, University of Pennsylvania Library).

{1812–1815}

"All the More Important Reports"

59. Brannan, John.

Official Letters of the Military and Naval Officers of the United States, during the War with Great Britain in the Years 1812, 13, 14 & 15: With Some Additional Letters and Documents Elucidating the History of That Period Collected and Arranged by John Brannan. *Washington City: Printed by Way & Gideon, for the editor, 1823. 510 p., 23 cm.*

"One of the most valuable and comprehensive collections of official dispatches on the American side . . . The papers are printed in verbatim, without comment, and comprise all the more important reports."—**Larned.**

Howes, B722. **Larned,** #1715. **Sabin,** #7411. **Shoemaker,** #11979. **NUC** (31). **OCLC** (106).

{1813}

Cooper Defends Elliott's Conduct and Cowardice or Treachery

60. Cooper, James Fenimore (1789-1851).

The Battle of Lake Erie, or, Answers to Messrs. Burges, Duer and Mackenzie by J. Fenimore Cooper. *Cooperstown: H.&E Phinney, 1843. iv, 117 p., illus., 19 cm.*

"It is a full explanation of the Battle of Lake Erie which took place on September 10, 1813, clearing Captain Elliott Perry's second in command, of the charge of either cowardice or treachery."—**Rosenbach.** "An exposition of disputed points in the battle of Lake Erie, intended not only to clear Capt. Elliott from charges reflecting upon his conduct, but to defend Cooper's *History of the War of 1812* against many hostile critics. The manoeuvres of the two fleets, and especially of the 'Niagara,' are given with great particularity, assisted by diagrams. . . . [I]t is a revelation of Cooper at the climax of the controversial period of his career."—**Larned.**

DAB (2), 400–406. **Larned,** #1721. **Rinderknecht and Bruntjen,** #43-1303. **Rosenbach,** #156. **Sabin,** #16415. **NUC** (37). **OCLC** (62).

Chesapeake and *Shannon* Engagement

61. Story, Joseph (1779-1845).

An Account of the Funeral Honours Bestowed on the Remains of Capt. Lawrence and Lieut. Ludlow, with the Eulogy Pronounced at Salem, on the Occasion, by Hon. Joseph Story. To Which Is Prefixed, an Account of the Engagement between the Chesapeake and Shannon, with Documents Relative to the Same, and Biographical and Poetical Notices . . . Boston: Printed by Joshua Belcher, 1813. 64 p., 22 cm.

"In a 15-minute battle *Chesapeake* was severely damaged and had 61 men killed and 148 wounded, including Capt. [James] Lawrence. Lawrence had sailed from Boston at the challenge of the British; his crew was green and his officers newly assigned. The British had a crew that had been aboard the ship for five years. It was no contest. Severely wounded, Lawrence called out, 'Don't give up the ship.' Lawrence was very well treated by his captors, in return for the compassion he had previously shown to Royal navy prisoners earlier in the war."—**Cooney.** The biography by Washington Irving, in this little known work is one of the scarcest of Irving's works.

Cooney, 36. **DAH** (2), 16. **Harbeck**, 18 (variant). **Howes** (not recorded). **Sabin**, #39355. **Shaw and Shoemaker**, #27647. **NUC** (10). **OCLC** (19).

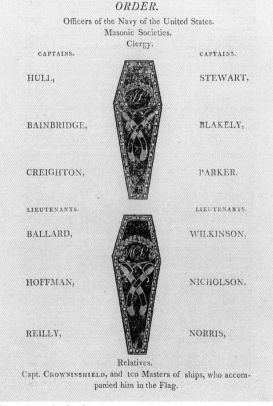

38

ute guns, rendered this part of the solemnities peculiarly grand and impressive. On the bodies being placed upon the hearses, they were covered with those colours which they had so signally honoured, and were conveyed at a suitable distance for the procession to form. At 1 o'clock the procession was formed agreeably to previous arrangements, in the following

ORDER.

Officers of the Navy of the United States.
Masonic Societies.
Clergy.

CAPTAINS.		CAPTAINS.
HULL,		STEWART,
BAINBRIDGE,		BLAKELY,
CREIGHTON,		PARKER.
LIEUTENANTS.		LIEUTENANTS.
BALLARD,		WILKINSON,
HOFFMAN,		NICHOLSON,
REILLY,		NORRIS,

Relatives.
Capt. CROWNINSHIELD, and ten Masters of ships, who accompanied him in the Flag.

Procession order for the funeral of Captain James Lawrence and Lieutenant Augustus C. Ludlow

Combat Poet of *Chesapeake* and *Shannon* Engagement

62. [Weaver, William Augustus] (1797-1846).

Journals of the Ocean; and Other Miscellaneous Poems: By a Seaman . . . New-York: G.C. Morgan, 1826. [1], [vii]-xv, [17]-228 (i.e., 226) p., 19 cm.

"In the poem 'Engagement Between the Chesapeake and the Shannon,' details of this famous battle can be found. Weaver had been wounded repelling boarders from the *Shannon* and was present when were uttered, the dying words from Lawrence' lip. . . .:'brave lads, don't give up the ship.'"—**Skallerup.**

Sabin, #102206. **Shoemaker and Cooper**, #27581. **Skallerup**, 65. **NUC** (8). **OCLC** (14).

See that your Honor you untarnish'd keep
And his who cri'd "O dont give up the ship.,

Book 1. Page 32.

Battle of Lake Erie
(frontispiece, entry 63)

{1813}

Epic Poem on Battle of Lake Erie
Illustrated with Battle Engraving

3. Woodworth, Samuel (1785–1842).

he Heroes of the Lake: A Poem, in Two Books Written in the utumn of 1813. *New York: Printed and published by Woodworth. 1814. 108 p., frontispiece, 15 cm.*

his preface, the author notes that he "is conscious that, ixing facts with fiction, has generally been considered aproper in an epic poem. He is convinced, however, that is objection is founded in nature, and, for reasons which ill appear in the work, has hazarded a violation of the le. The fictions themselves are founded on historical facts, ad here it may be proper to add, that in the introduction personages, in the episodes, character has been aimed , and not a particular history of their lives." Pages 79–108 e historical notes for this epic account in verse of the Bat- e of Lake Erie. The verse is organized into two books. The ontispiece is a charming, patriotic rendition of American d British warships engaged, the view dominated by the ern of USS *Lawrence*, a naval officer with drawn cutlass efiantly athwart the stern, and an American longboat with rge unfurled national banner and a standing naval officer the center. The view of naval battle was engraved by Chi- uet of New York City. It is apparently a depiction of Perry ansferring his flag to *Niagara*. "The battle began a quarter efore noon and lasted until 3 P.M. During its major part the runt was borne by the *Lawrence*. When the vessel had een shot to pieces, all her guns disabled, and of 103 men, ghty-three killed or wounded, Perry transferred his flag to e *Niagara*, which up to this time had taken but a small art in the battle."—**DAB.**

AB (7), 490–92. **Howes** (not recorded). **Sabin.** #31528. haw and Shoemaker (not recorded). **Wegelin,** #1296. UC (11). **OCLC** (Harvard University, Houghton Library; avy Department Library; University of Chicago).

{1814}

Navy Averts Utter Disgrace in Defense of Washington

64. Spectator (pseudonym).

An Enquiry Respecting the Capture of Washington by the British, on the 24th August, 1814; with an Examination of the Report of the Committee of Investigation Appointed by Congress. By Spectator. *Washington City: 1816. 32 p., 24 cm.*

"In July 1814 he [Commodore Joshua Barney] was called to aid in the defense of Washington, D.C. With a small fleet of armed barges he held off the advance of Admiral Sir George Cockburn's fleet, bearing General Robert Ross' army up Chesapeake Bay, for some weeks and, when the enemy eventually eluded him and threatened the capital, he abandoned the barges and marched his small force of about 500 sailors and marines back to Bladensburg, Mary- land, and placed his men, armed with a few ships' guns mounted on carriages, at the center of General William H. Winder's position. The battle on August 24 was a serious defeat for the Americans, who were saved from utter dis- grace only by the valiant resistance offered by Barney's small command."—**Webster. Sabin** notes this tract is "thought to be by John Armstrong," Secretary of War. Pages 19–23 of the tract contain information on Barney and the naval and marine force of 600 men.

Howes (not recorded). **Sabin,** #89139. **Shaw and Shoe- maker,** #38989. **Webster,** 24. **NUC** (8). **OCLC** (11).

{1814}

Peacock and *Epervier* Engagement
After Action Report

65. United States. Navy Department. Secretary.

Letter from the Secretary of the Navy, Transmitting the Offi- cial Account of the Capture of the British Sloop of War Eper- vier: By the United States' Sloop Peacock, Commanded by Captain Lewis Warrington, on the Twenty-ninth April Last. October 1, 1814. Printed by Order of the Senate . . . *Wash- ington City: R.C. Weightman, 1814, 8 p., 21 cm.*

Warrington (1782–1851) was a native of Williamsburg, Vir- ginia. He entered naval service during 1800, when appointed as midshipman. He rose to serve briefly as act- ing Secretary of the Navy in 1844. He is "remembered for his victory of April 29th, 1814, off Cape Canaveral, when he captured the British brig *Epervier*."—**DAB.** "This battle was hailed as a tribute to American gunnery. *Epervier* had 45 shot holes in her port side, and five feet of water in her hold when the 45 minute battle ended. *Peacock* received not one hit in her hull, and less than an hour after the engagement ended had repaired her rigging and was ready in all respects to fight again."—**USNI Almanac.**

DAB (Concise), 1146. **Shaw and Shoemaker,** #33265. **USNI Almanac,** 120. **Coletta,** 204. **NUC** (Clements Library, Library of Congress, University of Virginia Library). **OCLC** (63).

Official *Wasp* and *Reindeer* Engagement Report
Victor Subsequently Lost at Sea

66. United States. Navy Department. Secretary.

Letter from the Secretary of the Navy, Transmitting the Official Account of the Capture of the British Sloop Reindeer: By the United States' Sloop Wasp, Commanded by Captain Johnston Blakeley, on the Twenty-eighth June Last Printed by Order of the Senate of the United States. *Washington City: Printed by Roger C. Weightman, 1814. 13 p., folding table, 22 cm.*

In this action, the British warship surrendered 19 minutes after the United States sloop of war *Wasp* opened fire. The American commander, Johnston Blakely (1781–1814), following this victory, was lost at sea with his vessel. After engagement with the British brig *Atlanta* in September 1814, east of Madeira, *Wasp* is known to have sailed south, being last heard from on October 9 by Swedish brig *Adonus.*—**DAB.** The folding table is a list of British vessels captured by *Wasp.*

DAB (Concise), 81. **Shaw and Shoemaker,** #33266. **Maclay,** 601. **USNI Almanac,** 121. **NUC** (Clements Library, Library of Congress, Navy Department Library, University of Virginia Library). **OCLC** (64).

Naval Action on Lake Champlain, engraving

[1816]

Temple of American Naval Valor

67. [Kimball, Horace].

The Naval Temple: Containing a Complete History of the Battles Fought by the Navy of the United States. From Its Establishment in 1794, to the Present Time; Including the Wars with France, and with Tripoli, the Late War with Great Britain, and with Algiers. With Elegant Engravings, Representing Battles, &c. *Boston: B. Badger, 1816. vii, [2], [9]–258 p., engraved title page, 6 plates, 22 cm.*

The engraved plates are the "Triumphant return of the American Squadron under Com. Bainbridge from the Mediterranean 1815," "Capt. Sterrett in the Schr. Enterprise paying tribute to Tripoli, August 1801," two views of the Battle of Erie, "Naval Action on Lake Champlain," and "Battle of Plattsburg." At least one bibliographical description of this work cites as many as 20 plates; that number is incorrect. There is on the 1816 first edition a leaf entitled "Description of the Plates," which lists the plates above. In the second edition, also 1816, two additional plates, the "Bombardment of Fort McHenry" and the "U.S. Squadron Before the City of Algiers" appear. The printing described in the main entry is the first edition. It was reissued in 1816, 1831, 1836, 1837, 1840, 1857, and 1858.

Howes, K135. **Sabin,** #2696 (citing second edition of 322 pages). **Shaw and Shoemaker,** #38006. **NUC** (19). **OCLC** (18).

[1821]

Firsthand Account of Pirate Operations

68. Lincoln, Barnabas (1781–1850).

Narrative of the Capture, Sufferings and Escape of Capt. Barnabas Lincoln and His Crew, Who Were Taken by a Piratical Schooner, December, 1821, off Key Largo; Together with Facts Illustrating the Character of Those Piratical Cruisers. Written by Himself. *Boston: Printed by E. Lincoln, 1822. 40 p., 23 cm.*

This is a firsthand account of the kind of piractical activity that led to pirate suppression by employment of American naval forces. In 1816, responding to increasing frequency of pirate attacks in the West Indies, Congress passed legislation for punishment of pirate forces and for naval convoys of United States shipping. Operations against pirates were conducted from 1816 through 1829, "providing training for the Mexican War."—**DAH.** A March 3, 1818 congressional act followed that provided for a war on all piratical cruisers of the Spanish American colonies. On December 20, 1822, Congress authorized a West Indies squadron for repressing piracy, and affording effectual protection to the citizens and commerce of the United States. During naval operations in 1823 against pirates in the West Indies, the paddle-wheeler *Sea Gull* of three guns became the "first steamship in the world to enter combat."—**Sweetman.**

Cooney, 47, 49. **DAH (Concise),** 997. **Howes** (not recorded). **Sabin,** #41242. **Shoemaker,** #9273. **Sweetman,** 41. **NUC** (American Antiquarian Society, Library of Congress, New York State Library). **Neeser** (2), 8. **OCLC** (8).

[1823]

Land Assault on Puerto Rico Precipitates Porter's Court-Martial and Resignation

69. Beale, Robert.

A Report of the Trial of Commodore David Porter, of the Navy of the United States, Before a General Court Martial, Held at Washington, in July, 1825, by Robert Beale, Attorney at Law. To Which Is Added, a Review of the Court's Decision. *Washington City: 1825. iii, iv–viii, [1], 2–244, [1], 2–68 p., 23 cm.*

"In 1823 Porter, whose naval career had begun in 1796 and who had been on board the *Philadelphia* at Tripoli, was sent in command of a squadron to suppress piracy in the West Indies. One of his officers landed at Fajardo in Porto Rico, was imprisoned by the Spanish authorities on the charge of piracy, and Porter, without waiting for instructions or reporting the incident, forced the authorities to apologize (by sending an armed force ashore). For this he was recalled, court-martialed, and suspended for six months. With him on this expedition was his more famous son, David Dixon Porter, who later took part in Farragut's victory in the Civil War and helped capture Vicksburg."—**Rosenbach.** Porter commanded the West India Squadron from 1823 to 1825. As a consequence of this court-martial, which suspended him, Porter resigned and served as commander of the Mexican navy from 1826 to 1829.

Howes (not recorded). **Rosenbach,** #620. **Sabin,** #64222. **Shoemaker,** #19637. **NUC** (13). **OCLC** (36).

{1823–1825}

Suppression of Piracy in the West Indies

70. Strong, E. (publisher).

The Lives and Bloody Exploits of the Most Noted Pirates,
Their Trials and Executions, Including Correct Accounts of
the Late Piracies, Committed in the West Indias, and the
Expedition of Commodore Porter; Also Those Committed
on the Brig Mexican, Who Were Executed at Boston, in
1835. Embellished with Numerous Plates from Original
Designs. *Hartford, Conn.: E. Strong, 1836. [2], [5]–298 p.,*
illus., plates, 19 cm.

Pages 253–83 are "A Correct Account of the Late Piracies
Committed in the West Indies; and the Expedition of Commodore Porter." The foregoing appears on the front of the
initiating half title. The back of the half-title notes: "The
public mind has been much agitated by the depredations
of these enemies of all laws, human and divine. . . . Our
government has taken a forward step to arrest these free-
booters in their blood-thirsty projects, and no doubt the
expedition which was under the command of that gallant
officer, Commodore Porter, has done much towards
putting down this nefarious practice in the West-India
seas." The entire work carries many handsome engravings.
Earlier editions (1825, 1827, 1829, and 1834) have
appeared under the title, *The History of the Pirates.*

Howes (not recorded). **Rinderknecht,** #38559. **Sabin,**
#32197 (variant). **NUC** (Harvard University Library, Library
of Congress, New York Public Library, University of Pennsylvania). **OCLC** (12).

The Pirates flogging the Captain of a sloop. *Page* 155.

Piracy in the West Indies,
woodcut

[1825–1826]

Pursuit of Whaleship *Globe* Mutineers
First U.S. Naval Vessel to Visit Hawaii

71. Paulding, Hiram (1797-1878).

Journal of a Cruise of the United States Schooner Dolphin among the Islands of the Pacific Ocean; and a Visit to the Mulgrave Islands in Pursuit of the Mutineers of the Whaleship Globe, by Hiram Paulding. New York: G.C.&H. Carvill, 1831. 258 p., map (folding), 16 cm.

The author ended his service as a rear admiral. As a lieutenant, he served on board USS *Dolphin*, in this work telling "of his ship's adventurous pursuit of the mutineers from the whaler *Globe* in 1825–1826. On her way back to Callao from the Mulgrave Islands, where the mutineers were found, the *Dolphin* stopped at Honolulu, thus becoming the first naval vessel of the United States to visit Hawaii."—**Skallerup.** The folding map delineates the Mulgrave Islands as surveyed by *Dolphin*.

Bruntjen and Bruntjen, #8637. **Sabin,** #59186. **Skallerup,** 81. **Young,** 116–17. **Howes,** 131. **NUC** (8). **OCLC** (20).

[1832]

1832 Battle of Qualla-Battoo in Sumatra
First U.S. Warship Circumnavigation in Easterly Direction

72. Warriner, Francis (1805-1866).

Cruise of the United States Frigate Potomac Round the World, during the Years 1831-34. Embracing the Attack on Quallah-Battoo, with Notices of Scenes, Manners, etc., in Different Parts of Asia, South America, and the Islands of the Pacific, by Francis Warriner, Embellished with Engravings. New York: Leavitt, Lord & Co.; Boston: Crocker & Brewster, 1835. 366 p., illus, plates, 16 cm.

On August 28, 1831, President Andrew Jackson dispatched USS *Potomac*, 44 guns, under Captain John Downes to conduct operations against Sumatran pirates. "On this voyage she became the first U.S. warship to circumnavigate the earth in an easterly direction." On February 6, 1832, Commodore John Downes deployed from *Potomac* a force of 282 sailors and marines against Kuala Batu (Qualla Battoo) on the west coast of Sumatra. The attack was in response to plundering by the inhabitants of the American schooner *Friendship*. The American sailors and marines captured and burned the town and four forts. Two American sailors were killed and 11 naval personnel, including four marines, were wounded. Enemy losses included their chief warriors. On the following day shelling from *Potomac* destroyed a fifth fort.

Cooney, 53. **Rinderknecht,** #35267. **Sabin,** #101503. **Sweetman,** 44. **NUC** (10). **OCLC** (65).

[1834]

Sumatra Sailing Directions

73. Gillis, James Dunlap (1798-1835).

Sailing Directions for the Pepper Ports of the West Coast of Sumatra, North of Analaboo; to Accompany a Chart of That Coast. Salem, Mass.: John M. Ives, 1834. 31 p., 19 cm.

Following the naval assault of 1832 against Kuala Batu (Quallah Battoo), a second attack was launched. On January 1–2, 1839, in retaliation for the murder of the master of the American merchant vessel *Eclipse*, 360 sailors and marines from USS *Columbia*, 44 guns, and USS *John Adams*, 18 guns, were landed by Commodore George Read. Led by Commander T.W. Wyman and supported by naval shelling, the force reduced Kuala Batu. These 1834 sailing directions by Gillis were among the few American works available to naval forces.

Cooney, 56. **Rinderknecht and Bruntjen,** #24619. **Sabin** (not recorded). **NUC** (Boston Public Library, Library of Congress, Navy Department Library). **OCLC** (Harvard University, Houghton Library; Mariner's Museum; Navy Department Library).

Barbary States Relations

74. Greenhow, Robert (1800-1854).

The History and Present Condition of Tripoli, with Some Accounts of the Other Barbary States: Originally Published in the "Southern Literary Messenger." By Robert Greenhow. *Richmond: T.W. White, 1835. 80 p., 20 cm.*

"A history of the Barbary States and their relations with the United States to about 1830."—**Harbeck.** Greenhow served in the State Department, where "it was his duty to become familiar with all documents bearing on special problems in America's foreign relations, which led him, in 1835, to prepare his first work, *The History and Present Condition of Tripoli*."—**DAB.** This book by Greenhow and the book immediately below provide historical perspective on the Barbary states with whom the infant United States found itself engaged in hostilities as early as 1783. Prior to the American Revolution, the American colonies had relied on the naval might of Great Britain, and then annual payments to the Barbary powers (Algiers, Morocco, Tripoli, and Tunis), to secure unmolested passage of merchant shipping through the Mediterranean. By 1801 a series of expeditions by American naval squadrons had become necessary to suppress the Barbary powers before the War of 1812. Following that war, Decatur and Bainbridge were "ordered to the Mediterranean with an overwhelming force. . . . By June, 1815, . . . appearing off Algiers, he [Decatur] demanded and secured a treaty humiliating to the once proud piratical state—no future payments, restoration of all American property, the emancipation of all Christian slaves escaping to American men-of-war. . . . As Tunis and Tripoli were forced to equally hard terms and an American squadron remained in the Mediterranean, the safety of American commerce was assured."—**DAH.**

DAB (4), 580. **DAH (Concise),** 88–89. **Harbeck,** 13. **Rinderknecht,** #31937. **Sabin** (not recorded). **NUC** (Boston Public Library, Duke University, Huntington Library, Library of Congress, Massachusetts Historical Society, New York Public Library, University of California at Berkeley, University of Pennsylvania). **OCLC** (8).

Second Seminole War

75. [Potter, Woodburne].

The War in Florida: Being an Exposition of Its Causes, and an Accurate History of the Campaigns of Generals Clinch, Gaines, and Scott . . . by a Late Staff Officer. *Baltimore: Lewis and Coleman, 1836. viii, 184 p., 3 maps and plans, 19 cm.*

Development of American naval amphibious operations is rooted in both the Mexican War of 1846–1848 and the Second Seminole Indian War of 1835–1842. Prominent in the Seminole War was Lieutenant Levin M. Powell, USN. On March 17–28, 1836, he led from USS *Vandalia* a boat expedition of sailors and marines up the Manatee River and around the keys of Tampa Bay. On March 31, Powell joined Army forces at Charlotte Harbor for a joint operation up the Myacca River. The operation extended to April 27. On October 13, he led another boat expedition against Seminole Indians with sailors and marines from *Vandalia*, proceeding to Cape Florida, up the Miami River, and on to New River, and terminating on December 9. On October 25, Lieutenant J.H. Ward commanded a punitive expedition of three boats from USS *St. Louis* to Charlotte Harbor. That expedition terminated on November 9. Although primarily concerned with land forces, there is some note of Commodore Dallas, Lieutenant Levin M. Powell, and naval force support.

Cooney, 55. **Howes,** P515. **Rinderknecht,** #39688. **Sabin,** #64673. **NUC** (30). **OCLC** (70).

Slave Ship *Amistad* Mutiny

76. Thompson, Smith, and Judson, Andrew T.

The African Captives. Trial of the Prisoners of the Amistad on the Writ of Habeas Corpus, Before the Circuit Court of the United States, for the District of Connecticut, at Hartford; Judges Thompson and Judson. September Term, 1839. *New York: Published and for sale at 143 Nassau Street, 1839. vi, [7]–47 p., 21.5 cm.*

On August 26, 1839, USS *Washington* off New London, Connecticut, captured the Spanish schooner *Amistad.* Under the control of 54 slaves who had mutinied near Cuba and murdered part of the crew, the vessel was en route to Africa. The captives were landed on Long Island, New York, and tried in an American court which "held that it was not piracy for persons to rise up against those who illegally held them captive.... Former President John Quincy Adams represented the Africans before the Supreme Court."—**DAH.**

Cooney, 57. **DAH** (1), 114. **Rinderknecht** (not recorded). **Sabin,** #1337. **NUC** (not recorded). **OCLC** (24).

Wounded Veteran of the Fiji Island Interventions Seeking Public Sympathy for Claims of Seamen

77. Clark, Joseph G.

Lights and Shadows of Sailor Life, As Exemplified in Fifteen Years' Experience, Including the More Thrilling Events of the U.S. Exploring Expedition, and Reminiscences of an Eventful Life on the "Mountain Wave." By Joseph G. Clark. *Boston: B.B. Mussey, 1848. 322 p., frontispiece, illus., 19 cm.*

"In presenting this work to the public . . . I have been pursuing an object of the highest importance, which is the awakening of public sympathy to the nature and importance of the claims of seamen; this, in my estimation, may be best accomplished by a truthful and lucid exhibition of the 'lights and shadows of sailor life.'"—**Preface.** "Chapters on the Sandwich Islands and on the Pacific coast."—**Howes.** Clark was "badly wounded in the affair at Malolo in the Fijis, about which he gives an account."—**Lefkowicz.**

Howes, C442. **Lefkowicz** (*Catalogue Twenty-One*), #53. **Rosenbach,** #135. **Sabin,** #13322. **NUC** (not recorded). **OCLC** (18).

The attack on Joseph Clark and others at Malolo in the Fijis, engraving

Naval Casualties
Second Seminole War

78. Sprague, John Titcomb (1810–1878).

The Origin, Progress, and Conclusion of the Florida War: To Which Is Appended a Record of Officers, Non-Commissioned Officers, Musicians, and Privates of the U.S. Army, Navy, and Marine Corps, Who Were Killed in Battle or Died of Disease. As Also the Names of Officers Who Were Distinguished by Brevets, and the Names of Others Recommended; Together with the Orders for Collecting the Remains of the Dead in Florida, and the Interment at St. Augustine, East Florida, on the Fourteenth Day of August, 1842. By John T. Sprague. *New York: D. Appleton & Company; Philadelphia: G.S. Appleton, 1848. 557 p., [10] p. of plates, illus., map (folding), 23 cm.*

Naval operations against the Seminole Tribe continued into the 1840s. On April 16, 1840, sailors and marines from USS *Ostego*, two guns, were engaged for almost three hours against 50 to 80 Indians on the east coast of Florida. On December 31, 1840, a joint Army-Navy expedition was launched to surprise Seminole towns in the Everglades. On November 3–24, 1841, a joint force of 812 sailors and marines under Captain M. Burke, USN, Lieutenant J.T. McLaughlin, USN, and Lieutenant Ketchum, USMC, entered the Everglades to engage Seminoles. On November 27, 1841, Lieutenant John Rodgers led a 150-man naval brigade into the Everglades, the brigade operating there until December 23. On January 13–27, 1842, Lieutenant J.B. Marchand, USN, led a naval brigade from USS *Wave* against Seminoles. On February 15, 1842, Lieutenant John Rodgers, USN, from USS *Madison* led a naval brigade from Key Biscayne into the Florida interior, operating there until April 11. Pages 549–50 list the Navy and Marine Corps casualties. **Field** cites United States casualties as one for "every Indian taken or slain." The chronologically arranged chapters include "Lieutenant McLaughlin reports his passage up the Carlosahatchee river," "The Florida squadron commanded by Lieutenant McLaughlin, Report of Lieutenant J.T. McLaughlin, USN., commanding the Florida squadron," "The U.S. Marine Corps under Colonel Henderson," and "Death of Midshipman Niles, USN."

Cooney, 57–58. **Field,** #1475. **Larned,** #1963. **Sabin,** #89686. **NUC** (Library of Congress). **OCLC** (118).

Florida Squadron
Charged with Misuse of Medical Supplies

79. McLaughlin, John T. (d. 1847).

Memorial of John T. McLaughlin, Lieutenant U.S. Navy, to the House of Representatives, U. States, Washington, February 13, 1844. *[Washington City, 1844]. [1]-6 p., 21 cm.*

Deals with charges by William P.C. Barton, chief of the Bureau of Medicine and Surgery, "impugning the character and honor of the officers of the Florida Squadron, and charging upon them a misapplication of the Hospital stores of that Squadron."

Rinderknecht and Bruntjen (not recorded but see #44-3967). **Sabin** (not recorded). **NUC** (not recorded). **OCLC** (Navy Department Library).

{1844}
Naval Officer Account of Slave Trade Suppression

80. [Bridge, Horatio] (1806-1893).

Journal of an African Cruiser; Comprising Sketches of the Canaries, the Cape de Verds, Liberia, Madeira, Sierra Leone, and Other Places of Interest on the West Coast of Africa. By an Officer of the U.S. Navy. Edited by Nathaniel Hawthorne. New York & London: Wiley and Putnam, 1845. viii, [v]–vi, 179 p., 18 cm.

The journal covers the period June 5, 1843 through October 15, 1844. "It will not have escaped the reader's notice, that the foregoing journal of our cruise records not the capture of a single slave-vessel, either by our own ship or any other belonging to the American squadron. . . . The doctrines relative to the right of search, held by our Government and cordially sanctioned by the people, declare that the cruisers of no foreign nation have a right to search, visit, or in any way detain an American vessel on the high seas. Denying the privilege to others, we must of course allow the same inviolability to a foreign flag, as we assert for that of our own country. Hence, our national ships can detain or examine none but American vessels, or those which they find sailing under the American flag. But no slave-vessel would display this flag. The laws of the United States declare the slave-trade, if exercised by any of its citizens, to be piracy, and punishable with death; the laws of Spain, Portugal and Brazil, are believed to be different, or, at least, if they threaten the same penalty, are certain never to inflict it. Consequently, all slaves will be careful to sail under the flag of one of these latter nations, and thus avoid the danger of losing life, as well as property, in the event of capture."—**Chapter XXII.**

Howes (not recorded). **Rinderknecht and Bruntjen,** #45-1004. **Sabin** (not recorded). **Work,** 257. **NUC** (21). **OCLC** (54).

{1845}
Veteran of Four Naval Wars of the United States

81. Shaw, Elijah (b. 1771).

A Short Sketch of the Life of Elijah Shaw, Who Served for Twenty-one Years in the U.S. Navy, Taking an Active Part in Four Different Wars between the United States & Foreign Powers: Viz. I. With France in 1798; II. With Tripoli from 1802 to 1805; III. With England from 1812 to 1815; IV. With Algiers from 1815 to 1816: And Assisted in Subduing the Pirates, from 1822 to 1824. And in 1823 Entered On Board the "Old Ship Zion," Under a New Commander, Being in the 73d Year of His Age. 3d ed. *Rochester: E. Shepard, Mammoth Printing-House, 1845. iv, [5]–63, [1] p., illus., 17 cm.*

Shaw fought in the Quasi-War with France, during the Caribbean pirate suppression, against Algiers and Tripoli, and in the War of 1812. Fredriksen, noting Shaw as a veteran of the October 25, 1812 combat between USS *United States* and HMS *Macedonian*, quotes Shaw as follows: "On taking possession, the enemy was found fearfully cut to pieces, having received no less than a hundred round shot in his hull alone." By 1815 Shaw was serving on board USS *President*, which, during January of that year, was taken by a British squadron. That engagement is related "in detail," and there is also an account of Shaw's subsequent imprisonment at Bermuda. Shaw notes in the preface that he has written this account to stir patriotism in American hearts and to earn some money to repay the Monroe County House (New York State) where he had been forced by hard times to seek aid. Several attractive nautical woodcuts embellish the work. The verso of the title page carries a tabular description of the warship *Pennsylvania*, which is cited as the largest in the United States Navy. The table includes a list of provisions consumed in a year, including 114 tons 800 pounds of pork, 1,228 bushels of rice, 5,200 gallons of molasses, 2,600 gallons of vinegar, 258 tons 600 pounds of bread, 17½ tons of cheese, and 547,500 gallons of water.

Fredriksen, #460. **Howes,** S338. **Harbeck,** 97 (variant). **Rinderknecht and Bruntjen,** #45–5876. **Sabin,** #79905. **NUC** (Huntington Library, Library of Congress, Newberry Library, New York Public Library, Pennsylvania Historical Society, University of Virginia Library, Wisconsin Historical Society). **OCLC** (17).

{1846}

Texas Republic Navy

82. Buchanan, Franklin (1800-1874).

To the House of Representatives of the Congress of the United States: The Honorable Committee on Naval Affairs, upon the Memorial of E.W. Moore and Others, Representing Themselves To Be the Officers of the Navy of the Late Republic of Texas, Have Reported a Bill for Their Incorporation into the Navy of the United States. *[Washington?]: [1850?]. 13 p., 22 cm.*

"A claim in behalf of himself [Moore] and his fellow officers to incorporation into the federal navy was bitterly opposed by the federal naval officers. Finally, in 1857, Congress voted the Texan officers five years' pay."—**DAB.**

DAB (7), 120–21. **NUC** (not recorded). **OCLC** (Navy Department Library, United States Naval Academy, Yale University).

{1836–1846}

Texas Republic Navy

83. Moore, Edwin Ward (1810-1865).

A Brief Synopsis of the Doings of the Texas Navy under Command of Com. E.W. Moore: Together with His Controversy with Gen. Sam Houston, President of the Republic of Texas . . . *Washington: Printed by T. Barnard, 1847. 32 p., 25 cm.*

The Republic of Texas offered Moore command of its small navy. Moore's commission, which was not issued until July 20, 1842, gave him the rank of post captain commanding. In 1840–1841 he cruised the Mexican coast "to expedite the peace negotiations of the Texan diplomat James Treat. When these negotiations collapsed Moore not only swept Mexican commerce from the Gulf but also entered into a de facto alliance with Yucatecan rebels and captured the town of Tabasco . . . proceeded to New Orleans to refit his fleet for the enforcement of a blockade of Mexico, proclaimed by President Sam Houston in retaliation for Mexico's invasion of March 1842. . . . Moore had agreed with the authorities in Yucatan, in consideration of the payment of a sum of money sufficient to finish refitting the fleet, to attack the Mexican squadron blockading the Yucatan coast. In accordance with this agreement he attacked the squadron on April 30 and again on May 16, 1843, and in both engagements defeated it. . . . On June 1 Moore received a proclamation of Houston declaring that he was guilty of 'disobedience, contumacy, and mutiny' and suspending him from his command."—**DAB.**

DAB (7), 120–21. **Sabin,** #50351. **NUC** (not recorded). **OCLC** (Miami Dade Public Library, Navy Department Library, Quincy Library).

{1846–1847}

Future Confederate Admiral's Mexican War Service

84. [Semmes, Raphael]. (1809-1877).

Service Afloat and Ashore during the Mexican War: By Lieut. Raphael Semmes. *Cincinnati: Wm. H. Moore & Co., Publishers, 1851. xii p., blank leaf, [7]–480 p., map, 6 plates, 21 cm.*

"Commanding the brig *Somers* on the Mexican blockade, 1846, he [Semmes] lost the vessel in a tropical storm, but was exonerated of any blame. He served thereafter on shore at Vera Cruz and in the march to Mexico City, receiving several citations for gallantry."—**DAB.** Semmes became the outstanding Confederate naval officer, achieving the rank of admiral during the Civil War and writing a chapter on raider operations that catapulted him to legend.

DAB (Concise), 935. **Howes,** S288. **Sabin,** #79083. **Tutorow,** #3393. **NUC** (24). **OCLC** (121).

The United States Squadron, Landing the SEAMEN & MARINES, at the BRAZOS DE SANTIAGO, May 8th 1846.

U.S. sailors and marines landing at Brazos de Santiago, Mexican War, 1846, lithograph

{1846–1847}

Mexican War Operations

85. [Taylor, Fitch Waterman] (1803-1865).

The Broad Pennant: or, A Cruise in the United States Flag Ship of the Gulf Squadron, during the Mexican Difficulties; Together with Sketches of the Mexican War, from the Commencement of Hostilities to the Capture of the City of Mexico. By Rev. Fitch W. Taylor. *New York: Leavitt, Trow & Co., 1848. 415 p., frontispiece (folding), 20 cm.*

Tutorow cites this work for its coverage of naval operations on the eastern coast of Mexico. Taylor deals, among other subjects, with the second Alvarado Expedition and the Tabasco Expedition.

Howes (not recorded). **Sabin,** #94455. **Tutorow,** #3366. **NUC** (18). **OCLC** (61).

{1846–1847}

Landing of American Forces at Vera Cruz

86. Conner, Philip Syng Physick.

The Home Squadron under Commodore Conner in the War with Mexico, Being a Synopsis of Its Services. (With an Addendum Containing Admiral Temple's Memoir of the Landing of Our Army at Vera Cruz in 1847) 1846-1847. By Philip Syng Physick Conner. *[Philadelphia?]: 1896. 83, [1] p., 26 cm.*

"The plan of the Veracruz campaign was developed by Conner and Scott jointly."—**Webster.** "Written from his father's papers . . . with an appendix containing all the written orders issued by General Scott and Commodore Conner."—**Tutorow.**

Howes (not recorded). **Tutorow,** #3352. **Webster,** 78–79. **NUC** (16). **OCLC** (65).

{1847}

Firsthand Account of Siege and Bombardment of Vera Cruz

87. G[regor], J.M.

Siege and Bombardment of Vera Cruz, and Surrender of That City and the Castle of San Juan De Ulloa, to the American Forces, 29th March, 1847. By J.M.G., of the U.S. Frigate Potomac. *Norfolk, Va.: Printed by Wm. C. Shields, 1847. 16 p., front printed wrapper, 21.5 cm.*

The author took part in this action. He notes that his "only object is to give, at the request of a number of my shipmates, an accurate account of the siege and surrender of the city of Vera Cruz and castle of San Juan d'Ulloa, in which they, with the other crews of the Gulf Squadron, bore so conspicuous, effective, and honorable a part." He includes a list of those killed or wounded on March 24–25. He also tabulates the number of shot and shells fired during the bombardment by the Navy battery, the Army battery, and the Mosquito fleet.

Howes (not recorded). **Sabin** (not recorded). **Tutorow** (not recorded). **NUC** (not recorded). **OCLC** (Navy Department Library).

{1847}

China Intervention— A Key to the Adversary

88. [Shaw, Samuel] (1754-1794).

The Journals of Major Shaw, the First American Consul at Canton. With a Life of the Author, by Josiah Quincy. *Boston: W Crosby and H.P. Nichols, 1847. xiii, 360 p., portrait, 23 cm.*

Publication of this work followed just three years after the first hostile engagement of American forces in China (1844) and coincided with not only a need for charts such as that of 1855 prepared by Preble (see entry 91), but also an understanding of the China adversary and past experience with him. This volume, almost certainly, was intended to aid American naval and political leaders in understanding the enemy they would confront during any China interventions. Pages 131–213 are journals. "First Voyage to Canton." Pages 215–55 are "Second Voyage to Canton." The earlier part of the volume carries "The narrative of the military life of Major Shaw [and] is composed chiefly of letters written to his nearest relatives and friends, from his enlistment in the American army, at Cambridge, in December, 1775, to its final disbandment, at West Point, in January, 1784."—**Sabin.**

Howes (not recorded). **Sabin,** #79959. **NUC** (21 copies). **OCLC** (149).

{1848}

China Theater in 1848—
Background for Naval Officers

9. Ruschenberger, William Samuel Waithman (1807-1895).

Notes and Commentaries during a Voyage to Brazil and China, in the Year 1848 by W.S.W. Ruschenberger. *Richmond: Macfarlane & Fergusson, 1854. 219 p., 26 cm.*

A naval surgeon, Ruschenberger served as fleet surgeon of the East India Squadron (1847–1850). A man of learning and insightful observation, he attained wide recognition, serving from 1870 to 1872 as president of the Academy of Natural Sciences and from 1879 to 1883 as president of the College of Physicians, both in Philadelphia. He authored a number of works. This title is of interest because it gave American naval officers background information on China during a period of increasing naval activity there. The Navy Department copy is inscribed by the author on the title page.

Appleton (5), 348–49. **Howes** (not recorded). **Sabin**, 74190. **NUC** (Academy of Natural Sciences, Boston Public Library, Free Library of Philadelphia, Library Company of Philadelphia, Naval Observatory). **OCLC** (Academy of Natural Sciences, Navy Department Library).

{1855}

The African Squadron

90. [Foote, Andrew Hull] (1806-1863).

The African Squadron: Ashburton Treaty: Consular Sea Letters. Reviewed, in an Address by Commander A.H. Foote, U.S.N. *Philadelphia: William F. Geddes, Printer, Franklin Place, [1855]. [2], [3]–16 p., 22 cm.*

"... I will now express my views in reference to the recent action of the U.S. Senate on the subject of the African Squadron and the African Slave trade. I have before me a copy of the Instructions for the Senior officer of H.B. Majesty's cruisers, on the west coast of Africa ...which say: 'The commanding officers of her majesty's ships on the African Station, will bear in mind that it is no part of their duty to capture, or visit, or in any way interfere with vessels of the United States, *whether these vessels shall have slaves on board or not.*' These Instructions show that, as the African slave trade has been pronounced by the United States piracy *only in a municipal sense*—not piracy by the laws of nations, *bona fide* American vessels, irrespective of their character, are considered by the British government as well as our own to be in no sense amenable to foreign cruisers. But how is American nationality to be ascertained; for the slaver, even if not American, can easily hoist the American Flag; and therefore, unless the vessel is boarded, our colors may be made to cover the most atrocious acts of piracy.... We cannot believe that the people of the United States are unwilling to sustain an effective squadron on the African coast, while France and England have each well appointed fleets in that region."

Dumond (not recorded). **Howes** (not recorded). **Sabin**, #25014. **Work** (not recorded). **NUC** (14). **OCLC** (11).

{1856}

China Theater Sailing Directions
Prepared by First American to Command
China Landing Force

91. [Preble, George Henry] (1816-1885).

Sailing Directions for the Navigation of the Yang-Tze-Kiang to Wusung and Shanghai Prepared by Lieut. Preble, by Order of Commodore Joel Abbot. *[1856]. 9 p., original blank leaf, 22 cm.*

This is a rare and remarkable piece. It was George Henry Preble who commanded in 1844 the "first armed American landing in China in order to protect residents and American consulate at Canton."—**Cogar.** Sailing directions of this type, prepared by the man who set in history the beginning of a series of China interventions, were essential for American commercial and naval operations in China. On page 9 appears: "Examined and corrected—A True Copy. Geo. Henry Preble. *U.S. Ship Macedonian.* Singapore, April 2nd, 1856."

Cogar (1), 134–35. **NUC** (Yale University). **OCLC** (Navy Department Library).

{1856}
Canton Barrier Forts Assault

92. Hoppin, James Mason (1820-1906).

Life of Andrew Hull Foote, Rear-Admiral United States Navy. By James Mason Hoppin. *New York: Harper & Brothers, 1874. x, 411 p., illus., map, portrait, 22 cm.*

Foote "personally led an assault force against the barrier forts at Canton, China, in November 1856, driving the Chinese away and making the forts and their guns inoperable."—**Cogar.** On November 20–22, 400 Chinese and 7 Americans were killed during an engagement at Canton. The American landing party comprised 287 sailors and marines from USS *Levant*, 22 guns; USS *Portsmouth*, 20 guns; and USS *San Jacinto*, 6 guns. Following bombardment of Canton forts from the ships, the landing party captured one fort and then in small boats ascended the river, capturing a second fort and a battery. Two more forts were captured in subsequent fighting. Pages 106–27 describe operations against the barrier forts. Foote commanded naval operations on the upper Mississippi, Cumberland, and Tennesse rivers defending Forts Henry and Donelson.

Cogar (1), 63–65. **Cooney,** 73. **Larned,** #2176. **NUC** (27). **OCLC** (159).

Battle of Fort Donelson, engraving

{1856}

Rare Macao Printed Pamphlet on China Situation

93. Nye, Gideon (1812-1888).

The Rationale of the China Question: Comprising an Inquiry into the Repressive Policy of the Imperial Government, with Considerations of the Duties of the Three Treaty Powers, England, France & America, in Regard to It; and a Glance at the Origins of the First and Second Wars with China, with Incidental Notices of the Rebellion by an American. *Macao: 1857. [6], 41 p., printed wrappers, 27 cm.*

Coming shortly after the reduction of the barrier forts in 1856, this tract provides background on the political situation in China and the Western commercial powers. The title page cites this printing as "Third Edition." This copy is inscribed on the front flyleaf: "Admiral Rodgers with Mr. Nye's best compliments."

Sabin (not recorded). **NUC** (Essex Institute, Library of Congress, Yale University). **OCLC** (Boston Athenaeum, Harvard University Library, Navy Department Library, New York Public Library).

{1856}

First Navy Surgeon General
Firsthand Account of Capture of Canton Barrier Forts

94. Wood, William Maxwell (1809-1880).

Fankwei; or, The San Jacinto in the Seas of India, China, and Japan, by William Maxwell Wood. *New York: Harper & Brothers, 1859. viii , 1 l., [11]–545 p., 20 cm.*

Wood began his service with the Navy on May 10, 1829. He "served on the steamer *Poinsett* on the coast of Florida during the Seminole war in 1838–'41 . . . appointed fleet-surgeon of the Pacific squadron in 1843, and brought the first intelligence of the opening of the Mexican war . . . to Commodore Sloat . . . fleet surgeon of the East India squadron in 1856–'58 and present at the capture of the Barrier forts in Canton River, China. . . . On 1 July, 1869, he was appointed surgeon-general of the navy."—**Appleton.** The future surgeon general of the Navy divides the narrative of his voyage in USS *San Jacinto* into three parts: "The Voyage Out," "Siam and the Siamese," and "In China." The part on China constitutes pages 263–545, with pages 415–69 giving a detailed account from personal observation of and involvement in the capture of the barrier forts.

Appleton (6), 598. **Sabin** (not recorded). **NUC** (28). **OCLC** (78).

{1858}

Paraguay Punitive Expedition

95. Howard, Alexander.

Cruise of the U.S. Frigate Sabine. *Portsmouth: T.H. Godwin, 1861. 107 p., 20 cm.*

The 55-gun frigate *Sabine* was commissioned during August 1858 and assigned as the flagship of the Brazilian Squadron and Paraguay Punitive Expedition. Pages 9–22 relate to the Paraguay Punitive Expedition. "In February 1855, while on the Parana River, the *Water-Witch* was fired on from a Paraguayan fort; the vessel suffered considerable damage and one sailor was killed. On his return to the United States in May 1856 [Lt. Thomas Jefferson] Page began agitating for a punitive expedition. Such an expedition of 19 ships was sent out in October 1858 under Commodore William B. Shubrick, with Page . . . as fleet captain and second-in-command. The show of force produced a satisfactory diplomatic settlement."—**Webster.** After the Paraguay Expedition, *Sabine* went to the Mediterranean and then returned to the United States. This journal includes the Mediterranean cruise and the operations of *Sabine* in the American Civil War until July 4, 1861. The journal ends with a 16-page poem entitled "Description of a Man-of-War." A prefatory note states, "with the exception of schools and flogging, there has been no perceptible change in the Navy since the date of its [the poem's] composition." The poem originally appeared around 1841. The Navy Department copy of the *Sabine* journal belonged to Rear Admiral George Henry Preble and bears his signature on the title page.

Howes (not recorded). **Nevins** (not recorded). **Sabin** (not recorded). **Webster,** 305. **NUC** (Boston Public Library, Library of Congress, Navy Department Library). **OCLC** (Library of Congress, Navy Department Library).

The Mason and Slidell Affair

96. Anonymous.

A Legal View of the Seizure of Messrs Mason and Slidell. *New York: 1861. 27 p., 23 cm.*

"Signed Prolege."—**Harbeck.** "An argument that the capture of the Southern commissioners cannot be justified by international law."—**Nevins.** En route to London and Paris respectively, as Confederate commissioners, James Murray Mason of Virginia and John Slidell of Louisiana were on November 8, 1861, forcibly taken from the British ship *Trent* by a boarding party from USS *San Jacinto*, commanded by Captain Charles Wilkes. Mason and Slidell were imprisoned. England demanded an apology and the release of the Confederate diplomats, concurrently deploying 8,000 troops to Canada for its defense in the event of war with the United States. "Upon realizing that the alternative to surrender of the [Confederate] commissioners must be war with England, [Secretary of State] Seward, in a communication, December 26, 'cheerfully liberated' them."—**DAH.**

DAH (Concise), 965–66. **Harbeck,** 56. **Moebs** (*CSN*), 492. **Nevins** (1), 259. **Sabin** (not recorded). **NUC** (Greene County Historical Society, New York Historical Society, University of Texas at Austin, University of Virginia Library, Western Reserve Historical Society). **OCLC** (13).

Capture of Norfolk Navy Yard
Source of Legendary Confederate Ironclad *Merrimack*

97. United States. Navy Department. Secretary.

Destruction of the United States Vessels and Other Property at Norfolk, Virginia: Letter from the Secretary of the Navy, Transmitting, in Compliance with a Resolution of the House of Representatives of July 16, 1861, the Correspondence Relative to the Destruction of the United States Vessels and Other Property at the Navy Yard at Norfolk, Virginia. *[Washington: Government Printing Office, 1861]. 18 p., 24 p.*

On the night of Saturday, April 20, 1861, the United States naval authorities evacuated the navy yard at Gosport, Virginia, in one of the most extraordinary proceedings of the war. It was simply out of the power of the Confederates to capture the place. Yet federal authorities abandoned the yard in panic, allowing the Confederates to take possession immediately of the yard and its 1,195 large caliber guns. These guns furnished the batteries from Norfolk to New Orleans. The "steam frigate *Merrimac* [later renamed CSS *Virginia*] was scuttled and sunk, and burned. . . . She was raised, and the powder in her magazine (put up in air-tight copper tanks) was found to be in good condition; and it was afterwards used by her in her engagements [in Hampton Roads]."—**Parker.**

Moebs (*CSN*), 91. **Parker** (*Recollections of a Naval Officer, 1841–1865*), 246–50. **NUC** (Hoover Institution on War, Revolution and Peace, Virginia State Library). **OCLC** (College of William and Mary, Library of Virginia, Navy Department Library, United States Army Military History Institute, University of Rochester).

Flag Officer Du Pont's Blockading Instructions
Adding African Americans to the Squadron

98. United States. Navy. South Atlantic Blockading Squadron.

Blockading Instructions. General Order No. 1. Flag Ship *Wabash*, Hampton Roads, October 24, 1861. *[Hampton Roads, Virginia], [1861]. 2 conjugate leaves, 24 cm.*

Printed on blue lined paper, the front of the first leaf carries under bold heading, the blockading instructions. The front of the second leaf carries an instruction on reporting and a modification. The instructions, signed in type by Flag Officer S.F. Du Pont, are eight in number and include: "3d. Protect our commerce from the depredations of privateers, and as a matter of course, capture them, and all other vessels of the enemy, whenever you can do so without being seduced away from your station." Other instructions cover neutral or foreign vessels, contraband goods, vessels leaving insurgent ports without legal clearances, and port closings by proclamation. The Navy Department copy has with it the flagship printed general orders 5–8, 11–15, 18–25, 27–33 and a circular. June 19, 1863, is the date of the last order. The general orders were printed on board USS *Wabash* at Port Royal Harbor, South Carolina. They are primarily administrative in nature, with one exception, General Order No. 11:

"The hot season on this coast now approaching, renders it desirable that acclimated persons be employed on board of the ships of this Squadron in such duties as involve much exposure to sun and heat, such as boat service and work in the engine rooms. The Commanding Officers are therefore authorized to enlist 'contrabands,' with their consent, on their respective vessels, rating them as Boys at $8, $9, and $10 per month, and one ration—this privilege to be exercised with sound discretion."

The term "contrabands" refers to African Americans.

OCLC (Navy Department Library).

{1861}

Commander of West India Squadron Court-Martialed

9. [Browning, O.H., and Hill, Britton A.].

Defence of Com. Charles Wilkes, U.S.N., Late Acting Rear Admiral, in Command of the West India Squadron, Read before a General Court Martial, on Charges Preferred by the Secretary of the Navy. Washington: McGill & Witherow, Printers, 1864. 56 p., 23 cm.

"In 1861 [Wilkes], commanded *San Jacinto* which stopped British mail steamer *Trent* in West Indies, taking off the Confederate agents James Mason and John Slidell. Seen by many as a hero, but the '*Trent* Affair' caused much international tension between the U.S. and Great Britain. Holding several more commands during the Civil War, was subsequently court-martialed for disobedience, disrespect, insubordination, and conduct unbecoming an officer owing to his comments against Secretary of the Navy Gideon Welles. Found guilty and sentenced to public reprimand and suspended three years, a sentence reduced to one year."—**Cogar.**

Cogar (1), 209–11. **Howes** (not recorded). **Sabin** (not recorded). **NUC** (14). **OCLC** (21).

{1861–1863}

Operations of USS *Susquehanna*

100. Burton, Amos.

A Journal of the Cruise of the U.S. Ship Susquehanna: During the Years 1860, 1861, 1862 and 1863 by Amos Burton. *New York: Edward O. Jenkins, 1863. 177 p., 23 cm.*

Assigned to the North Atlantic Blockading Squadron in 1861, *Susquehanna* participated in the August 1861 Hatteras Inlet Expedition. In October 1861 she was deployed to South Carolina waters. During April 1862 she was ordered to Hampton Roads, Virginia, to strengthen the North Atlantic Blockading Squadron, and in May was ordered to the West Gulf Blockading Squadron. She was decommissioned on May 14, 1863.

DANFS (6), 685–86. **Howes**, B1029. **Sabin,** #9489. **NUC** (Boston Public Library, New York Public Library, Western Reserve Historical Society). **OCLC** (Boston Athenaeum Library, Navy Department Library, New York Public Library, University of California Santa Barbara, University of West Florida Library, Western Reserve Historical Society).

{1861–1863}

Gunboat Operations on the Western Waters

101. [Walke, Henry].

Naval Scenes on the Western Waters: The Gunboats Taylor, Carondelet and Lafayette. *[1863?]. [2], [29]–71 p., 20 plates (many folding), 22 cm.*

This work in its complete form should follow *U.S. Naval Court Martial of Commander Henry Walke* with pagination [2], [3]–25 p., which carries a February 7, 1861 date and signature of Isaac Toucey with the "Charges and Specifications." This work was probably published by Walke to redeem his reputation after his court-martial. Paged continuously, and printed on matching paper, the two sections have sometimes been cataloged separately. The after action reports on the Mississippi Flotilla are illustrated with lithographed monocolor sketches, most likely by Walke who was an artist. The text is nearly identical to accounts in his *Naval Scenes and Reminiscences of the Civil War in the United States, on the Southern and Western Waters during the Years 1862 and 1863* (New York, 1877), which has more sophisticated colored plates.

Nevins (1), 237. **Sabin** (not recorded). **NUC** (Illinois Historical Society, Navy Department Library, New York Public Library, Public Library of Cincinnati & Hamilton Co.). **OCLC** (Illinois State Library, Navy Department Library, Public Library of Cincinnati & Hamilton Co., University of Arkansas).

First Battle Between Ironclads
Gunner's Account of *Monitor* and *Merrimack* Engagement

102. Curtis, Richard.

History of the Famous Battle between the Iron-Clad Merrimac C.S.N. and the Iron-Clad Monitor and the Cumberland and Congress of the U.S. Navy, March the 8th and 9th, 1862 As Seen by a Man at the Gun. *[Norfolk, Va.: Press of S.B. Turner & Son, 1907]. 2 p. l., [4]–17 p., portrait, 18 cm.*

Fought on March 9, 1862, this was "history's first battle between ironclad ships. . . . The duel between the ironclads introduced a new era of naval warfare."—**Boatner.** "Some time in January, 1862 the writer of this book was transferred from Co. A, 32nd Regt., Va. Vols., then stationed at Yorktown, Va., to the C.S. Navy, and for the *Merrimac* I am the only enlisted man of her crew now living in Norfolk or its vicinity. Mr. Wesley Messick, now living on Back River, Va., was also one of her crew."—**Preface.** The title page includes a photograph of Curtis in uniform.

Boatner, 560–61. **Nevins** (not recorded). **NUC** (Huntington Library, University of Virginia Library, Virginia State Library). **OCLC** (Library of Virginia, Navy Department Library, Virginia Historical Society Library).

Instructions to Warships for Slave Trade Suppression

103. United States. President (1861-1865: Lincoln).

A Proclamation [of Treaty . . . for the Suppression of the African Slave Trade]. *[Washington, D.C.]: Navy Dept., 1862. [1], [2]–15 p., 17.5 cm.*

Implements the treaty to suppress the slave trade with "Instructions for the Ships of the United States and British Navies Employed to Prevent the African Slave Trade," pages 7–9.

NUC (not recorded). **OCLC** (Brown University Library, Navy Department Library).

Confederate and Union Sides of Hampton Roads Battle

104. [Worden, John Lorimer] (1818-1897).

The Monitor and the Merrimac; Both Sides of the Story, Told by Lieut. J.L. Worden, U.S.N., Lieut. Greene, U.S.N., of the Monitor, and H. Ashton Ramsay, C.S.N., Chief Engineer of the Merrimac. *New York: Harper, 1912. xi, 72 p., frontispiece, 18 cm.*

"Worden and Greene's post-action report (when Lincoln visited the *Monitor*), and Ramsay's essay written fifty years later."—**Nevins.** This copy is the first printing of this work with the accounts of these three participants.

Nevins (1), 239. **NUC** (16 copies). **OCLC** (91).

Commander of Union Ironclad *Monitor* Reports on His Battle in *Merrimack*

105. [Worden, John Lorimer] (1818-1897).

Report of Capt. John L. Worden, U.S.N., on Fight between the Monitor and Merrimack, Mar. 9, 1862. *[United States, 1868]. 13 leaves, 27 cm.*

"For 3 hours the ships exchanged shells. Worden, wounded and partially blinded, was forced to consign his command to his lieutenant, Samuel D. Greene."—**Faust.** "The strategic victory of the *Merrimack* in buying time for the Confederacy to shift forces from the Potomac to defend Richmond is an American classic illustration of the influence of sea power upon history."—**DAH.**

DAH (Concise), 622–23. **Faust,** 843. **NUC** (not recorded). **OCLC** (Navy Department Library).

Slave Trade Suppression Viewed by an African American

106. Du Bois, William Edward Burghardt (1868-1963).

The Suppression of the African Slave-Trade to the United States of America, 1638-1870, by W.E. Burghardt Du Bois. *New York, London [etc.]: Longmans, Green and company, 1896. xi, 335 p., diagrams, 23 cm.*

"This is a laborious and careful compilation of provincial, state and federal enactments in relation to the suppression of the slave trade. It shows great industry in the collection of facts and the examination of sources"—**Larned.** On March 3, 1819, Congress provided for the use of U.S. naval forces to suppress the African slave trade. The African Squadron was established in 1820. By 1823 it had been deactivated, but individual ships were intermittently deployed off Africa. During 1842, the squadron was reactivated. On March 25–29, 1845, Lieutenant S.F. Blunt commanding a joint force of six boats from USS *Truxtun* and HMS *Ardent*, captured the American slaver *Spitfire* in the Rio Pongas, West Africa. On November 30, 1845, commanding USS *Yorktown*, Commander C.H. Ball captured the American slaver *Pon* off Kabenda, Africa. On August 21, 1858, the future legendary Confederate raider Lieutenant John N. Maffitt, commanding USS *Dolphin*, captured the slave ship *Echo*, with 300 slaves on board, off Cuba. On May 23, 1860, Maffitt, now commanding USS *Crusader*, captured another slave ship, *Bogata*, with 500 slaves on board, off the coast of Cuba. On July 23, 1860, Maffitt, struck again, capturing the slave ship *William R. Kirby* at Aguila, Cuba. On October 10, 1860, Captain T.A. Dorwin, commanding USS *San Jacinto*, captured the slave ship *Bonito*, with 622 slaves on board, in the South Atlantic.

Cooney, 60, 74-76. **Howes,** D522. **Larned,** #1882. **Sweetman,** 39-40. **NUC** (40). **OCLC** (191).

Pursuit of the First English-Built Confederate Steam Cruiser

107. Preble, George Henry (1816-1885).

The Chase of the Rebel Steamer of War Oreto, Commander J.N. Maffitt, C.S.N., into the Bay of Mobile, by the United States Steam Sloop Oneida, Commander Geo. Henry Preble, U.S.N., September 4, 1862. *Cambridge: Printed for private circulation, 1862, 60 p., 24 cm.*

Oreto was the name used to identify CSS *Florida* during her construction in England. "The *Florida*.—The first of the Confederate steam cruisers built in England...bore the dock-yard name of the *Oreto*.... In March, 1862, she was ready to go to sea.... She sailed from Liverpool [for the Bahamas], March 22d."—**Scharf.** Arriving in Mobile harbor from Havana, on September 4, 1862, *Florida* had eluded the Union pursuit and "entered as a warship."—**Wise.** The Confederate commander was former U.S. Navy Lieutenant John Newland Maffitt who came to be known as the "Prince of Privateers." "In an audacious dash...[Maffitt] braved a hail of projectiles...and raced through them...for a hero's welcome by Mobile. *Florida* had been unable to fight back not only because of sickness (aboard) but because rammers, sights, beds, locks and quoins had, inadvertently, not been loaded in the Bahamas."—**Moebs.**

Moebs (*CSN*), 105, 114, 238, 324, 505. **Nevins** (1), 231. **Sabin,** #12217. **Scharf,** 790. **Spencer,** 43. **Wise,** 265. **NUC** (9). **OCLC** (23).

[1862]

Original Manuscript Defense of
Preble's 1862 Service
Terminated by Dismissal for Escape of CSS *Florida*

108. Preble, George Henry (1816-1885).

Geo. Henry Preble's Services with the West. Gulf Blockading Squadron from Jan 14. 1862 to Oct 12. 1862 in Command of the U.S. Steam Gunboat Katahdin & U.S. Steam Sloop Oneida, with Commentary Letters from Admiral Farragut. Vice Adm. Porter, Rear Admiral Bailey, H.H. Ball, Palmer, Commodore Alden and Others, &c. &c. *[U.S. Navy Yard, Charlestown Massachusetts, March 1, 1870]. 49 p. (primarily manuscript with some printed clippings pasted in), 24.5 cm.*

Secretary of the Navy Gideon Welles relieved Preble of command of USS *Oneida* for failure to stop CSS *Florida* from entering Mobile harbor. Prior to the *Florida* incident, Preble's service had been distinguished and extensive. It was Preble who in 1844 had commanded the first troops engaged in hostile action in China. Preble had been one of the gunboat captains in the April 24, 1862 engagement with and destruction of the Confederate fleet when Farragut ascended the Mississippi River to capture New Orleans. Preble put together the album described in the main entry above to defend himself following his dismissal (later reversed) for failing to stop *Florida* under command of John Newland Maffitt, popularly known as the "Prince of Privateers," when Maffitt was successful in bringing *Florida* past the blockade and into Mobile harbor. Among the evidence collected in this album is a printed letter from Maffitt stating: "Dear Preble, . . . [Y]ou performed your duty well. Your fire was formidable; the hull of the 'Florida' was perforated a number of times, one man killed and eleven wounded, all or nearly all our rigging, standing and running, was shot away, boats damaged, hammocks torn out of their nettings, and had I not sent the crew below, the casualties would have been severe. Nothing but the superior speed of the 'Florida' saved her from destruc-

tion. . . . When I heard of the conduct of the Department in regard to you, I was much astonished." This album is primarily in Preble's handwriting and bears his engraved bookplate, which Preble has signed. The materials in the album date from 1862 into 1870.

OCLC (Navy Department Library).

Bookplate and title page

{1862}

Fall of New Orleans

109. United States. Navy. Western Gulf Blockading Squadron.

Reports of the Naval Engagements on the Mississippi River, Resulting in the Capture of Forts Jackson and St. Philip and the City of New Orleans, and the Destruction of the Rebel Naval Flotilla. *Washington: Government Printing Office, 1862. 107 p., illus., 23 cm.*

On April 24, 1862, as the Union fleet under Admiral Farragut advanced up the Mississippi River toward New Orleans, eight Confederate vessels were lost in an engagement with Farragut's fleet as it passed Forts Jackson and St. Philip. "In the action *Manassas* attempted to ram USS *Pensacola* which turned in time to avoid the blow and deliver a broadside at close range. *Manassas* then ran into murderous fire from the whole line of the Union fleet. She then charged USS *Mississippi* and delivered a long glancing blow on her hull, firing her only gun as she rammed. Next she rammed USS *Brooklyn*, again firing her gun, and injuring her rather deeply, but not quite enough to be fatal. . . . Her [CSS *McRae*] last fight was a gallant defense of Forts Jackson and St. Philip on 24 April 1862. In the engagement the conduct of her officers and crew was reported 'rarely surpassed in the annals of warfare.' With their ship cut to ribbons they fought on and would not surrender in an unequal contest which was conducted simultaneously against several Union warships and which left most of her crew dead or injured on her deck. . . . [Tug CSS *Mosher*] was towing a fire boat against a heavy sloop-of-war, probably USS *Hartford*, when she received a broadside shot and sank instantly. . . . [E]mployed as a telegraph station . . . the steamer [CSS *Star*] was destroyed by a Federal gunboat during the action. . . . In the engagement *Stonewall Jackson* rammed USS *Varuna*, which had already been struck by *Governor Moore*. With *Varuna's* shot glancing off her bow, *Stonewall Jackson* backed off for another blow and struck again in the same place, crushing *Varuna's* side. The shock of the blow turned the Confederate vessel, and she received five 8-inch shells from *Varuna*, abaft her armor. *Varuna* ran aground in sinking condition, and *Stonewall Jackson*, chased by USS *Oneida* coming to *Varuna's* rescue, was driven ashore and burned."—**DANFS.**

DANFS (2), 546, 548, 550, 569. **Moebs** (*CSN*), 107–8. **Nevins** (1), 236. **NUC** (Boston Public Library, Clements Library, Library of Congress, Louisiana State University, Navy Department Library, Ohio State University, University of Virginia Library). **OCLC** (9).

{1862–1863}

Extensive Unpublished Civil War Sailor's Diary

110. Lacy, Milo.

Milo Lacy's Log Book. *[1862–1863]. 3 manuscript vols., 100; 176; 224 p., 19 cm.*

This log book is a significant and unpublished diary of a United States sailor who began service in the waters of Newport News, Virginia, on board USS *Tennessee*. The diary begins with May 13, 1862: "Left McGregor, Iowa, for Omaha, N.T. with the intention of crossing the plains in the escort company, which is to start from the latter place in a short time to protect the emigration for California and Oregon." The first 20 pages are related to that episode and experiences in Nebraska Territory. On August 26, 1862, Lacy decided to join the United States Navy. On September 26, 1862, he joined the crew of *Tennessee*. His diary is an account of subsequent service in the waters of Virginia, North Carolina, and into Louisiana. The details of his service and notation of ships encountered are impressive. The final entry is September 26, 1863.

OCLC (Navy Department Library).

{1862–1864}

Porter's Mississippi River Squadron

111. United States. Navy. Mississippi River Squadron.

General Orders, Mississippi Squadron, Rear Admiral D.D. Porter, Commanding, from October 16th, 1862, to October 29th, 1864. *St. Louis: R.P. Studley and Co., Printers, 1865. 136 p., 22 cm.*

"In October 1862 he [Porter] took command of the Mississippi Squadron and assumed responsibility for the Mississippi and its tributaries north of Vicksburg. In cooperation with the Federal army he was involved in the capture of Arkansas Post January 1863 and then Vicksburg in July. For the latter action he was promoted to rear admiral."—**Faust.**

Faust, 594. **NUC** (Navy Department Library). **OCLC** (Duke University Library, Harvard University Library, Navy Department Library, University of Southern Mississippi).

{1862–1865}

Ram Fleet on Mississippi River
Destruction of Confederate Fleet in Battle of Memphis

112. [Crandall, Warren Daniel] (b. 1838).

History of the Ram Fleet and the Mississippi Marine Brigade in the War for the Union on the Mississippi and Its Tributaries. The Story of the Ellets and Their Men. Written and Published under the Auspices of Their Society of Survivors. Two Parts in One Volume. *St. Louis: [Press of Buscahrt brothers], 1907. 464, [28] p., illus., 22 cm.*

"The basic account."—**Coletta.** "Visiting the besieged city of Sebastopol during the Crimean War, Ellet became convinced that a naval siege could be broken by the use of 'ram-boats'....In March 1862 Secretary of War Edwin M. Stanton commissioned Ellet a colonel subject only to his own authority. Working under deadlines imposed by Stanton, Ellet converted 9 old steamboats into a ram fleet. Though Ellet realized his unarmed rams seemed weak, he believed that audacity in striking the enemy would compensate for this. The test came during the Battle of Memphis, which resulted in the destruction of the Confederate fleet and the surrender of the city...6 June."—**Faust.**

Coletta, #1338. **Faust,** 238–39. **Howes,** C857. **Nevins** (not recorded). **NUC** (15). **OCLC** (53).

{1863}

Instrumental in the Taking of Vicksburg

113. United States. Navy. Mississippi River Squadron.

Internal Rules and Regulations for Vessels of the Mississippi Fleet in the Mississippi River and Tributaries. *Cincinnati, Rickey & Carrol [for the Mississippi Squadron], [1863?]. 36 p. forms, 23 cm.*

"Preface signed by David D. Porter, rear admiral commanding Mississippi squadron."—**NUC.** "As commander of Mississippi River Squadron, [Porter] cooperated with army in taking various areas...including Vicksburg in July 1863."—**Cogar.** In his prefatory note, Porter orders that these rules and regulations be "hung up in some conspicuous place...never to be taken away from the vessel when a Commander leaves." Coverage includes "Mess Arrangements," "Colors," "Reports," "Officers" "Watches," "Military Etiquette," "Answers to Hails," "Hours for Boats," "Routine of Drill for the Week," "Orders," "Yeoman," "Ship's Corporal," and "Additional Orders." There is also detailing of ordnance stations, personnel serving those stations, and individual arms to be carried by personnel serving the ordnance.

Cogar (1), 131–33. **DAH (Concise),** 647. **Nevins** (not recorded). **NUC** (Illinois Historical Society, Minnesota Historical Society, Navy Department Library). **OCLC** (Boston University Library, Duke University Library, Illinois State Historical Society, Minnesota Historial Society Library, Navy Department Library, Public Library of Cincinnati & Hamilton Co.).

[1864]

Only Overseas Naval Battle of Civil War

114. Edge, Frederick Milnes.

The Alabama and Kearsarge: An Account of the Naval Engagement in the British Channel, on Sunday, June 19th, 1864, from Information Furnished to the Writer by the Wounded and Paroled Prisoners of Alabama..., and the Officers of the United States' Sloop-of-War Kearsarge, and Citizens of Cherbourg. By Frederick Milnes Edge. *London: W. Ridgway, 1864. 48 p., 20 cm.*

"An excellent report written shortly after the action; based on personal interviews and inspections by the author."— **Nevins.** Under the command of Raphael Semmes, CSS *Alabama* "became the terror of American vessels.... [S]he sank, burned, or captured more than sixty ships."—**DAH.** This legendary engagement was the only ship-to-ship battle of the Civil War in overseas waters.

DAH (Concise), 23. **Howes,** E45. **Nevins** (1), (listing the 1908 reprint). **Sabin,** #21842. **NUC** (9). **OCLC** (9).

[1864–1865]

Civil War Surgeon

115. Batten, John Mullin (1837-1916).

Reminiscences of Two Years in the United States Navy. By John M. Batten. Printed for the Author. *Lancaster, Pa.: Inquirer printing and publishing co., 1881. 125 p., 19 cm.*

Nevins cites Batten as a surgeon on the gunboat *Valley City* in North Carolina waters from April 1864 to the end of the war. This is the first printing. An enlarged edition of 320 pages was published in 1896.

Howes, B236. **Nevins** (1), 218. **Young,** 10–11. **NUC** (19 copies). **OCLC** (56).

[1864–1865]

Pacific Squadron Commander's Incoming Correspondence

116. [Pearson, Rear Admiral George Frederick].

Album of 210 Manuscript Letters of One or More Pages Being the Incoming Correspondence of the Commander, United States Pacific Squadron from September 24th, 1864 through December 4th, 1865. *1864–1865. 31 cm.*

Pearson served as the Pacific Squadron commander, October 1864–December 1866. This album of his incoming correspondence contains letters and instructions primarily from the Navy Department and the Mare Island Navy Yard, but it also includes letters from the State Department, U.S. District Attorney's Office (Northern California), United States consular offices and legations, U.S. Army Department of Pacific, California gubernatorial office, and private citizens.

Cogar (1), 125–26.

{1871}

243 Koreans Dead
11 Awards of Medal of Honor

117. Anonymous.

A Narrative of the French Expedition to Corea in 1866, the U.S. Expedition in 1871, and the Expedition of H.M.S. "Ringdove" in 1871. *Shanghai: Printed at "The North-China Herald" Office, 1871. 27 p., 23 p.*

An American naval force consisting of USS *Monocacy*, USS *Palos*, and four steam launches arrived at the mouth of the Han River on May 26, 1871. Under the command of Rear Admiral John Rodgers, the force had been sent in retaliation for the murder of the entire crew of the armed schooner *General Sherman*, a United States merchant vessel attempting to open Korea to trade. On June 1, 1871, as the American force under Commodore Rodgers proceeded up the Salee River, it was fired upon by masked batteries on both sides of the river. Fire was returned and the batteries were silenced, two Americans being wounded. On June 10–11, 243 Koreans were killed in an engagement with 650 sailors and marines landed from Commodore Rodgers' expeditionary force. Five Korean forts were reduced. During this battle, feats of valor by American forces resulted in the award of 11 Congressional Medals of Honor. On July 3, 1871, United States forces were withdrawn. Not until 1882 would a treaty be signed with Korea resolving the isolation of Korean ports from international trade.

Cooney, 170. **DAH (Concise),** 519–20. **Sweetman**, 93. **NUC** (Navy Department Library). **OCLC** (Navy Department Library, University of California at Santa Barbara).

{1871}

Korean Intervention
After Action Report

118. Rodgers, John (1812-1882).

Expedition to Corea. Report of Rear-Admiral John Rodgers. *[In* Annual Report of the Secretary of the Navy on the Operations of the Department for the Year 1871. *Washington: Government Printing Office, 1871. 275–313]. 23 cm.*

This essential and detailed account of the intervention begins with June 3, 1871, and ends with July 5.

Cooney, 170. **DAH (Concise),** 519–20. **Sweetman**, 93.

{1871}

Order Awarding 11 Medals of Honor for
Korean Intervention

119. United States. Navy Department. Secretary.

General Order No. 169. Navy Department, Washington, February 8, 1872. Medals of Honor Are Hereby Awarded to the Following-Named Seamen and Marines, Who Have Distinguished Themselves in Battle, or Extraordinary Heroism in the Line of Their Profession: In the Attack on and Capture of the Corean Forts, June 11, 1871 . . . [Geo. M. Robeson, Secretary of the Navy]. *[Washington: 1872]. [1]–3 p., 18 cm.*

This original general order announces the award of the Congressional Medal of Honor to 11 seamen and marines who exhibited extraordinary bravery in the taking of the Korean forts. Each recipient is named and his rank is given together with some description of his heroism. Eight of the recipients were from USS *Colorado*. On page 2, under the caption "In The Attack on the Corean Forts," appear the names of 13 sailors and marines from USS *Alaska* and 18 from USS *Benicia* "who, although not recommended for the higher distinction of Medals of Honor, are entitled to great credit for their good and brave conduct." The men from *Alaska* are specifically noted as having "captured flags inside Fort McKee." The men from *Benicia* are cited generally as having "captured flags."

NUC (Boston Public Library, Brown University, Columbia University, Huntington Library, Library of Congress, Yale University). **OCLC** (Navy Department Library).

{1871}

Broadside Tributes
Poem Printed in U.S. Flagship *Colorado*
Noting Korean Intervention

120. Willis, George R. (d. 1884).

God Speed, Rear Admiral John Rodgers, Homeward Bound. [U.S. Flag Ship *Colorado*, May 15, 1872]. *Broadside with ornamental borders, 21 cm.*

Complimented by

[United Service Magazine, June, 1882]. When Rear-Admiral John Rodgers Died a Great Spirit Was Quenched. Son of One of the Most Distinguished of Our Naval Heroes . . . Fought a Good Fight at Fort Darling, One of the Least Known of Naval Engagements, and Yet One of the Hottest Affairs of the Rebellion . . . Illustrating in His Daily Walk the Spirit of Bayard Taylor's Noble Lines—"The bravest are the tenderest, the loving are the daring." *[United States, 1882]. Broadside surrounded by bold black mourning borders, 22 cm.*

Broadside, a leaf of paper with printing on one side only, offers an exciting field for the researcher. Often little known and rare because of their fragile nature, they can give insights into the past not found in books and pamphlets. These two broadsides, separated by 11 years, express the sentiment captured by Rear Admiral John Rodgers, as leader of the squadron intervening in Korea in 1871 and in death in 1882. The first of the two was probably printed on board U.S. flagship *Colorado* in 1872 as Rodgers made his way home, just short of a year after leading the Korean Intervention of 1871. The poet, identified only by the initials "G.R.W." (George R. Willis) is cited in the **NUC** under the pseudonym "Tom Stopper-Knot" and

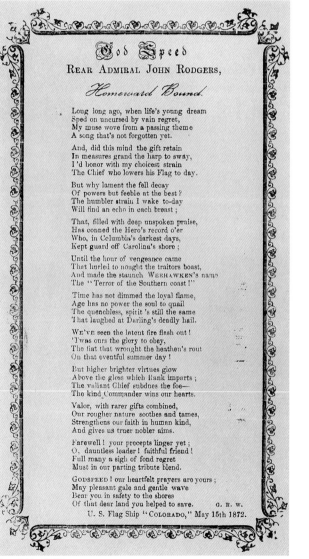

Broadside, 1872

credited with an 1877 book of poems from USS *Tennessee,* of which only the New York Public Library copy is recorded. His ode to Rodgers is in 11 stanzas, each of four lines. One stanza makes note of Rodgers' Korean leadership: "We've seen the latent fire flash out! 'Twas ours the glory to obey, / The fiat that wrought the heathen's rout / On that eventful summer day!'"

NUC (neither broadside recorded). **OCLC** (Navy Department Library, University of California).

{1871}

650 Sailors and Marines Reduce Five Korean Forts

121. Willis, George R. (d. 1884).

The Story of Our Cruise in the U.S. Frigate "Colorado," Flagship of the Asiatic fleet—1870-'71-'72, by George R. Willis. [1873?]. 149 p., illus., 19 cm.

During the reduction of the Korean forts on June 10–11, acts of valor by American seamen and marines resulted in 11 awards of the Congressional Medal of Honor. Eight of the recipients were members of the USS *Colorado* crew. Three of Willis' chapters recount the participation of *Colorado* in the 1871 Korean Intervention: Chapter 11, "The Expedition to Corea"; Chapter 12, "The Flag Insulted!"; and Chapter 13, "The Insult Avenged."

NUC (Library of Congress, Navy Department Library). **OCLC** (American Antiquarian Society, Navy Department Library, New York Historical Society Archives).

{1873}

Hawaii Intervention in Wake of King's Coronation

122. Cummings, Henry.

A Synopsis of the Cruise of the U.S.S. "Tuscarora," from Date of Her Commission to Her Arrival in San Francisco, Cal. Sept. 2d, 1874. Compiled by Henry Cummings. *San Francisco: Cosmopolitan Printing Co., 1874. 61 p., tables, 23 cm.*

As a consequence of riots following coronation of the king, a force of 150 officers and men from USS *Portsmouth* and USS *Tuscarora* landed at Honolulu. Pages 36–41 give an account of this application of naval forces. One of the Navy Department's two copies bears an inscription to the historian, Brantz Mayer, dated San Francisco 1874, from Lieutenant Commander Theodore F. Jewell, the executive officer of *Tuscarora*.

Cooney, 171. **Howes** (not recorded). **NUC** (Free Library of Philadelphia, Library of Congress, Navy Department Library). **OCLC** (15).

{1885}

Flagship of the Panamanian Intervention Expedition

123. Hatton & Hart (photographers).

Scenes On Board a Man-of-War. U.S. Flag-Ship Tennessee *New York: Hatton & Hart, Photo., 15 City Hall Square [c1887]. 20 original mounted photographs, blue cloth covered boards with beveled edges and gilt illustration and entitlement of front board, 28.5 x 38 cm.*

This is apparently an unrecorded album of original photographs. USS *Tennessee* had been the *Madawaska* until May 15, 1869. During the period September 1884 to June 1886, *Tennessee* was the flagship of the North Atlantic Squadron under Rear Admiral James Edward Jouett (1828–1902). It was Jouett who "commanded force sent to Isthmus of Panama in 1885 that quashed rioting there and restored transit across the isthmus."—**Cogar.** The 20 original photographs in this album include one of Admiral Jouett and one of a landing party, the men in that photograph probably veterans of the 1885 land force under Commander McCalla that restored order. The other photographs are primarily on-board depictions of various sections of the crew and include one of the color guard with a gatling gun.

Cogar (1), 86–87. **NUC** (not recorded). **OCLC** (Navy Department Library).

pprentices

*iremen with ship's
ascot and a young
irl (entry 123)*

Occupation of Panama City by the "Fighting Admiral"

124. [McCalla, Bowman Hendry] (1844-1910).

Report of Commander McCalla upon the Naval Expedition to the Isthmus of Panama, April, 1885. *[Washington: Government Printing Office, 1885]. 44 p., 3 maps (2 folding), 2 plans, 23 cm.*

McCalla "frequently led troops into combat during his career, thereby gaining the reputation as a fighting admiral. In 1885, led a landing party of Bluejackets and marines which quickly occupied Panama City and helped quell trouble there."—**Cogar**. McCalla's report as seen here is a detailed account of the personnel, equipment, and operational aspects of the Navy and Marine intervention force, numbering some 280 sailors and 459 marines. He provides the names of the participants and their officers.

Cogar (2), 181–82. **NUC** (Library of Congress, Navy Department Library). **OCLC** (Navy Department Library, New York Public Library).

{1891}

"Fighting Bob" Intervenes at Valparaiso

125. United States. President (1889–1893: Harrison).

Message of the President of the United States Respecting the Relations with Chile: Together with the Diplomatic Correspondence, the Correspondence with Naval Officials, the Inquiry into the Attack on the Seamen of the U.S.S. Baltimore in the Streets of Valparaiso, and Evidence of Officers and Crew of the Steamer Keweenaw Respecting the Ill-treatment of Patrick Shields by the Chilean Police. *Washington: Government Printing Office, 1892. xiv, 664 p., illus., 23 cm.*

This extensive report covers the imposition of American naval forces in the aftermath of an attack on the *Baltimore's* seamen in Valparaiso. The incident was dealt with by Robley Dunglison Evans (1846–1912), nicknamed "Fighting Bob." In the Civil War, he had "commanded a company of marines during assault on Fort Fisher, NC . . . receiving severe wounds. . . . In Aug 1891, captained gunboat *Yorktown* sent to Valparaiso, Chile, where he skillfully handled the diplomatic crisis over the killing of two American sailors from USS *Baltimore* and the use of the American legation as an asylum for political refugees."—**Cogar.**

Cogar (2), 84–85. **NUC** (Boston Public Library, Harvard University Library, John Crerar Research Library, Library of Congress, Pan American Library Union, University of New Mexico). **OCLC** (32).

{1893}

USS *Boston* Supports Settlers against New Constitution

126. Young, Lucien (1852–1912).

The Boston at Hawaii; or, The Observations and Impressions of a Naval Officer during a Stay of Fourteen Months in Those Islands on a Man-of-War, by Lucien Young. *Washington, D.C.: Gibson Bros., 1898. xi, 311 p., illus., 19 cm.*

"While with the *Boston*, he [Young] participated in protecting American interests during the Hawaiian Revolution in 1893."—**Cogar.** On January 16, following Queen Liliukalani's proclamation of a new constitution intended to reduce American influence, the American settlers in Hawaii revolted. The settler uprising was successful following the landing of a force of 150 sailors and marines from USS *Boston* at Honolulu. In 1899, the author revised, enlarged, and reissued the above work as *The Real Hawaii: Its History and Present Condition, Including the True Story of the Revolution.*

Cogar (2), 314–15. **Sweetman,** 100. **NUC** (20 copies). **OCLC** (49).

Lucien Young, U.S. Navy

{1898}

Spanish Account of Destruction of Her West Indies Squadron

127. Cervera y Topete, Pascual (1839–1909).

The Spanish-American War. A Collection of Documents Relative to the Squadron Operations in the West Indies. Arranged by Rear-Admiral Pascual Cervera Y Topete. Translated from the Spanish. Office of Naval Intelligence. *Washington: Government Printing Office, 1899. 165 p., 25 cm.*

Admiral Cervera obtained permission, for his own vindication, to publish these documents, which consist chiefly of communications between himself, the Spanish minister of marine, and the captain-general of Cuba. They cover a period from November, 1897, to the Admiral's return to Spain, and afford a pretty complete history of Spanish naval operations in the West Indies. They show that Cervera protested vigorously against taking his fleet thither, expected nothing but disaster from its feebleness and ill-equipped condition, and sailed out of Santiago harbor only because expressly so ordered by his superior, Captain-General Blanco. The appendix contains the instructions for Camara's 'squadron of reserve,' which never got any further than Port Said."—**Larned.**

Larned, #2424. **NUC** (9). **OCLC** (31).

North Atlantic Squadron by Henry Reuterdahl (entry 129)

{1898}

First Combat Employment of Naval Reserves

128. Doubleday, Russell (b. 1872).

A Gunner Aboard the "Yankee"; from the Diary of Number Five of the Afterport Gun; the Yarn of the Cruise and Fights of the Naval Reserves in the Spanish-American War ed. by H.H. Lewis; with Introduction by W.T. Sampson. *New York: Doubleday & McClure Company, 1898. xv, 312 p., frontispiece, 26 plates (some colored), 21 cm.*

"[T]he experience of a member of the New York Naval Reserve . . . based upon the personal diary of the . . . author."—**Larned.** "As the Commander-in-Chief of the American Naval squadron blockading Santiago and the Cuban coast, the auxiliary cruiser *Yankee*, manned by the New York Naval Reserve, came immediately under my observation. . . . The young men forming the ship's company . . . were called into service several weeks prior to any other Naval Reserve battalion; . . . they have made the name of their ship a household word throughout the country, and have proved that the average American, whether he be clerk or physician, broker, lawyer, or merchant, can . . . prove a capable fighter for his country even amid such strange and novel surroundings as obtained in the naval service."—**Rear Admiral W.T. Sampson.**

Larned, #2428. **Venzon,** 208. **NUC** (16). **OCLC** (74).

Superb Colored Battle Prints in Folio Size

129. Herrick, E.R. & Company (publisher).

Lest We Forget. *New York: E.R. Herrick & Company, 70 Fifth Ave., [1898]. 3 p. l., 16 colored plates in folio size (some double-page), pictorial boards, 31.5 x 49 cm.*

This work is illustrated with dramatic chromolithographs, many naval, which include "The North Atlantic Squadron and Torpedo Flotilla at Sea" (double-page), "How the Battle Ship Indiana Looks in Action," "Night at Hampton Roads," "In Fighting Trim" (double-page), "Shelling a Harbor to Clear Out Submarine Mines, Etc.," "First Attack by Admiral Sampson on San Juan, Porto Rico, May 12," "A Torpedo Boat Destroyer in Action," and "Destruction of Cervera's Fleet."

Bennett (not recorded). **McGrath** (not recorded). **NUC** (Library of Congress, Pennsylvania Historical Society). **OCLC** (Brown University, Connecticut State Library, New York Public Library, New Mexico State University Library, Navy Department Library, Quincy University).

A Henry Reuterdahl chromolithograph depicting a fanciful combat scene of the Spanish-American War period

Destruction of USS *Maine*
Setting Off the Events Leading to Spanish-American War

130. [Sigsbee, Charles Dwight] (1845-1923).

The "Maine" an Account of Her Destruction in Havana Harbor, the Personal Narrative of Captain Charles D. Sigsbee, U.S.N. *New York: Century, 1899. xiv, 270 p., facsimiles, illus., plates, 21 cm.*

It was the explosion on February 15, 1898, that was responsible for "setting off the chain of events that resulted in the Spanish-American War."—**Cogar.** As commanding officer of *Maine*, Sigsbee "was convinced [the] explosion [was] caused by [an] exterior mine. Includes eight appendices with technical description of the *Maine*, reports of the U.S. and Spanish Courts of Inquiry, McKinley's message and Powelson's report on the identification and burial of the dead."—**Venzon.**

Cogar (2), 253–55. **Venzon,** #464. **NUC** (27). **OCLC** (118).

Commemorative Spanish-American War brochure cover

Rare Battle Report Printed in Hong Kong
USS *Baltimore* in the Battle of Manila Bay

131. [Silk, C.A., and Vanderveer, Jean J.].

Spanish-American War, 1898: The U.S.S. "Baltimore," at the Battle of Manila Bay (Philippine Islands), May 1st, 1898. *Hong Kong: Printed by Kelly & Walsh, Limited, Queen's Road and Duddell Street, 1898. [9], 10–39, [1] p., frontispiece (portrait), illus., map (folding), 13 plates, 27 cm.*

This is a handsomely printed memento of the service of USS *Baltimore* in the historic Battle of Manila Bay. The text is entirely in blue ink and each page is surrounded by a red border. Textual illustrations are views of *Baltimore* and are also printed in blue. The 13 full-page plates are nostalgic photographs depicting the crew and officers. The frontispiece is a portrait of Admiral George Dewey. This copy bears a presentation card from Jean J. Vanderveer who authored the work together with C.A. Silk, both of whom participated in the Battle of Manila Bay. The introductory leaf is signed in print by Silk and Vanderveer who note: "The events recorded are as we saw them on board this good ship, true to life; the photographs of the men as we know them, fore and aft." This copy is in the original, flexible leather binding with gilt stamped entitlement, profile of *Baltimore*, and lining of margins. There is also a Buffalo, New York printing which may have been printed in 1898. Of it, the **NUC** locates just the Library of Congress copy.

Venzon (not recorded). **NUC** (Bancroft Library of University of California at Berkeley, Library of Congress). **OCLC** (Bancroft Library of University of California at Berkeley, Library of Congress, Navy Department Library).

Official Report on Sinking of USS *Maine*

132. United States. Naval Court of Inquiry upon Destruction of Battleship Maine.

Message from the President of the United States; Transmitting the Report of the Naval Court of Inquiry upon the Destruction of the Battle Ship Maine in Havana Harbor, February 15, 1898, Together with the Testimony Taken Before the Court. *Washington: U.S. Government Printing Office, 1898. 307 p., illus., (some folding), 23 cm.*

USS *Maine* "was ordered from Key West, Florida, to Havana, Cuba, during that island's revolt against Spanish rule, as an 'act of friendly courtesy.' Spanish authorities in Havana objected to the arrival of the *Maine.* For three weeks the ship lay moored to a buoy 500 yards off the Havana arsenal. There was considerable ill feeling against the United States among the Spaniards, but no untoward incident took place until 9:40 P.M. on February 15, when two explosions threw parts of the *Maine* 200 feet in the air and illuminated the whole harbor.... The forward half of the ship was reduced to a mass of twisted steel; the after section slowly sank.... Separate investigations were soon made by the American and Spanish authorities. Their conclusions differed: the Spaniards reported that an internal explosion, perhaps spontaneous combustion in the coal bunkers, had been the cause; the Americans, that the original cause had been an external explosion that in turn had set off the forward magazines.... Without doubt the catastrophe stirred up national feeling over the difficulties in Cuba, crystallized in the slogan 'Remember the *Maine*,' and was a major factor in bringing the United States to a declaration of war against Spain on April 25 (retroactive to April 21)."—**DAH.**

DAH (4), 227. **NUC** (13). **OCLC** (17).6

Printed On Board U.S. Flagship *New York*
American Order of Battle at Santiago

133. United States. Navy. North Atlantic Squadron.

North Atlantic Station. U.S. Flagship New York (1st Rate), Key West, Florida, March 21, 1898. Squadron General Order No. 2. *[Key West, Fla.: 1898]. [2] p., 21 cm.*

Following the item in the main entry above is Squadron General Order No. 1, dated March 26, 1898, thus after No. 2; the May 2, 1898 instructions for the blockade of Cuba; Admiral Sampson's May 7, 1898 second and third plan of battle; Sampson's May 10, 1898 supplementary order of battle (2 copies); Squadron General Orders No. 8 and No. 9, which are the June 4 and 7 signals for the squadron; 33 issues of the *Squadron Bulletin* printed on board flagship USS *New York*; and 16 folding pages of cruising orders, cruising diagrams, ordnance practice reports, and war plans. The 33 issues of the *Squadron Bulletin* date from June 16, 1898, through August 13, 1898. They are an early and firsthand source on squadron activities and operations.

OCLC (George Washington University Library, Navy Department Library).

Combat Operations at Manila Bay
Rough Log Book of USS *Petrel*

134. United States Ship *Petrel.*

Bureau of Equipment. Form No. 21. Rough Log Book. U.S.S. Ship Petrel Month of May 1898. *[Manila Bay, Philippine Islands], 1898. 67 unnumbered pages of which 64 carry manuscript entries, 43 cm.*

This is the rough log of USS *Petrel* for the entire month of May 1898. "Withdrawing from Hong Kong in April 1898 *Petrel* became part of Dewey's fleet in the campaign against Manila. On 1 May, after Dewey's squadron had defeated the heavy Spanish ships, *Petrel* entered the inner harbor and lowered a boat to destroy 6 Spanish ships there. *Petrel* then steamed to the navy yard at Cavite and forced its surrender. Sent into Cavite to destroy any Spanish ships seeking refuge there 2 May, *Petrel* sent a party ashore which seized the arsenal at Cavite and returned with 2 tugs, *Rapido* and *Hercules*, plus 3 additional launches. *Petrel* continued operations in the Philippines throughout 1898 and 1899."—**DANFS.**

DANFS (5), 277. **OCLC** (Navy Department Library).

{1898}

"Hoisting the First U.S. Flag over Puerto Rico"

135. [Wainwright, Richard] (b. 1849).

Log of the U.S. Gunboat Gloucester, Commanded by Richard Wainwright, and the Official Events of Her Cruise during the Late War with Spain. *Annapolis, Md.: U.S. Naval Institute, 1899. 188 p., frontispiece, plates, 23 cm.*

Serving on board USS *Gloucester* was future Rear Admiral Harry McLaren Pinckney Huse (1858–1942). It was Huse who "commanded a landing force from the *Gloucester* to Guanica, Puerto Rico, on 25 July 1898, securing a landing place for the army, bringing down the Spanish flag, and hoisting the first U.S. flag over Puerto Rico."—**Cogar.** "Reprint of the deck log from refit to September 4, 1898, describing Cervera's breakout, and the capture of Guanica, Puerto Rico."—**Venzon.**

Cogar (2), 139–41. **Venzon,** #575. **NUC** (Boston Public Library, Cleveland Public Library, Library Company of Philadelphia, Library of Congress, Navy Department Library, Pennsylvania Historical Society, Spokane Public Library, U.S. National War College). **OCLC** (33).

{1898}

Battle of Manila Bay
Shipboard Printed Account from
Admiral Dewey's Flagship

136. Young, Louis Stanley (editor).

The Bounding Billow. Published in the Interest of American Men-o'-Warsmen. Published at Intervals on U.S.F.S. Olympia. Manila, Philippine Islands, June, 1898. Vol. I. No. 5. The Battle of Manila Bay. "We Came! We Saw! We Conquered!" "'Twas for Cuba and Our Honor, to Avenge Our Heroes Slain. That Victory Wreathed Our Banner When We Fought the Ships of Spain." *U.S.F.S. Olympia, Manila, Philippine Islands, June, 1898. [2], 3–16 p., illus., 21 cm.*

The *Bounding Billow* "ceased publication with no. 7, Nov./ Dec. 1898."—**NUC.** This is a historic piece, one of major proportions. Printed on board the flagship of Admiral Dewey (USS *Olympia*), it carries a firsthand account of the American victory in the Battle of Manila Bay. "The victory at once made the United States one of the principal powers in the East."—**DAB.** It was *Olympia* that led American forces in that battle. Pages 2–8 are a detailed account of this historic naval action. Page 15 is given entirely to a poem by the editor of this newspaper, Louis Stanley Young. The poem is entitled "The Battle of Manila Bay." Page 16 is a map of the scene of action in Manila Bay.

NUC locates four holdings of which some lack this issue (Columbia University, University of Michigan, Wisconsin State Historical Society, Yale University). **OCLC** (Chattanooga Hamilton Historical Society, Library of Congress, Navy Department Library, Utah State Historical Society, Wisconsin State Historical Society).

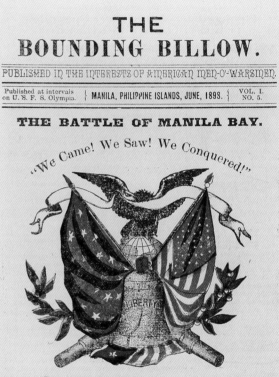

U.S.F.S. Olympia *shipboard publication*

Firsthand Account of River Operations

137. Fiske, Bradley Allen (1854-1942).

War Time in Manila [by] Rear-Admiral Bradley A. Fiske, U.S.N., Navigator of the U.S.S. *Petrel* and *Monadnock* during the Time. *Boston: R.G. Badger, [c1913]. 276 p., plates, 20 cm.*

Petrel, a gunboat of 900-ton displacement, participated in the taking and occupation of Iloilo, Philippine Islands, February 10–12, 1899. On February 21, she arrived off Cebu, which was taken without resistance. By September 1899, "the mountains surrounding the town and garrison at Cebu heated up as rebels continued to threaten the city from large numbers of forts and smaller entrenchments built into the high elevations looking down on Cebu."—**Williams.** On station at Cebu, *Monadnock* supported the Army with naval bombardment and a signal party sent ashore. *Petrel* later in 1899 participated in operations to recover the gunboat *Urdaneta*, following loss of the gunboat to hostile action. *Urdaneta* was the "only naval vessel lost in the Philippine Insurrection."—**Sweetman.** Its commander, Naval Cadet Welborn C. Wood (USNA 1899), was killed by enemy fire as was part of the crew, the remainder falling captive to insurgents. This account by Fiske includes combat operations of *Monadnock* around Fort San Antonio, Pasai, Tondo, Malabon, Caloocan, and Paranaque.

Sweetman, 112. **Williams,** 137–64. **NUC** (14). **OCLC** (56).

American Bombardment of Samoa
Report Printed On Board USS *Philadelphia*

138. Kautz, Albert (1839-1907).

Report of Affairs in Samoa by Rear Admiral Albert Kautz, U.S. Navy to the Secretary of the Navy. *[Samoa?]: U.S.S. Philadelphia Flagship Print, [1899]. 44 p., map, 3 photographs, 34 cm.*

On January 16, 1878, the United States signed a treaty of friendship with Samoa that provided the harbor of Pago Pago as a naval station and coaling facility. On January 24, 1879, Germany signed with Samoa a treaty of friendship that provided the harbor of Apia as a naval and coaling station. The death of King Malietoa Talayou on November 8, 1880 brought civil war. By July 12, 1881, the three powers involved in Samoa (Germany, Great Britain, and the United States) recognized a new king. The remainder of the 1880s and the 1890s saw more civil war and squabbling between these three contending powers in Samoa. On March 15, 1899, British and U.S. warships jointly bombarded Apia as a protest against a king installed under German support. This report is key to that action and is a rare source on it. The copy held by the Navy Department Library was acquired in the early 1930s and is a facsimile by some early photocopying process. The **NUC** does locate two copies (Library of Congress and Navy Department Library) of a tract with a similar title but covering a shorter period (March 6–April 1).

Langer, 939. **NUC** (Library of Congress, Navy Department Library). **OCLC** (Navy Department Library facsimile copy).

Detachment at the British Consulate in Samoa, 1899

Philippine Insurrection
Gunboat Rescue Operation

39. Sonnichsen, Albert (1878-1931).

Ten Months a Captive among Filipinos; Being a Narrative of Adventure and Observations during Imprisonment on the Island of Luzon, P.I. By Albert Sonnichsen. *New York: C. Scribner's Sons, 1901. xiii, 388 p., frontispiece, map, 21 cm.*

On November 25, 1899, the gunboats *Callao* and *Samar* and USS *Oregon* supported a landing party of 142 sailors and 50 marines at Vigan on the upper east coast of Luzon, Philippine Islands. During this operation some of the crew of the gunboat *Urdaneta*, taken prisoner in September 1899, were repatriated as was Lieutenant James C. Gilmore and some of his crew from USS *Yorktown*, who had been involved in operations in April 1899, ordered by Admiral Dewey "to rescue a number of Spanish soldiers and two priests surrounded by a large force of nationalists at Baler." Gilmore and his men were captured by insurgents during the rescue operation. Prior to recovery of the prisoners of war, the landing party of 192 sailors and marines was met by Albert Sonnichsen, "an escaped prisoner who carried with him a message from Gilmore. Sonnichsen led a party from the *Oregon* in search of Gilmore."—**Williams.** Pages 38–88 relate to this episode.

Williams, 181–82. **NUC** (24). **OCLC** (67).

"Boxer" Insurgents Driven from Peking

140. Dix, [Charles Cabry].

The World's Navies in the Boxer Rebellion (China 1900) by Lieut. C.C. Dix, R.N. *London: Digby, Long & Co., 1905. viii, [9]–319 p., frontispiece, plates, 21 cm.*

Chinese insurgent forces known as "Boxers" and sworn to expel foreigners from Chinese soil precipitated the commitment of naval forces for protection of legations at Peking. On May 24, 1900, a detachment of sailors and 28 marines was landed at Taku from USS *Oregon*. Commanded by Captain John T. Myers, their mission was to establish a defensive force for legations under Boxer siege at Peking. On May 29, under the command of Captain Newt H. Hall, USMC, 26 marines from USS *Newark* were landed at Taku. On May 31, the combined force of sailors and marines from *Newark* and *Oregon* arrived in Peking to form an international legation guard to oppose Boxer forces. During the period June 10–26, a force of 112 Americans under Captain B.H. McCalla, commanding officer of *Centurion*, fought as part of the 2,078-man allied force under Admiral Edward Seymour, RN, attempting to reopen the railway between Tientsin and Peking. On June 14, 425 officers and men were dispatched from Cavite, Philippine Islands, for Taku, China. USS *Brooklyn* and *Newark* transported these reinforcements for operations against Boxer insurgents. On June 17, USS *Monocacy* under Commander F.M. Wise was fired upon by the Taku Fort at Ton Chu, China. In an attempt to avoid entanglement with international operations against Boxer insurgents, Wise did not return fire. On June 22, a force of 130 marines under Major L.W.T. Waller, in cooperation with 400 Russian troops, engaged Chinese imperial forces outside Tientsin. The marines and Russians were surrounded and almost overpowered. On August 14, American and allied forces took Peking, ending the Boxer Rebellion. Major Waller and his 482 marines were among the allied forces under Admiral Edward Seymour, RN, that entered Peking. On September 28, all expeditionary forces in China were ordered by the Secretary of the Navy to return to Cavite, Philippine Islands. Although a general work, the index includes entries on American arms and equipment, assistance, troops, and warships. There is also specific mention of Captain McCalla: "Two companies of *Centurion's* men and some thirty Americans, the whole under the direction of Captain M'Calla, USN (a fine old Civil War veteran), were sent to turn the enemy's flank, which was done most successfully."

Cooney, 195–98. **NUC** (Boston Public Library, Duke University, Essex Institute, Florida State University, Navy Department Library, New York Public Library, Stanford University). **OCLC** (16).

Royal Welsh Fusiliers on board Fame *(entry 140)*

The "Fighting Admiral" Leads Ashore

141. [McCalla, Bowman Hendry] (1844-1910).

Memoirs of a Naval Career by Bowman H. McCalla. *Santa Barbara, Calif.: 1910. 4 parts, approximately 1,000 pages, illus., 28 cm.*

McCalla "frequently led troops into combat during his career, thereby gaining the reputation as a fighting admiral. . . . During the Boxer Rebellion in China of 1900, he commanded a landing party as part of the column of the Royal Navy designed to relieve the legations in Peking. Wounded three times during the expedition."—**Cogar.** More than 150 pages of Part 4 of McCalla's memoirs deal with his participation in the Boxer Rebellion. The unpublished memoirs exist in the form of several copies of a typescript. The Navy Department Library holds one such copy bound in four parts (volumes).

Cogar (2), 181–82. **NUC** (not recorded). **OCLC** (Navy Department Library).

Bombardment of the Taku Forts in China

142. United States. Navy Department. Secretary.

Bombardment of the Taku Forts in China. Letter from the Secretary of the Navy, Transmitting, in Response to the Inquiry of the House, Copies of Communications between the Navy Department and Rear Admiral Kempff in Relation to the Bombardment of the Taku Forts in China. *[Washington: Government Printing Office, 1902]. 32 p., map (folding), 22.5 cm.*

An essential source on this intervention in China, this detailed presentation of real-time communications covers June 5, 1900, through September 6, 1900. Pages 25–32 of the Secretary's letter carry some 19 communications that deal with after-action analysis of the intervention. The large foldout map is entitled "Pei-Ho or Peking River." Issued as House Document No. 645 (57th Congress, 1st Session).

OCLC (Navy Department Library).

Second American Naval Biographical Dictionary

143. Bailey, Isaac.

American Naval Biography Compiled by Isaac Bailey. *Providence (R.I.): Published by Isaac Bailey, near Turk's head, 1815. iv, [5]–257, [1] p., 19 cm.*

This is the only printing. The biographies are Thomas Truxtun (pp. 5–13), Edward Preble (pp. 14–51), Alexander Murray (pp. 51–64), John Rodgers (pp. 64–68), Isaac Hull (pp. 69–76), Stephen Decatur (pp. 77–95), Jacob Jones (pp. 94–103), James Lawrence (pp. 104–25), William Bainbridge (pp. 125–55), John Barry (pp. 156–66), Nicholas Biddle (pp. 167–78), David Porter (pp. 179–98), Charles Morris (pp. 199–204), William Henry Allen (pp. 205–23), Oliver H. Perry (pp. 224–30), William Burrows (pp. 231–42), Thomas Aylwin (pp. 242–47), and Thomas Macdonough (pp. 248–54).

Howes, B31. **Harbeck,** 69. **Sabin,** #2734. **NUC** (10). **OCLC** (93).

Joshua Barney and the Defense of Washington

144. Barney, Mary.

A Biographical Memoir of the Late Commodore Joshua Barney: From Autobiographical Notes and Journals in Possession of His Family, and Other Authentic Sources Edited by Mary Barney. *Boston: Gray and Bowen, 1832. xvi, 328 p., leaf of plates, portrait, 22 cm.*

"In the form of a memoir with original material scattered here and there through the text, in notes, and in an appendix. Interesting, but full of prejudice."—**Larned.** "In July 1814 he [Barney] was called to aid in the defense of Washington, D.C. With a small fleet of armed barges he held off the advance of Admiral Sir George Cockburn's fleet, bearing General Robert Ross's army, up Chesapeake Bay, for some weeks and, when the enemy eventually eluded him and threatened the capital, he abandoned the barges and marched his small force of about 500 sailors and marines back to Bladensburg, Maryland, and placed his men, armed with a few ships' guns mounted on carriages, at the center of General William H. Winder's position. The battle on August 24 was a serious defeat for the Americans, who were saved from utter disgrace only by the valiant resistance offered by Barney's small command."—**Webster.**

Howes, B160. **Larned,** #1234. **Rosenbach,** #48. **Sabin** (not recorded). **Webster,** 24. **NUC** (31). **OCLC** (93).

"Gallant Seamen" Celebrated in Song

145. Bartgis, M.E. (publisher).

The Naval Songster, Containing a Collection of the Best Selected American Naval Songs, Relating to the Victories Which Our Gallant Seamen Have So Gloriously Achieved during the Present War. *Frederick Town, Md.: Printed by M.E. Bartgis, 1814. [6], 77, [2] p., 16 cm.*

Among the songs are "Rise Columbia, Brave and Free"; "A Naval Ode" by James C. Holland, S.C.; "Hull's Naval Victory"; "The Tough Yankee Tar!" "America, Commerce & Freedom"; "American Perry Song"; "The Wasp and Frolic"; "A New Song, on Commodore Perry's Victory"; "John Bull & Brother Jonathan or the Seven Naval Victories"; "Constitution and Guerriere, A New Patriotic Song"; "Impromptu on the Capture of the Epervier by the Peacock"; "Macdonough's Victory"; and "Verses, On the Numerous Naval Victories of Republican America."

Shaw and Shoemaker, #32218. **Howes** (not recorded). **Sabin** (not recorded). **NUC** (Maryland Historical Society, Navy Department Library). **OCLC** (Cambridge University, Navy Department Library).

6 THE NAVAL SONGSTER.

Brave Jones then he anſwer'd, " as ſoon as you like."
Saying " Fire away boys, we'll ſoon make them ſtrike."
    Fal de rad el al, &c.

Then down came her colors, and George's croſs fell,
Leaving but a few the ſad ſtory to tell ;
Some went to Old Davy—ſome got the Cholic
Says our brave boys, " It was only a Frolick."
    Fal de rad el al, &c.

On board of a ſhip, Macedonian by name,
In old John Bull's iſland a ſhip of great fame,
Theſe brave fellows now are determin'd to dreſs,
Thoſe bloodhounds who would our bold ſeamen impreſs
    Fal de rad el al, &c.

Here's a health to brave Jones and all his bold crew,
What all good Americans ſurely would do :
We'll drink to his valor, his fame and renown,
And ſpeak of his gallantry all thro' the town.
    Fal de rad el al &c.

[This is one of the ſucceſsful Prize Poems for which the editors of the Port Folio gave a premium of one hundred dollars.]

RISE COLUMBIA, BRAVE AND FREE.

A Naval Ode by James C. Holland, S. C.

When Freedom firſt the triumph ſung,
 That cruſh'd the pomp of Freedom's foes,

THE NAVAL SONGSTER. 7

The Harps of Heav'n reſponſive rung,
 As thus the choral numbers roſe :

Riſe, Columbia ! brave and free !
 Thy thunder, when in battle hurl'd,
Shall rule the billows of the ſea,
 And bid defiance to the world.

Supremely bleſt by Fate's decree,
 Thy hardy tars, in battle brave,
Shall plume thy wings, and keep the free,
 As is the motion of thy wave :

 Riſe, Columbia ! &c.

The Stars that in thy Banner ſhine,
 Shall rain deſtruction on thy foes,
Yet light the brave of every clime,
 To kindred friendſhip and repoſe :

 Riſe, Columbia ! &c.

The ſtorms that on thy ſurges rock,
 Around thy Flag ſhall idly ſweep,
Proof to the tempeſt's fierceſt ſhock,
 Its Stripes ſhall awe the vaſſal deep

 Riſe, Columbia ! &c.

Encircled with a flood of light,
 Thy Eagle ſhall ſupremely riſe,
Lead thee to victory in fight,
 And bear thy glory to the ſkies :

 Riſe, Columbia! &c.

Prize Poem, by James C. Holland

Conquest of California

146. [Bayard, Samuel John] (d. 1879).

A Sketch of the Life of Com. Robert F. Stockton; with an Appendix, Comprising His Correspondence with the Navy Department Respecting His Conquest of California; and Extracts from the Defence of Col. J.C. Fremont, in Relation to the Same Subject; Together with His Speeches in the Senate of the United States, and His Political Letters. *New York: Derby & Jackson, 1856. 210, 131 p., portrait, 24 cm.*

Naval forces under Stockton were prominent in Mexican War operations in California. On August 5, 1846, Santa Barbara was captured by a landing party of sailors and marines from USS *Congress*, 44 guns, Commodore Robert F. Stockton commanding. On August 13, a joint Army-Navy force under command of Commodore Stockton and Major John Fremont captured Los Angeles. Garrisoned by a Marine force led by Lieutenant Gillespie, Mexican forces retook Los Angeles on August 30. On December 29, 1846, Stockton led sailors and marines from San Diego on an expedition to retake Los Angeles. The expeditionary force was constituted from USS *Cyane, Congress*, and USS *Portsmouth*. En route to Los Angeles on January 8, Commodore Stockton's expeditionary force engaged and dislodged 600 Mexican troops entrenched along the San Gabriel River. On January 9–10, 1847, Commodore Stockton's 700-man expeditionary force engaged a Mexican force of 800 men near La Mesa, California. Following two and half hours of fighting, the Mexicans withdrew. American forces took Los Angeles the following day.

Cooney, 61–64. **Howes,** B259. **Sabin,** #91904. **Tutorow,** #3743. **NUC** (21). **OCLC** (134).

First Jewish Captain
Restored to Captain's Rank by Congressional Inquiry

147. [Butler, Benjamin Franklin] (1795-1858).

Defence of Uriah P. Levy, Before the Court of Inquiry, Held at Washington City, Nov. and Dec., 1857: In Pursuance of the Act of Congress, Entitled "An Act to Amend an Act Entitled 'An Act to Promote the Efficiency of the Navy,'" Approved Jan. 16, 1857 Prepared and Read by His Senior Counsel B.F. Butler, of New York; with an Abstract of the Proceedings and Testimony, and an Appendix Containing the Documents Referred To in the Defence. *New York: Bryant, 1858. vii, 169 p., 22 cm.*

Levy's "service was marked by frequent bitter altercations: he was court-martialed six times, cashiered twice from the service (in 1819 and 1842) and then reinstated, and involved in at least one duel, which resulted in the death of his opponent. Most of these conflicts were brought about by the contempt in which he was held by many of his associates in the navy—for not only had he risen to command from the ranks, but he was also a Jew, one of the very few Jewish officers in the service. . . . He was promoted to captain in March 1844 but for the next decade . . . was unable to obtain a command; in 1855, as a consequence, he was dropped from the captains' list. A successful appeal before a congressional board of inquiry in 1857 restored him to rank and . . . he was shortly promoted to commodore and in 1860 was commander of the Mediterranean Squadron."— **Webster.**

Webster, 237. **Sabin** (not recorded). **NUC** (Boston Public Library, Drexel Institute, New York Public Library, Southern Illinois University, Washington Square Library). **OCLC** (Harvard Law Library, Navy Department Library, Southern Illinois University, University of Missouri Law Library, University of Pennsylvania Center for Judaic Studies Library).

Navy Chaplain Governs Monterey Province in 1846

148. Colton, Walter (1797-1851).

Three Years in California by Walter Colton. *New York: A.S. Barnes; Cincinnati: H.W. Derby, 1850. 456 p., facsimile (folding), 12 plates, 19 cm.*

"Colton was Alcalde (governor) of Monterey; his narrative is interesting and valuable."—**Howes. Edel** cites Colton as 'the most commanding figure in all the history of the corps of chaplains. . . . In 1845, while attached to the frigate *Congress*, he made a cruise to California . . . on July 28, 1846, was made alcalde (governor) of the province of Monterey. . . . It was a letter from Walter Colton, published in the Philadelphia North American, which first announced the discovery of gold in California and precipitated the gold rush of 1849 . . . aside from the forceful character of his preaching, and the excellent work he was able to do in opposing such customs as flogging and the rum issue in the naval service, he became a national figure because of his connection with the growth and development of the free institutions of the newly acquired territory of California." "Gives an excellent notion of some aspects of the [Mexican] war."—**Larned.**

Edel, 881–83. **Howes,** C625 (noting also issued as *The Land of Gold*). **Larned,** #2000. **Sabin,** #14800. **NUC** (33). **OCLC** (109).

Legendary Civil War Commando

149. Edwards, Eliza Mary Hatch.

Commander William Barker Cushing of the United States Navy. *London, New York: F. Tennyson Neely, [c1898]. 202 p., 22 cm.*

Cushing (1842–1874), forced to resign from the U.S. Naval Academy for a prank and casual attention to academics, found his way into the operational Navy during the Civil War. During the war, he performed "brilliant feats in blockade duty and in shore raids. On October 27, 1864, he and a volunteer crew took a steam launch armed with a bow torpedo up the Roanoke River to Plymouth, North Carolina. Under a hail of fire he rammed and sank the last Confederate ironclad, the *Albemarle* . . . [and] captured Plymouth. . . . His launch was blown up and he and one of his crew were the only ones to escape death or capture, swimming down the river to safety. The exploit brought him the thanks of Congress. . . . Between major adventures he had continued to take, seemingly routinely, one prize ship after another. Although on several occasions he was long under enemy fire, he received not a scratch through the entire war and many times was the only survivor of an encounter. Such fortune, together with his courage and daring, fostered among his men an almost superstitious trust in him, and prompted Secretary of the Navy Gideon Welles to refer to him as 'the hero of the war.' "—**Webster.**

Moebs (*CSN*), 308. **Harbeck,** 76. **Webster,** 89–90. **NUC** (Boston Public Library, Case Western Reserve University, Duke University, Library of Congress, New York Public Library, University of Virginia Library, Western Reserve Historical Society). **OCLC** (49).

"Fighting Bob" Leads Assault on Fort Fisher

150. [Evans, Robley Dunglison] (1846-1912).

A Sailor's Log; Recollections of Forty Years of Naval Life, by Robley D. Evans . . . *New York: D. Appleton and Company, 1901. ix, 467 p., plates, 22 cm.*

"Nicknamed 'Fighting Bob'. . . [Evans] commanded a company of marines during the assault on Fort Fisher, North Carolina, on 15 January 1865, receiving serious wounds in the attack."—**Cogar. Nevins** cites this work as including "a graphic description of the landing force in that campaign." Pages 83–100 give Evans' account of his participation in the assault on Fort Fisher.

Cogar (1), 84–85. **Nevins** (1), 223. **NUC** (36 copies). **OCLC** (254).

First Naval Biographical Compilation

151. Folsom, Benjamin (1790-1833).

A Compilation of Biographical Sketches of Distinguished Officers in the American Navy, with Other Interesting Matter . . . By Benjamin Folsom. *Newburyport: Published by the compiler, 1814. 187, [1] p., frontispiece (folding), 24 cm.*

This is the only printing of the earliest compilation of biographies on American naval officers cited by **Harbeck**. Subjects of this work are Captain Isaac Hull, Commodore Stephen Decatur, Captain Jacob Jones, Commodore William Bainbridge, Captain James Lawrence, Commodore John Rodgers, Captain William H. Allen, Lieutenant William Burrows, Commodore Oliver Hazard Perry, Commodore Alexander Murray, Lieutenant John C. Aylwin, and Lieutenant James M. Broom. Pages 173–79 provide obituaries together with some verse memorialization. The frontispiece engraving by Bowen depicts the action between *Constitution* and *Guerriere*.

Harbeck, 70. **Howes,** F224. **Sabin,** #24960 (paginating 127 pages). **Shaw and Shoemaker,** #31494. **NUC** (Boston Public Library, Library of Congress, Massachusetts Historical Society, Naval Observatory Library, University of Virginia Library). **OCLC** (19).

U.S. brig Perry *confronting a slave trader, lithograph*

Suppression of the African Slave Trade

152. [Foote, Andrew Hull] (1806–1863).

Africa and the American Flag. By Commander Andrew H. Foote . . . *New York [etc.]: D. Appleton & Co., 1854. 390 p., frontispiece (colored), map, plates (colored), 20 cm.*

"Lieut. Foote commanded the U.S. brig *Perry*, 1850–51, on the coast of Africa, with orders to break up the slave trade carried on in vessels flying the American flag. . . . The last half of the book is practically a copy of the log of the ship during the cruise to capture slavers. The narrative is clear, concise, and includes many thrilling incidents."—**Larned.** Foote was "zealous in putting down the slave trade, a goal he made almost a crusade with subsequent public lectures and his book *Africa and the American Flag, 1854.*"—**Webster.**

Dumond, 52. **Larned,** #1886. **Sabin,** #25013. **Webster,** 126. **Work,** 259. **NUC** (30). **OCLC** (144).

Founder of First Naval Officers' School and First Naval Medical School

153. Harris, Thomas (1784-1861).

The Life and Services of Commodore William Bainbridge, United States Navy. By Thomas Harris, M.D. *Philadelphia: Carey, Lea & Blanchard, 1837. xvi, [17]–254 p., portrait, 21 cm.*

Thomas Harris, the second chief of the Bureau of Medicine and Surgery, established the first Navy medical school. Located at the Philadelphia Navy Yard, the school was intended to train newly appointed medical officers. Commodore William Bainbridge founded the first naval officers' training school at Charlestown Navy Yard in Massachusetts on December 10, 1815.

Coletta, #731. **Harbeck** (73). **Howes** (not recorded). **Rosenbach,** #44. **Sabin,** #30526. **USNI Almanac,** 199–200. **NUC** (24). **OCLC** (65).

African American Commander

154. Healy, M[ichael] A[ugustine] (1839-1904).

Report of the Cruise of the Revenue Marine Steamer Corwin in the Arctic Ocean in the Year 1884. By Capt. M.A. Healy. *Washington: Government Printing Office, 1889. 128 p., frontispiece, plates (some colored), 30 x 24 cm.*

Healy's "first major command was the Thomas Corwin in which he cruised up and down the North Pacific and the Arctic, engaging in spectacular rescue operations and in pioneer explorations of hitherto unknown territory in Alaska. In 1884 and 1885 he published *The Cruise of the Corwin* reporting these explorations."—**Logan.** Michael Augustine Healy (1839–1904) was born into bondage on the plantation of his father, Michael Morris Healy, in Jones County, Georgia, near the city of Macon. His mother was an enslaved African American, Mary Eliza Smith. At the age of nine, Michael Healy was sent by his father to be with his older brothers at Holy Cross College in Worcester, Massachusetts, thus emancipating him. During 1854, Michael ran away from school to follow the sea, serving as a cabin boy. Brought back by his brothers in 1855, he attended school in Montreal, but again ran away. Returned to his family, he was sent to school in Belgium, and once more he ran away. At this point—his father dead—his brothers left him undisturbed to follow the sea. In Australia, at the outbreak of the Civil War, he did not enter military service. In 1865, he joined the forerunner of the United States Coast Guard, the U.S. Revenue Cutter Service. It was in this organization that he would gain prominence as a naval officer, ending as seventh ranked captain in the U.S. Revenue Cutter Service. Across the years he served on the cutters *Active, Moccasin, Reliance, Rush,* and *Vigilant.* He commanded the U.S. Revenue Cutter *Thomas Corwin* in operations in the North Pacific, the Arctic, and in Alaskan waters. Subsequently, he commanded the USRC *Bear,* operating with her off the West Coast of the United States and functioning as the main federal law enforcement officer in the coastal waters of the Alaska Territory. Recipient of many citations for bravery, he was a strict disciplinarian. In 1889, 1891, and 1896, he was court-martialed for "excessive cruelty to seamen." Logan states that Healy is believed to have been a model used by Jack London when writing *The Sea Wolf.* Michael Augustine Healy was the brother of Patrick Francis Healy (1834–1910), an African American Jesuit priest and president of Georgetown University in Washington, D.C. Issued as House Miscellaneous Document 602 (50th Congress, 1st Session).

Logan, 303–30 **Howes** (not recorded). **Matthews** (not recorded). **Moebs** (*Black Soldiers*), #3174 **Work** (not recorded). **NUC** (19). **OCLC** (75).

Legendary Hero Eulogized by Renowned Author

155. [Irving, Washington] (1783-1859).

Biography of James Lawrence, Esq., Late a Captain in the Navy of the United States: Together with a Collection of the Most Interesting Papers, Relative to the Action between the Chesapeake and Shannon, and the Death of Captain Lawrence, &c., &c. Embellished with a Likeness. New-Brunswick, [N.J.]: Printed and published by L. Deare, at Washington's head, 1813. 244 p., portrait, 14 cm.

"Disobeying specific orders with respect to *Chesapeake's* mission, he [Lawrence] put to sea on June 1 to engage HMS *Shannon*, then blockading Boston. In an action that lasted less than fifteen minutes, the *Shannon* was victorious and Lawrence was mortally wounded. His words, 'Don't give up the ship,' said to have been uttered when he was carried below, became a popular slogan."—**DAH.** In February 1804 Lawrence had distinguished himself as "second-in-command in the daring raid into Tripoli harbor to burn the captured frigate *Philadelphia*."—**Webster.**

DAH (Concise), 550–51. **Howes,** I82. **Sabin,** #39356. **Shaw and Shoemaker,** #27952. **Webster,** 227. **NUC** (12). **OCLC** (24).

Barbary War Commander

156. [Kirkland, John Thornton] (1770-1840).

Life of Commodore Preble. [n.p.1810?] 30 p., [3] p.of plates, 24 cm.

This short biography of Maine native Commodore Edward Preble was originally published in two parts in the May and December 1810 issues of *Portfolio.* The Library's copy includes three plates. Two plates are portraits: one is an engraving by T. Kelly, and the other is attributed to S. Harris, sculptor. The third plate is an illustration of the 1804 medal struck in Preble's honor.

Howes, K192. **Sabin,** #38003. **Shaw and Shoemaker,** #20501. **NUC** (American Antiquarian Society, Harvard University Library, Library of Congress). **OCLC** (8).

Victor of Lake Erie
"We Have Met the Enemy and They Are Ours."

157. Mackenzie, Alex[ander] Slidell (1803-1848).

Life of Commodore Oliver Hazard Perry. New York: Harper & Brothers, 1840. 2 vols., [14], 322; 270 p., portrait, 16 cm. First edition.

"This victory [Lake Erie] regained the Michigan-Detroit territory for the United States and had a marked effect on peace negotiation."—**USNI Almanac.**

DAB (7), 490–92. **Howes,** M134. **Sabin,** #43422. **USNI Almanac,** 119. **Webster,** 318. **NUC** (16). **OCLC** (79).

Leader of "the Most Daring Act of the Age"

158. Mackenzie, Alexander Slidell (1803-1848).

Life of Stephen Decatur, a Commodore in the Navy of the United States by Alexander Slidell Mackenzie. *Boston: C.C. Little and J. Brown, 1846. [14], 433 p., facsimiles, 24 cm.*

On February 16, 1804, it was Decatur who carried out the raid on Tripoli harbor, which Admiral Lord Nelson would call "the most bold and daring act of the age." In this action, Decatur commanded eight Americans who surreptitiously entered Tripoli harbor on board *Intrepid* and destroyed the American frigate *Philadelphia,* which had fallen into enemy hands. The *Dictionary of American Biography* notes that Folsom's 1813 and Waldo's 1821 biographical treatments of Decatur "were superseded by Capt. A.S. Mackenzie's *Life of Stephen Decatur...* which has remained standard." This is the only 19th-century printing. Some copies were issued on large paper.

DAB (3), 189. **Howes,** M136. **Sabin,** #43424. **Webster,** 97–98. **NUC** (17). **OCLC** (34).

Signed Copy of Maury's Petition to Congress

159. Maury, M[atthew] F[ontaine] (1806-1873).

The Petition of M.F. Maury to the Senate and House of Representatives in Congress ... *[Observatory, Washington, January, 1856.] 17 p., 21.5 cm.*

Signed by Maury, this is a significant document in the history of Maury's salvaging of his naval career. "With his scientific reputation secure, however, he was placed in a humiliating position by a board of naval officers convened by act of Congress in 1855 to 'promote the efficiency of the navy.' Meeting in secret, the board recommended that certain officers be dropped from the navy, others be placed on furlough, and others still on leave of absence. Maury's name was included in the third list, ostensibly because the injury to his leg unfitted him for sea duty. It is not improbable, however, that his fame, gained on shore, did not endear him to many officers who found themselves assigned to less pleasant service afloat."—**DAB.**

DAB (6), 430. **Sabin,** #46974 (under). **NUC** (Library Company of Philadelphia, Library of Congress, Stanford University, University of Cincinnati, University of Virginia Library). **OCLC** (Mariner's Museum, Stanford University, United States Naval Academy, University of Cincinnati).

Mission to Simon Bolivar Suppression of New York City Draft Riots

160. Meade, Rebecca Paulding.

Life of Hiram Paulding, Rear-Admiral, U.S.N., by Rebecca Paulding Meade. *New York: The Baker & Taylor Co., 1910. ix, 321 p., illus., 19 cm.*

Paulding's career illustrates the varied roles in which Navy personnel and forces were employed. "In 1824, [Paulding] carried despatches from Callao, Peru, deep into the Andean Mountains to Simon Bolivar.... Sailors and marines under his command helped to quell the New York Draft Riots in 1863."—**Cogar.** "Draft riots broke out in response to the Union's first national conscription act, passed 3 March 1863."—**Faust.** "Emphasizes Paulding's early career, but has some material about his service during the early part of the Civil War at Washington, Norfolk, and the New York Navy Yard."—**Nevins.** Pages 19–24 carry an account of Paulding's 1824 mission to Simon Bolivar. Pages 263–65 relate to the draft riots in New York City.

Cogar (1), 124–25. **Faust** (*Historial Times*), 225. **Nevins** (1), 229. **NUC** (9). **OCLC** (58).

Frontispiece

Many Portraits of Naval Officers

161. Peterson, Charles Jacob (1819–1887).

The American Navy: Being an Authentic History of the United States Navy, and Biographical Sketches of American Naval Heroes, from the Formation of the Navy to the Close of the Mexican War, by Charles J. Peterson. Illustrated with Over One Hundred Fine Engravings. *Philadelphia: J.B. Smith & Co., 1856. xiii, 545 p., frontispiece, illus., plates, portraits, 23 cm.*

Peterson begins with colonial times and ends with the Mexican War. All of that accomplished in the first 48 pages! The focus of this work is really biographical. Pages 49–545 present, with many portraits, 36 biographical sketches of American naval officers. This volume was first published in 1852 as *A History of the United States Navy.* Although Peterson's history appeared in five other printings, all are scarce.

Sabin, #61228. **Howes** (not recorded). **NUC** (Navy Department Library, New Hampshire Public Library, University of Chicago). **OCLC** (Navy Department Library, New York Public Library, State Historical Society of Wisconsin).

Paul Revere's Grandson
Dual and Controversial Career

162. Revere, Joseph Warren (1812–1880).

Keel and Saddle: A Retrospect of Forty Years of Military and Naval Service, by Joseph W. Revere. *Boston: J.R. Osgood and company, 1872. xiii, 360 p., 20 cm.*

The story of Joseph Warren Revere is one that suggests the curious turns of history. Grandson of Paul Revere, he entered the Navy as a midshipman during April 1828 and saw varied service with it until 1850. During the Civil War, as a general officer, he was relieved of duty for cowardice. In 1845 he was "assigned to the California coast, where, in command of a landing party from the *Portsmouth,* he raised the flag at Sonoma on July 9, 1846, fought in Stockton's force at the San Gabriel River, and participated in subsequent naval activities on the Mexican west coast. . . . [A]t the close of 1851 he accepted an offer to organize the artillery of the Mexican army, and served as colonel till the following spring, being badly wounded in February during an insurrection in Morelia, Mexico. . . . [For actions] at Chancellorsville . . . May 3, 1863 . . . General Sickles sharply censured him and relieved him of command. He was court-martialed and dismissed, but the sentence—severe in view of his previous record for ability and gallantry—was revoked on September 10, 1864, by President Lincoln, and his resignation accepted."—**DAB.**

DAB (8), 513–14. **Warner,** 395–96. **Webster,** 347. **NUC** (22). **OCLC** (109).

Commander of Troops in Reduction of Korean Forts

163. Schroeder, Seaton (1849-1922).

A Half Century of Naval Service, by Seaton Schroeder. *New York: London: D. Appleton and Company, 1922. ix, [1], [2], 443, [1] p., plates, 21 cm.*

Subsequently to rise to rear admiral rank, Schroeder "served under Commodore John Rodgers on the 1871 expedition against Korean forts, participating in a landing party and in several of the actions."—**Cogar.** Chapter 2 (Asiatic Station—Korean Expedition) gives a good account of this application of American naval power in Korea in 1871.

Cogar (2), 249–50. **NUC** (16). **OCLC** (105).

One of George Washington's First Six Captains

164. Tuckerman, Henry T[heodore] (1813-1871).

The Life of Silas Talbot, a Commodore in the Navy of the United States, By Henry T. Tuckerman. *New York: J.C. Riker, 1850, 137 p., 15 cm.*

"On June 5, 1794, President Washington chose him [Talbot] third in a list of six captains of the new navy then under organization."—**DAB.** "Originally intended to have been included in *Spark's American Biography* series, the publication of which was suspended . . . A scarce biography."—**Lefkowicz.**

Coletta, #797. **DAB** (9), 280. **Harbeck,** 98. **Howes,** T402. **Lefkowicz** (*Catalog Twenty-One*), #300. **Sabin** (not recorded). **Webster,** 427. **NUC** (14). **OCLC** (38).

Case of the Future "Prince of Privateers"

165. United States. Navy Department. Court of Inquiry.

The Case of Lieut. J.N. Maffitt, U.S.N. Before Naval Court of Inquiry, No. 1. *Baltimore: Printed by Joseph Robinson, 185? 76 p., 22 cm.*

The subject of naval inquiries and courts-martial of officer is large and fascinating. The intriguing nature of these lega proceedings is apparent in the case of John Newland Maf fitt (1819–1886) who served in the Confederate States Nav from 1861 to 1865, gaining legendary status and the nick name of the "Prince of Privateers."

NUC (Pennsylvania Historical Society). **OCLC** (Mariner Museum, Navy Department Library, United States Nav Academy).

Commodore Barron on Trial
Following Service in the French Navy

166. United States. Navy Department. Court of Inquiry.

Proceedings of a Court of Enquiry, Held at the Navy Yard, Brooklyn, New York, upon Captain James Barron of the United States' Navy, in May, 1821. *Washington City: Printed by Jacob Gideon, junior, 1822. 2, [1], 4–111 p., 24 cm.*

In this rare document, the court considered charges that Barron had made derogatory statements about the United States government and that he was absent from duty following a five-year period of suspension for his losing *Chesapeake* to HMS *Leopard*. During his suspension, Barron served at high rank in the French navy.

DAB (1), 649–50. **Howes**, B179. **Sabin,** #3644. **NUC** (College of William and Mary, Free Library of Philadelphia, Library of Congress, Miami University at Oxford, Pennsylvania Historical Society, Yale University). **OCLC** (13).

First African American Awarded Medal of Honor

167. United States. Navy Dept.

The Secretary of the Navy hereby awards Medals of Honor to the following named petty officers, seamen, &c., who have "distinguished themselves by gallantry in action and other seamanlike qualities . . ." *[Washington: The Dept.], 1864. 4 p., 18 cm.*

The earliest awarding of the Congressional Medal of Honor to an African American serving with naval forces of the United States was made to Robert Blake of USS *Marblehead*. The citation appears on pages 3–4 of the noted order: " . . . Robert Blake, Contraband, U.S. steamer *Marblehead*, in the engagement with rebel batteries on Stono river, December 25, 1863. . . . Robert Blake, serving as powder-boy, displayed extraordinary courage, alacrity, and intelligence in the discharge of his duties under trying circumstances, and merited the admiration of all."

Moebs (*Black Soldiers*), #6-17. **NUC** (Clements Library, New York Public Library). **OCLC** (Navy Department Library).

Commanders as Authors and Scholars
Pioneer Work on Writings of American Naval Personnel

168. Young, Lucien (1852-1912).

Catalogue of Works by American Naval Authors. Compiled by Lieutenant Lucien Young. Bureau of Navigation, Navy Department. *Washington, D.C.: [Government Printing Office], 1888. 149 p., 25 cm.*

This excellent source on the writings of American enlisted and commissioned naval personnel includes periodical publications and is heavy on technical and scientific publications. Probably the first work of its type, it deserves the attention of a present-day naval history enthusiast who could fill in the gaps and add annotations. The result would be a formidable work.

NUC (Free Library of Philadelphia, Library Company of Philadelphia, Library of Congress, Navy Department Library, Pennsylvania Historical Society, University of Virginia Library). **OCLC** (17).

The guard signal hoisted over the following numbers is to indicate that those numbers are there employed as distinguishing pennants.

The private signal of the squadron is the answering pennant over the ensign at the mast head.

No 4 — Act at discretion
5 — Action prepare for
6 — " Commence
7 — " Close
12 — Withdraw from
13 — Act as already ordered —
15 — Action continue
21 — Ahead go and look out for danger having the signal for danger bent to let it be known

Confederate States' signal flags (entry 172)

Veteran of the *Monitor* and *Merrimack* Engagement

169. Association of Survivors of the Confederate States Navy.

First Annual Report of W.F. Clayton, Secretary of the Association of Survivors of the Confederate States Navy. *Florence, S.C.: Time-Messenger Print, 1900. 11 p., 14 cm.*

Clayton takes note of the "extreme ignorance of the people regarding the Confederate States Navy" and consequently outlines a plan to bring forth documentation of "the many acts of daring of that little band....That history is locked in the breasts of the survivors; nearly all our records were destroyed when Richmond was evacuated. . . . Shall oblivion claim it, or will we do our duty to posterity and to our immediate off-springs, by divulging it?" Secretary Clayton had fought in the historic Battle of Hampton Roads, Virginia (March 8–9, 1862), when the Union ironclad *Monitor* engaged the Confederate ironclad *Merrimack*. This engagement, which inaugurated a new era of naval warfare, was one of just three full-dress naval ship-to-ship battles of the war. Clayton's wartime experiences were published during 1910 as *A Narrative of the Confederate Navy*. The Navy Department copy of his report appears to be the only one located.

Moebs (*CSN*), 104, 425. **NUC** (not recorded). **OCLC** (Navy Department Library).

First Compilation of Confederate Naval Laws

170. Confederate States of America. Army and Navy. Laws.

Laws for the Army and Navy of the Confederate States. *Richmond: Printed By Ritchie & Dunnavant, 1861. [2], [3]–98 p., 23 cm.*

Pages 87–98 carry an index. Pages 25–32 carry "AN ACT to provide for the organization of the Navy," which bears an approval date of March 16, 1861. Specific sections under the Index that relate to naval affairs are "Blockade," "Dock Yards," "Floating Defences of Mississippi," "Gun-Boats," "Inventor of New Armed Vessels," "Light-House Bureau," "Marine Corps," "Maritime Law," "Neutral Flag," "Navy Department," "Prizes," "Privateers," and "Sea Service, and Seamen."

Crandall, #33. **Moebs** (*CSN*), #3. **Parrish and Willingham,** #46. **NUC** (17). **OCLC** (13).

Leadership of Secretary of Navy Mallory Questioned

171. Confederate States of America. Congress. Investigation. Navy Department Affairs. Evidence.

Report of Evidence Taken Before a Joint Special Committee of Both Houses of the Confederate Congress, to Investigate the Affairs of the Navy Department. P. Kean, Reporter. *Richmond, Va.: Geo. P. Evans & Co., Printers, "Whig" Building, [1863?]. [2], [3]–472 p., plate, 22 cm.*

Congressman Foote of the House of Representatives had offered a resolution declaring that the "Navy Department, under its present head, had not the confidence of the country." Consequently, Congressman Barksdale offered a resolution requiring that "a Joint Select Committee of five on the part of the Senate, and five on the part of the House, be appointed to investigate the administration of the Navy Department, under its present head, with power to send for persons and papers, and to report the results of said investigation to the two Houses respectively." The resolution for investigation was adopted on August 27, 1862. The House appointed Barksdale, Boyce, Dupre, Foote, and Lyons to serve. The Senate appointed Clay, Hunter, Maxwell, Phelan, and Semmes. The investigation was conducted from September 4, 1862, through March 24, 1863. This report is the complete record of the committee's meetings and the documentation it considered. The volume is illustrated with a lithographed plate showing the positions of Union and Confederate gunboats at Fort Jackson and Fort St. Philip on the Mississippi River below New Orleans.

Crandall, #90. **Moebs** (*CSN*), #61. **Parrish and Willingham,** #261. **NUC** (29). **OCLC** (30).

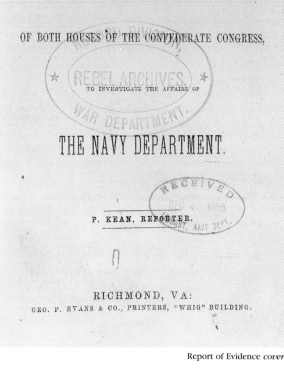

REPORT OF EVIDENCE

TAKEN BEFORE A

JOINT SPECIAL COMMITTEE

OF BOTH HOUSES OF THE CONFEDERATE CONGRESS,

TO INVESTIGATE THE AFFAIRS OF

THE NAVY DEPARTMENT.

P. KEAN, REPORTER.

RICHMOND, VA:
GEO. P. EVANS & CO., PRINTERS, "WHIG" BUILDING.

Report of Evidence *cover*

Unrecorded Confederate Code Book

172. Confederate States of America. Navy Department. Manual.

Telegraphic Dictionary, Navy of the Confederate States. *Richmond, Va.: Tyler, Wise & Allegre, 1861. 395 p., 3 p. manuscript additions, 20 cm.*

Bound in before the work is *Signals for the Use of the Navy of the Confederate States, 1861* (Richmond: Enquirer Book and Job Press, Tyler, Wise & Allegre, [1861]), leaf with manuscript entries on verso, [3], 4–9 p., plate of hand-drawn and hand-colored signal flags, 8 lined leaves (some with manuscript entries), 20 cm. This separate work is **Parrish and Willingham,** #1715 and carries the signals relating to compass, course, situation, action, etc. The manuscript entries are additions to the printed signal numbers, consisting of one to four digits, which could be constructed by number signal flags and correspond to an action, direction, situation, etc. The *Telegraphic Dictionary* presents a three to four digit number code for thousands of words.

Parrish and Willingham (not recorded). **NUC** (not recorded). **OCLC** (Navy Department Library).

Veteran of Combat with Tucker's Naval Brigade

173. Confederate States of America. Navy Department. Ordnance Instructions.

Ordnance Instructions for the Confederate States Navy Relating to the Preparation of Vessels of War for Battle, to the Duties of Officers and Others When at Quarters, to Ordnance and Ordnance Stores, and to Gunnery. London: Saunders, Otley, & Co., [Printed by Spottiswoode and Co.], 1864. 160 leaves, [21] leaves of plates, illus., 28 cm.

Printed in England, where renowned Confederate warships such as CSS *Alabama* had been constructed, this copy belonged to Midshipman Francis L. Place of Louisiana and is signed by him. Place fought in the land battle of Sayler's Creek, Virginia (April 6, 1865), with a division under General Custis Lee that formed the rear guard of General Robert E. Lee's Army of Northern Virginia as it retreated following the fall of Richmond.

Moebs (*CSN*), 177, 250. **NUC** (10). **OCLC** (19).

First Compilation of Confederate Naval Regulations

174. Confederate States of America. Navy Department. Regulations.

Regulations for the Navy of the Confederate States. 1862. Richmond: Macfarlane & Fergusson, printers, 1862. [i]–[iii]–iv, [1], 2–239 p., 17.5 cm.

On the title page, below the entitlement, appears a short letter from Secretary of the Navy S.R. Mallory. Dated April 29, 1862, it notes approval of the Regulations by President Davis and states, "They will accordingly be strictly obeyed, and nothing contrary to them will be enjoined or permitted in any portion of the naval forces of the Confederate States by the officers thereof." Pages [iii]–iv constitute an index. Page [1] is blank. Chapters cover "Rates of vessels of the navy and complements" (1); "Rank and command" (2); "General regulations" (3); "Appointments and promotions" (4); "Military honors and ceremonies" (5); "The commander-in-chief of a fleet or squadron" (6); "Commanders of squadrons and divisions of fleet" (7); "Commanders of vessels" (8); "Commander of a steam vessel" (9); "Executive officer" (10); "Lieutenants and Watch officers" (11); "Master" (12); "Passed Midshipman" (13); "Midshipman" (14); "Boatswain, gunner, carpenter, and sailmaker" (15); " Chief engineer" (16); "Fleet surgeon" (17); "Surgeon" (18); "Passed and other assistant surgeons" (19); "Paymaster" (20); "Chaplain" (21); "Master-at-arms" (22); "Yeoman" (23); "Petty officers and persons of inferior ratings" (24); "Marines—Marines in vessels" (25); "Officer of orders and detail" (26); "General muster-book" (27); "Pay and allowances" (28); "Furloughs and leaves of absence" (29); "Recruiting service" (30); "Honorable discharges" (31); "Receiving vessels" (32); "Surveys" (33); "Correspondence and reports" (34); "Approval of requisitions and accounts" (35); "Officers' apartments, sleeping births [*sic*] and messes" (36); "The commanding officer of a station" (37); "Navy yards—commanding officer" (38); "Navy yards—second in command" (39); "Navy yards—lieutenants" (40); "Navy yards—naval constructor" (41); "Navy yards—chief engineer" (42); "Navy yards—master workmen" (43); "Navy yards—paymaster" (44); "Navy yards—navy storekeeper" (45); "Navy yards—clerk of the yard" (46); "Navy yards—marines in navy yards" (47); "Convoys" (48); and "Prizes and prize money" (49). Pages 231–39 constitute an appendix and provide formats for reports, etc. There is apparently a variant that collates: iv, 216. That variant is **Crandall,** #884, and **Parrish and Willingham,** #1710.

Crandall, #885. **Moebs** (*CSN*), #40. **Parrish and Willingham,** #1711. **OCLC** (12).

Monitor and *Merrimack* Battle Report

175. Confederate States of America. President.

Message of the President. Executive Department, April 10, 1862. To the Senate and House of Representatives of the Confederate States: I Herewith Transmit to Congress a Communication from the Secretary of the Navy, Covering a "Detailed Report of Flag Officer Buchanan, of the Brilliant Triumph of His Squadron Over the Vastly Superior Forces of the Enemy, in Hampton Roads, on the 8th and 9th of March Last." Jefferson Davis. *[Richmond, Va.: 1862]. [2], [3]–4, [5]–13 p., original blank leaf, 22 cm.*

This work is a significant Confederate publication with pages 5–13 carrying the *Report of Flag Officer Buchanan.* Dated, "Naval Hospital, Norfolk, March 27th, 1862" and signed by Buchanan, it details the combat between the ironclads CSS *Virginia* (*Merrimack*) and USS *Monitor* on March 9, 1862 and that of the previous day between *Virginia* and the Union fleet at Hampton Roads, Virginia. This battle that changed naval warfare forever is considered a classic in American naval warfare: "The strategic victory of the *Merrimack* (*Virginia)* in buying time for the Confederacy to shift forces from the Potomac to defend Richmond is an American classic illustration of the influence of sea power upon history."—**DAH.**

Boatner, 94. **Crandall,** #874. **DAH (Concise),** 622–23. **Harwell** *(Hundred),* #17. **Parrish and Willingham,** #1699. **Wakelyn,** 116 (Buchanan). **OCLC** (9).

Confederate Steam Ram *Atlanta*

176. [Davis, Robert Stewart].

History of the Rebel Steam Ram "Atlanta," Now on Exhibition at the Foot of Washington Street, for the Benefit of the Union Volunteer Refreshment Saloon, Philadelphia, with an Interesting Account of the Engagement Which Resulted in Her Capture. *[Philadelphia: Printed by Geo. H. Ives, N.E. Corner of Walnut and Dock Streets, 1863. 12 p. (including original illustrated and printed wrappers), 15 cm.*

A very rare tract, it was issued to promote the exhibition in Philadelphia of the Confederate steam ram *Atlanta* in 1863. She had been captured in the Port Royal Sound of South Carolina during 1863. The tract provides a detailed description of the warship, the verso of the front wrapper carrying a full-page profile plan of her. Robert S. Davis, a reporter for the *Philadelphia Inquirer,* also wrote in the tract a long description describing *Atlanta's* capture. Present during the capture, he witnessed the entire engagement. The verso of the rear wrapper carries a full-page "View of the Union Volunteer Refreshment Saloon," at the Foot of Washington Street, Philadelphia.

Nevins (1), 222. **Sabin,** #32202. **NUC** (10). **OCLC** (14).

Confederate Steam Ram *Atlanta*
Joint Exhibition with the Newly Patented Gatling Gun

177. [Davis, Robert Stewart].

History of the Rebel Steam Ram "Atlanta," Now on Exhibition at Foot of Washington Street, for the Benefit of the Union Volunteer Refreshment Saloon. It Gives Us Great Pleasure to Announce That We Have Procured the Rebel Steam Ram Atlanta, from the United States Government, for a Short Period . . . This Ship Is Reported to Have Been Built by the Voluntary Sale of the Jewelry of Southern Ladies, at a Cost of $1,500,000 . . . The "Atlanta" Is Now Doing a Noble Work, in Replenishing the Funds of an Institution, Organized for the Purpose of Feeding Union Soldiers. *[Philadelphia: Committee of the Union Refreshment Saloon, 1863]. [3], 4–6, p. [2] p. of plates, 24 cm.*

The tract in the preceding entry is presented here in large format. In this issue, the verso of the plate leaf carries a large profile illustration from port side of *Atlanta.* The front side of the plate leaf presents a fine view of "The Gatling Gun or Battery," which was patented on November 4, 1862. Capable of firing 150 to 200 balls per minute at a range of up to a mile and a quarter, this new weapon was on exhibition with the Confederate ram *Atlanta.*

Nevins (not recorded). **Sabin** (not recorded). **NUC** (not recorded). **OCLC** (Navy Department Library).

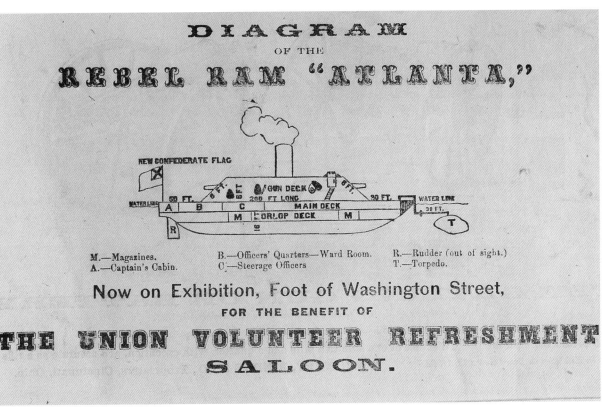

Starboard diagram of
Atlanta *(entry 177)*

Veteran of *Alabama* and *Kearsarge*
Battle off French Coast

178. Kell, John McIntosh (1823–1900).

Recollections of a Naval Life, Including the Cruises of the Confederate States Steamers, "Sumter" and "Alabama." By John McIntosh Kell . . . *Washington: The Neale Company, 1900. 307 p., frontispiece (portrait), 23 cm.*

Before the Civil War, Kell had served in the United States Navy, achieving the rank of Lieutenant. As a Confederate naval officer, he rose to command of CSS *Richmond* in the James River Squadron. On April 19, 1864, Kell fought off the coast of Cherbourg, France, on board CSS *Alabama* against USS *Kearsarge*, in the only formal battle that was fought overseas during the Civil War.

Howes, K39. **Moebs** (*CSN*), 229, 431. **NUC** (23). **OCLC** (142).

"Last Truly Classic Cruise of Private-Armed Sea Power"

179. Murphy, D.F.

These Jeff Davis Cases. Full Report of the Trial of William Smith for Piracy, As One of the Crew of the Confederate Privateer, The Jeff Davis. Before Judges Grier and Cadwalader, in the Circuit Court of the United States, for the Eastern District of Pennsylvania, Held at Philadelphia, in October, 1861, by D.F. Murphy. *Philadelphia: King & Baird, Printers, 1861. [7]–100 p., 23 cm.*

These cases are a complete record of the trial of Smith for charges of piracy as a result of service on board the C.S. privateer *Jefferson Davis,* formerly the slave ship *Echo.* Commissioned on June 18, 1861, she put to sea from Charleston, South Carolina, on June 28. Of her subsequent operations, the *Dictionary of American Naval Fighting Ships* notes that under the command of Louis M. Coxetter, "a name soon to be placed high on the list of 'pirates' most wanted by the U.S. Navy, although he treated his prisoners well, by their own account . . . Coxetter took 9 sail in 7 weeks in 'the last truly classic cruise in the history of private-armed sea power.'"—**DANFS.**

DANFS (2), 539. **Moebs** (*CSN*), 337, 467. **Sabin,** #51456. **NUC** (14). **OCLC** (28).

Seamanship for Confederate Midshipmen

180. Parker, W[illia]m H[arwar].

Questions on Practical Seamanship; Together with Harbor Routine and Evolutions. Prepared for the Midshipmen of the C.S. Navy, by Wm. H. Parker, Commanding C.S. School-Ship Patrick Henry. *Richmond: Macfarlane and Fergusson, Printers, 1863. [4], [5]–92, ii p. 22 cm.*

According to his preface, dated September 28, 1863, Parker prepared the work from notes he made as an instructor in Naval Tactics and Seamanship at the United States Naval Academy, Annapolis. He states that most of his notes were left at the Academy, and consequently the work is incomplete. He advises that "at some future day," he hopes to "issue it in a more creditable manner." The book is in four parts: "Rigging Questions On" (pp. [5]–7), "Harbor Routine" (pp. 8–42), "Evolutions" (pp. 45–61), and "Master's Duties" (pp. 62–92). An index constitutes pages i–ii. Part I is entirely a series of questions without prefatory discussion. The other parts are a combination of prefatory discussion and questions. In some cases he is very detailed, as in his explanation of two methods for determining deviation in a compass.

Crandall, #2467. **Parrish and Willingham,** #1705. **NUC** (Duke University, Emory University, Library of Congress, National Archives, New York Public Library). **OCLC** (Buffalo and Erie County Public Library, Navy Department Library, New York Public Library).

Confederate Naval Raid on Portland, Maine

181. Read, Charles W.

Reminiscences of the Confederate States Navy. [*In* Southern Historical Society Papers, *1876, v. 1, 333–62.].*

"Basic to any study of his exploits."—**Smith.** On board C.S. schooner *Archer,* Read led a raid against Portland, Maine, on June 27, 1863, during which he captured the USRC *Caleb Cushing.* His other operations against the East Coast included the destruction of some 16 ships and bonding of 6. He was widely involved in the naval operations of the war.

Moebs (*CSN*), 132, 471. **Smith** (*American Civil War Navies*), #2006. **Webster,** 342–43.

Classic Work by Confederate Navy Combat Veteran

82. Scharf, J[ohn] Thomas (1843-1898).

History of the Confederate States Navy from Its Organization to the Surrender of Its Last Vessel: Its Stupendous Struggle with the Great Navy of the United States; the Engagements Fought in the Rivers and Harbors of the South, and upon the High Seas; Blockade-Running, First Use of Iron-clads and Torpedoes, and Privateer History, by J. Thomas Scharf. *New York: Rogers & Sherwood; San Francisco: A.L. Bancroft & Co.; etc., etc.], 1887. 824 p., 42 plates, 24 cm.*

This classic is "still unsurpassed in its wealth of information."—**Harwell.** The author was a combat veteran of the Confederate Navy. His service included the Savannah Squadron and the capture of USS *Underwriter* (February 2, 1864). **Larned** cites Scharf for "having been himself one of the pupils of the Naval Academy at Richmond, and having borne a creditable part in some of the famous exploits of his service." This first edition was followed in 1894 by an Albany printing.

Harwell (*Tall Cotton*), #162. **Howes,** S147. **Larned,** #2313. **Loebs** (*CSN*), 258, 426. **Neeser,** #8574. **NUC** (39). **OCLC** (20).

Alabama crew (v.2), lithograph

The Confederate Naval Life Classic

183. Semmes, R[aphael] (1809-1877).

The Cruise of the Alabama and the Sumter. From the Private Journals and Other Papers of Commander R. Semmes, C.S.N., and Other Officers. *London: Saunders, Otley & Co., 1864. 2 vols., [16], 411; [12], 436 p., 7 plates, 21 cm.*

"Among several accounts of life in the Confederate Navy . . . stands out as the classic . . . the outstanding edition is that issued in London in two volumes by Saunders, Otley, and Co. in 1864."—**Harwell.**

Harwell (*Tall Cotton*), #165. **Howes,** S285. **Sabin,** #79076. **NUC** (12). **OCLC** (120).

Last Warship to Lower Confederate Flag
Only Confederate Warship to Circumnavigate Globe

184. United States. Department of State.

Rebel Pirate Shenandoah: Message from the President of the United States, in Answer to a Resolution of the House of Representatives of the 8th Instant, Relative to the Reported Surrender of the Rebel Pirate Shenandoah. *[Washington: Government Printing Office, 1866]. 25 p., 25 cm.*

"The *Shenandoah* came out of the Straits on June 29th, and while running towards the California coast spoke, on August 2nd, the British bark *Baracouta*, 14 days from San Francisco, from whose captain Waddell learned of the capture of President Davis, and the capitulation of the remaining military forces of the Confederacy. The *Shenandoah's* guns were at once dismantled, ports closed, funnels whitewashed, and the ship transformed, so far as external appearance went, into an ordinary merchantman. . . . Waddell decided to give the ship up to British authorities, and brought her into Liverpool on November 6th, not a single vessel having been spoken during the long voyage from the North Pacific."—**Scharf.** "The *Shenandoah* finally lowered its flag, the last to fly over a Confederate combat unit, on November 6, 1865."—**Sifakis.** "The *Shenandoah* has the distinction of being the only Confederate ship to circumnavigate the globe while flying the Confederate States of America's flag."—**Moebs.** Includes correspondence from the U.S. minister to Great Britain, the U.S. consul at Liverpool, and the British Foreign Office.

Howes (not recorded). **Moebs** (*CSN*), 181. **Scharf,** 811. **Sifakis,** 680. **NUC** (New York Public Library, Pennsylvania Historical Society). **OCLC** (Marshall University, Navy Department Library, New York Public Library, Smith College, United States Naval Academy).

Lady Prisoner on Famous
Confederate Warship

185. Williams, Martha [Noyes]
"Mrs. H. Dwight Williams."

A Year in China; and a Narrative of Capture and Imprisonment, When Homeward Bound, On Board the Rebel Pirate Florida. By Mrs. H. Dwight Williams. With an Introductory Note by William Cullen Bryant. *New York: Hurd and Houghton, 1864. xvi, 362 p., 19 cm.*

This work is notable for its account of Mrs. William's captivity on board CSS *Florida* under the command of Captain John Newland Maffitt, perhaps the most flamboyant of the Confederate raider captains. Pages 302–46 are given to that experience. Mrs. Williams, wife of the commissioner to the port of Swatow, China, was taken from the merchant ship *Jacob Bell*. *Harper's Pictorial Weekly* gave a full-page illustration of the capture of *Jacob Bell*, captured in the West Indies on February 12, 1863.

Howes (not recorded). **Moebs** (*CSN*), 505–6. **Nevins** (not recorded). **Sabin** (not recorded). **NUC** (26). **OCLC** (66).

Naval Academy Textbook

186. Coffin, John Huntington Crane (1815-1890).

Navigation and Nautical Astronomy. Prepared for the use of the U.S. Navy Academy. *New York: D. Van Nostrand, 1865. 2 prelim. l., ii, [7]–283 p., diagrams, 20 cm.*

"This treatise was originally prepared by Prof. Chauvenet to be used in manuscript by the students of the Naval Academy. . . . It has been my purpose . . . to prepare a more complete work, or to supplement it with a treatise on navigation. J.H.C. Coffin."—**NUC.** Coffin "was appointed professor of mathematics in the U.S. navy, and in that capacity served on the *Vandalia* and the *Constitution*, in the West India Squadron, at Norfolk navy-yard, and on the Florida surveys, until 1843, when he was placed in charge of the U.S. naval observatory in Washington, remaining until 1853. Afterward he was intrusted with the department of mathematics, and subsequently that of astronomy and navigation, at the U.S. naval academy."—**Appleton.** This is the second edition, fifth printing.

Appleton (1), 675. **NUC** (Library of Congress, Naval Observatory, Navy Department Library). **OCLC** (15).

Scarcity of American-Born Seamen in 1840
Calling for Naval Schools and an Apprentice System

187. [Goin, Thomas] (1803-1847).

Remarks on the Home Squadron, and Naval School, by a Gentleman of New-York, Formerly Connected with the City Press. *New-York: Printed by J.P. Wright, 1840. xii, 40 p., 23 cm.*

"The object of this pamphlet is to call the attention of Congress to the very important fact of the great scarcity of American-born seamen, both in our vessels of war and in our merchant service; to show a few of the great evils resulting to us even in a time of peace from this circumstance, and the greater evils that would result to us from the same, in time of war; to point out in a plain and concise manner how these evils may be remedied by the practical operation of Naval Schools and the Apprenticeship System."—**Preface**.

Rinderknecht and Bruntjen, #40-2669. **Sabin,** #69465. **NUC** (Library of Congress, Navy Department Library, New York Public Library). **OCLC** (8).

Earliest History of United States Naval Academy

188. Marshall, Edward Chauncey (b. 1824).

History of the United States Naval Academy, with Biographical Sketches, and the Names of All Superintendents, Professors and Graduates, to Which Is Added a Record of Some of the Earliest Votes by Congress, of Thanks, Medals, and Swords to Naval Officers, by Edward Chauncey Marshall. *New York: D. Van Nostrand, 1862. 156, 12 p., illus., 2 plates, 19 cm.*

"Still quite useful for those interested in the institution's early days."—**Lefkowicz.**

Howes, M311. **Lefkowicz** (*Catalog Twenty-One*), #205. **Sabin,** #44770. **NUC** (15). **OCLC** (48).

Naval Library and Institute

189. Naval Library and Institute.

Statutes of the Naval Library and Institute. *Boston: D. Clapp, 1842. 7 p., 16 cm.*

The Naval Library and Institute, founded on February 25, 1842, and the Naval Lyceum, founded eight years earlier, were the predecessor organizations to the U.S. Naval Institute, founded in October 1873 and has, since 1874, published the prestigious *U.S. Naval Institute Proceedings*. The Naval Library and Institute had as its objectives "to form a collection of works on General and Naval Literature and Science; to supply a place of deposit for paintings, engravings, maps and charts; for cabinets of curiosities of natural history; for models of naval architecture and machinery connected with the naval profession." Its constitution was accepted on May 27, 1842, and Commodore John Downes was elected as its president. Publications of the Naval Library and Institute are few and rare. The **NUC** locates just three: *Annual Report* (Library Company of Philadelphia, Library of Congress, and New Hampshire State Library); 1860 *By-Laws* (Library of Congress); and an 1867 printing of *Statutes* (Library of Congress and Pennsylvania Historical Society).

Howes (not recorded). **Rinderknecht and Bruntjen** (not recorded). **Sabin** (not recorded). **Skallerup,** 179–84. **NUC** (not recorded). **OCLC** (Navy Department Library).

Seamanship As Taught at Annapolis

190. Totten, B[enjamin] J. (1806–1877).

Naval Text-Book. Letters to the Midshipman of the Unite[d] States Navy on Masting, Rigging, and Managing Vessels o[f] War. Also, a Set of Stationing Tables; a Naval Gun Exercise[;] and a Marine Directory, by B.J. Totten. *Boston: C.C. Littl[e] and J. Brown, 1841. xv, 430p., illus., plate, 22 cm.*

"Lieutenant Benjamin J. Totten's *Naval Text-Book* (1841[)] which was available in the ship's library of 1841–1843, an[d] was probably used in the schools also, was of unique or[i]gin. In compiling his book, Totten used as source materia[l] the manuscript copies of questions and answers which mi[d]shipmen had prepared (such as Midshipmen Foote an[d] Davis had done in 1827) in order to pass their examinatio[n.] This information, Totten observed, had always been 'greed[-]ily sought for the candidates.'"—**Skallerup.** "Contains tech[-]nical details on seamanship as taught at the Naval Academ[y] during the Civil War."—**Nevins.**

Harbeck, 129. **Howes** (not recorded). **Rinderknecht an[d] Bruntjen,** #41-5177. **Sabin** (not recorded). **Nevins** (1[.] 236. **Skallerup,** 158. **NUC** (John Crerar Research Librar[y,] Library of Congress, New York Public Library, Victori[a] Provincial Library in Canada). **OCLC** (12).

First Regulations
"Annapolis" as United States Naval Academy

91. United States. Naval Academy. Secretary.

Rules and Regulations for the Government of the Naval Academy at Annapolis, Md. Prepared by a Board of Navy Officers . . . and Approved by Wm. Ballard Preston, Secretary of the Navy. *Washington: C. Alexander, printer, 1850. 46 p., 22 cm.*

On October 10, 1845, the "Naval School" was opened at Annapolis, Maryland. Its students underwent two years of training there and three years of apprenticeship at sea. On July 1, 1850, the "Naval School" was redesignated the United States Naval Academy. These regulations and rules are the first for "Annapolis" under the designation of United States Naval Academy."

Kane, 404. **Sweetman,** 50–51. **NUC** (Harvard University Library, Library of Congress). **OCLC** (9).

1824 Catalogue of the Navy Department Library

192. United States. Navy Department.

Catalogue of the Library of the Navy Department, 1824. *Washington: [Navy Dept.], 1824. [25] p., 26 cm.*

This reference is the earliest recorded catalog found in the Navy Department Library. The manuscript includes a list of books arranged alphabetically by title, with information on the number and size of volumes. The library collection still includes many books listed in the catalog such as Machiavelli's *The Art of War*, published in Albany, New York, by Henry C. Southwick in 1815; Joseph Huddart's *The Oriental Navigator or, New Directions for Sailing to and from the East Indies*, published in London by Robert Laurie and James Whittle, 1794; and Moritz von Kotzebue's *Narrative of Journey into Persia, in the Suite of the Imperial Russian Embassy, in the Year 1817*, published in Philadelphia by M. Carey and son, 1820. The 1829 *Catalogue of the Navy Department Library* is similar in format to the 1824 but lists prices and "missing" items as well. It also includes a list of maps, charts, paintings and engravings, many of which were later transferred to the Library of Congress.

OCLC (Navy Department Library).

Shipboard Libraries

193. United States. Navy Department. Bureau of Equipment.

Catalogue of the Ship's and Crew's Libraries of the U.S.S. Amphitrite. *Washington: Government Printing Office, 1896. [28] p., 24 cm.*

Bound with *Catalog of the Ship's and Crew's Libraries* for USS *Columbia* (1895), USS *Minneapolis* (1895), and USS *Raleigh* (1895), as well as Bureau of Equipment Form No. 36, *Model Ship's Library* [1895] and Bureau of Equipment Form No. 37, *Model Crew's Library* (1895).

OCLC (Navy Department Library).

Boy Recruiting and Training in 1875

194. United States. Navy Department. Bureau of Equipment and Recruiting.

Regulations for the Enlistment, Government, and Instruction of Boys On Board of the U.S. Naval Training Ships, As Authorized by the Circular of the Navy Department, Dated April 8, 1875. Bureau of Equipment and Recruiting, Navy Department. *Washington: U.S. Government Printing Office, 1878. 60 p., 23 cm.*

Provides a detailed look at daily routines and instructional courses as well as recruiting procedures.

NUC (Library of Congress and Navy Department Library). **OCLC** (Navy Department Library, Duke University, Rutherford B. Hayes Presidential Center Library).

Warship's 1860 Circulating Library

195. United States. Navy. Warship.
U.S. Sloop Narragansett.

U.S. Steam Sloop Narragansett's Circulating Library. *Norfolk, Va.: Argus Print, [1860]. [3], 4–15 p., including printed wrappers with front bearing illustration of* Narragansett, *22 cm.*

The front printed wrapper contains the rules and regulations of this shipboard library. Pages [3]–4 list the library's subscribers by name and rank or rate. Pages [7]–15 list, in short title format, the 302 titles constituting the vessel's library.

OCLC (American Antiquarian Society, Navy Department Library).

CIRCULAR

RELATING TO THE

ENLISTMENT OF BOYS

IN THE

U. S. NAVAL SERVICE.

NAVY DEPARTMENT,
WASHINGTON, *April* 8, 1875.

A limited number of boys between the ages of *sixteen and seventeen years* will be enlisted under the provisions of the following Acts of Congress; viz, Revised Statutes of the United States:

"SECTION 1418. Boys between the ages of sixteen and eighteen years may be enlisted to serve in the Navy until they shall arrive at the age of twenty-one years, &c., &c."

"SECTION 1419. Minors between the ages of sixteen and eighteen years shall not be enlisted for the naval service without the consent of their parents or guardians."

"SECTION 1420. No minor *under the age of sixteen years*, no insane or intoxicated person, and no deserter from the naval or military service of the United States, shall be enlisted in the naval service."

These boys will be sent on board of suitable vessels, to be trained for the naval service, under the following regulations:

Every boy previous to being enlisted must satisfy the Examining Board of Officers—

1st. That he is of robust frame, intelligent, of perfectly sound and healthy constitution, free from any physical defects or malformation, and not subject to fits.

2d. That he is able to read and write.

In special cases, where the boy shows a general intelligence and is otherwise qualified, the Examining Board, if they think fit, may enlist him, notwithstanding his knowledge of reading and writing is imperfect.

3d. That he is of proper age.

No boy less than *sixteen* nor over *seventeen* years of age will be accepted.

Navy Department circular relating to enlistment of boys (entry 194)

1845 Philadelphia Naval School Gunnery Book

196. Ward, James H[armon] (1806–1861).

An Elementary Course of Instruction on Ordnance and Gunnery. Prepared for the Use of the Midshipmen at the Naval School, Philadelphia: Together with a Concise Treatise on Steam. Adapted Especially to the Use of Those Engaged in Steam Navigation, by James H. Ward. *Philadelphia: Carey and Hart, 1845. viii, 109, 59 p., illus., diagrams, tables, 23 cm.*

"Ward was recognized as one of the most scholarly officers in the navy, and after delivering a series of lectures in 1844–1845 at the naval school in Philadelphia and publishing them in the later year as *An Elementary Course* . . . he became executive officer (later commandant of cadets) and head of the ordnance and gunnery department at the new Naval school (subsequently Naval Academy) at Annapolis, Maryland, when it opened in October 1845."—**Webster.** On June 26, 1861, while commanding a small craft flotilla on the Potomac River, Ward became the first United States naval officer to be killed in action.

Rinderknecht and Bruntjen, #45-6710. **USNI Almanac.** 196. **Webster,** 462. **Sabin** (not recorded). **NUC** (Library Company of Philadelphia, Library of Congress, Navy Department Library, Pennsylvania Historical Society). **OCLC** (Library of Congress; Navy Department Library; New York Public Library; University of California at Berkeley, Bancroft Library; United States Military Academy; University of Delaware).

First Navy Steamship to Circumnavigate Globe

197. Allen, George L.

The Pilgrimage of the Ticonderoga by George L. Allen. *[1880?]. 85 p., illus., 18 cm.*

On December 7, 1878, USS *Ticonderoga* sailed from Hampton Roads, Virginia to circumnavigate the globe. On November 9, 1880, she became the "first U.S. navy steamship to sail around the world."—**Cooney.** Chapters cover "Outward Bound" (1), "Maderia" (2), "Sierra Leone" (3), "Monrovia" (4), "Down the Coast" (5), "St. Helena" (6), "Cape Town" (7), "East Coast of Africa" (8), "Searching for Commerce among the Arabs" (9), "Bombay" (10), "Singapore" (11), "Hong Kong" (12), "Japan" (13), "Nagasaki" (14), "The Japs" (15), "Across the Pacific" (16), "Honolulu" (17), and "End Ho" (18). Pages 78–80 provide a list of ports visited.

Cooney, 172. **NUC** (Pennsylvania Historical Society). **OCLC** (Naval Postgraduate School; Navy Department Library; New York Historical Association; Society of California Pioneer Library; University of California at Berkeley, Bancroft Library).

Jeannette 1881–1882 Arctic Expedition
Changed the Map of the Arctic

198. Bliss, Richard W. (1879-1881).

Our Lost Explorers: The Narrative of the Jeannette Arctic Expedition As Related by the Survivors, and in the Records and Last Journals of Lieutenant De Long. Revised by Raymond Lee Newcomb. *Hartford, Conn.: American Publishing Company; San Francisco, A.L. Bancroft & Co., 1882. 479 p., incl. frontispiece, illus., map, plates, 23 cm.*

George Washington De Long (1844–1881) graduated from the U.S. Naval Academy in 1865 and led the *Jeannette* expedition to the Arctic, 1879–1881. His journal was published in 1883. *Jeannette* left San Francisco on July 8, 1879 for a "dash through Bering Strait to the Pole." On September 5, caught in an ice pack, the vessel "drifted to the northwest for over twenty-one months," before being crushed by ice floes in June 1881. Prepared for the emergency, De Long and his men abandoned ship taking provisions and boats with them. For over two months, De Long and his men "fought their way over a frozen sea" to open water. But by the "end of October, the entire command succumbed one by one to starvation and exposure. . . . [Their voyage] established the existence of a northwestward polar drift and at the same time changed the map of the Arctic."—**DAB.**

DAB (3), 228. **USNI Almanac,** 155–56. **NUC** (20). **OCLC** (107).

First Steam-Powered American Warship to Cross Atlantic

199. Bolton, William.

A Narrative of the Last Cruise of the U.S. Steam Frigate Missouri: From the Day She Left Norfolk, Until the Arrival of Her Crew in Boston, Including a Full and Circumstantial Detail of the General Conflagration, Which Took Place at Gibraltar, Resulting in Her Total Loss. Interspersed with Explanatory Remarks by William Bolton, One of the Crew. *Philadelphia: Printed at the Southeast Corner of Second and Market St., 1844. iv, [5]–32 p., original front printed wrapper, 21.5 cm.*

On August 25, 1843, USS *Missouri* arrived at Gibraltar, thus becoming the first United States Navy steam-powered ship to cross the Atlantic Ocean. She was destroyed by fire the next day. The first printing in Boston is dated 1843. As many as four editions are believed to have been printed that year.

Cooney, 59. **Rinderknecht and Bruntjen,** #44-855. **Sabin,** #6250. **Howes** (not recorded). **NUC** (this edition not recorded). **OCLC** (Navy Department Library).

"Please Send Back to De Long"

200. [Bryan, R.W.D.].

Polar Exploration. U.S. Naval Observatory, Washington, D.C., January 25, 1877. *[Washington: 1877]. [1], 2–10 p., 22.5 cm.*

Bryan writes that he is "opposed to all spasmodic efforts to reach the Pole. . . . There have been comparatively few well organized Polar expeditions. . . . They have gone at erratic intervals, knowing comparatively nothing of the laws that govern the Arctic seasons. . . . The only legacies that can be considered of absolute value which these expeditions have left to the world are the feats of heroism and endurance that send the enthusiastic glow of admiration through the heart of humanity. . . . [I]t is important that the efforts toward the Pole be continuous. Let a vessel be always ready at some advance post to push forward whenever an opportunity offers." Issued in caption-title format, this copy bears in manuscript at its head: "Please send back to De Long." The reference is to George Washington De Long (1844–1881) who in 1873 had been "assigned to the *Juniata* which was soon afterwards sent to the Arctic in search of the missing steamer *Polaris*. The adventures of this trip fired his enthusiasm for further Arctic research. . . . After several years of planning . . . secured the Arctic steamer *Pandora*, re-christened her the *Jeannette*, and fitted her out for the dash through the Bering Strait to the Pole. . . . Although the *Jeannette* expedition failed in its original purpose, it established the existence of a northwestward polar drift and at the same time changed the map of the Arctic by delimiting the size of Wrangel Island and by discovering the small group of islands now named for its courageous commander."— **DAB.** De Long died during the expedition.

DAB (3), 227–28. **NUC** (not recorded). **OCLC** (Navy Department Library).

United States Exploring Expedition, 1838–1842

201. Colvocoresses, George Musalas (1816–1872).

Four Years in a Government Exploring Expedition; to the Island of Madeira, Cape Verde Islands, Brazil . . . By Lieut. Geo. M. Colvocoresses. *New York: Cornish, Lamport & co., 1852. 371 p., frontispiece, plates, 19 cm. First edition.*

"Compiled from a journal . . . which the author kept in obedience to a 'General order' from the Navy department."— **Preface.**

Sabin, #14907. **Young,** 24–25. **NUC** (27). **OCLC** (55).

Southern Hemisphere Astronomical Expedition

202. Gilliss, James Melville (1811–1865).

The U.S. Naval Astronomical Expedition to the Southern Hemisphere, during the Years 1849-'50-'51-'52. *Washington: A.O.P. Nicholson, printer, 1855–1856. 4 vols., frontispiece, illus., maps (part folding), plans, plates (some colored), 30 x 23 cm.*

"On August 16, 1849, Lieutenant J.M. Gilliss, USN, left New York as a passenger on board the merchant steamer *Empire City*. Gilliss had orders from the Secretary of the Navy, dated November 16, 1848, to erect an observatory and other buildings necessary to conduct a series of observations on Mars and Venus in order to obtain a new, or to confirm the old, measurement of solar parallax."—**Ponko.**
It was Gilliss who published the first American volume of astronomical observations.

Ponko, 93–107. **Sabin,** #27419. **USNI Almanac,** 152–53. **Webster,** 142. **NUC** (32). **OCLC** (149).

Equatorial telescope (v.3), lithograph

Chilean parrot (v.2), lithograph, drawn by W. Dreser

North Pacific 1853–1856 Exploring Expedition
Main Contemporary Narrative

203. Habersham, A[lexander] W[ylly] (1826–1883).

My Last Cruise; or, Where We Went and What We Saw: Being an Account of Visits to Malay and Loo-Choo Islands, the Coasts of China, Formosa, Japan, Kamschatka, Siberia, and the Mouth of the Amoor River. By A.W. Habersham . . . *Philadelphia: J.B. Lippincott & Co., 1857. 1 p. l., 507 p., frontispiece, 29 plates, 22 cm.*

"In August 1852, Congress appropriated $125,000 'for prosecuting a survey and reconnaissance for naval and commercial purposes, of such parts of the Bering Straits, of the North Pacific Ocean and of the China Seas, as are frequented by American whaleships and by trading vessels in their routes between the United States and China'. . . . [S]ome of the officers and men of the expedition did manage to interest themselves in the sights and everyday life in China. One of these was Lieutenant A.W. Habersham, who . . . recorded his observations of the Hong Kong area. . . . This account and a German language work by Wilhelm Heine are the main published contemporary narratives of the expedition."—**Ponko.**

Ponko, 206–30. **Sabin,** #29466. **NUC** (18). **OCLC** (47).

Jeannette Search Expedition
of 1882–1884
Photographic Plates of Russian Ceremonial Tribute

204. [Harber, Giles Bates] (1849-1925).

Letter from the Secretary of the Navy: Transmitting Report of Lieut. G.B. Harber, U.S.N., Concerning the Search for the Missing Persons of the Jeannette Expedition, and the Transportation of the Remains of Lieutenant-Commander De Long and Companions to the United States. *[Washington: Government Printing Office, 1884]. 75 p., map (folding), 4 plates, 23 cm.*

Harber "commanded the search expedition for survivors of the *Jeannette* Expedition from 1882–1884, returning with the bodies of ten members of the expedition."—**Cogar.** The four plates depict the ceremonial tent, guards, and railcar provided by Russia for the remains of Commander De Long and companions as they were transported back to the United States through Russia.

Cogar (2), 121–22. **Howes** (not recorded). **NUC** (Rutherford B. Hayes Presidential Center Library, Library of Congress, New York State Library, Toronto Public Library, U.S. Geological Survey Library, University of British Columbia). **OCLC** (18).

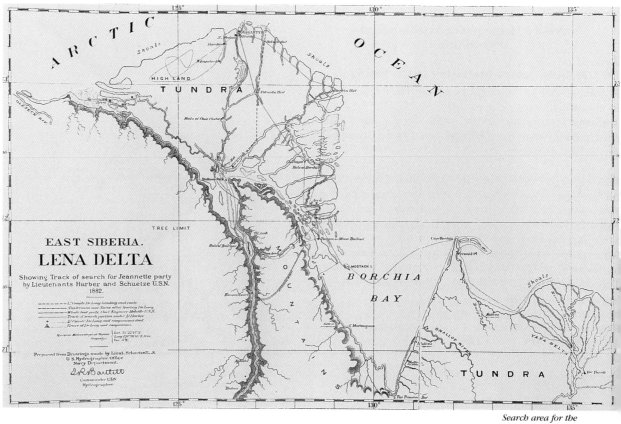

Search area for the
Jeannette *Party*

African American Commander

205. Healy, M[ichael] A[ugustine] (1839-1904).

Report of the Cruise of the Revenue Marine Steamer Corwin in the Arctic Ocean in the Year 1885. By Capt. M.A. Healy. Washington: Government Printing Office, 1887. 102 p., frontispiece, plates (some colored), maps (part folding), diagrams, 30 x 24 cm.

Michael Augustine Healy (1839–1904) was born into bondage on the plantation of his father, Michael Morris Healy, in Jones County, Georgia, near the city of Macon. His mother was an enslaved African American, Mary Eliza Smith. At the age of nine, Michael Healy was sent by his father to be with his older brothers at Holy Cross College in Worcester, Massachusetts, thus emancipating him. During 1854, Michael ran away from school to follow the sea, serving as a cabin boy. Brought back by his brothers in 1855, he attended school in Montreal, but again ran away. Returned to his family, he was sent to school in Belgium, and once more he ran away. At this point—his father dead—his brothers left him undisturbed to follow the sea. In Australia at the outbreak of the Civil War, he did not enter military service. In 1865, he joined the forerunner of the United States Coast Guard, the U.S. Revenue Cutter Service. It was in this organization that he would gain prominence as a naval officer, ending as seventh ranked captain in the U.S. Revenue Cutter Service. Over the years he served on the cutters Active, Moccasin, Reliance, Rush, and Vigilant. He commanded the USRC Thomas Corwin in operations in the North Pacific, the Arctic, and in Alaskan waters. Subsequently, he commanded the USRC Bear, operating with her off the West Coast of the United States and functioning as the main federal law enforcement officer in the coastal waters of the Alaska Territory. Recipient of many citations for bravery, he was a strict disciplinarian. In 1889, 1891, and 1896, he was court-martialed for "excessive cruelty to seamen." Logan states that Healy is believed to have been a model used by Jack London when writing The Sea Wolf. Michael Augustine Healy was the brother of Patrick Francis Healy (1834–1910), an African American Jesuit priest and president of Georgetown University in Washington, D.C. Issued as House Executive Document 153 (1st Session, 49th Congress).

Howes (not recorded). **Logan**, 303–4. **Moebs** (Black Soldiers), #318. **Matthews** (not recorded). **Work** (not recorded). **NUC** (13). **OCLC** (54).

Caused Mark Twain to Become River Pilot and Writer

206. Herndon, W[illia]m Lewis (1813-1857).

Exploration of the Valley of the Amazon, Made under the Direction of the Navy Department, by Wm. Lewis Herndon and Lardner Gibbon. Washington: R. Armstrong [etc.], public printer, 1854. 2 vols., illus., 52 plates plus separate atlas with 5 maps (folding), 22 cm.

"The first Navy expedition to this area . . . account of his journey has remained ever since a foundation for other expedition reports . . . furnished much information on that mysterious area, and one interesting and little known sidelight: Mark Twain said that it was his reading of Herndon's account of the expedition which led him to his life as a steamboat pilot and later, writer."—**USNI Almanac.** "[C]ontains minute, accurate, and very interesting accounts of the aborigines of the Andes, and the Amazon and its tributaries."—**Sabin.**

Larned, #4077. **Sabin,** #31524. **USNI Almanac,** 152. **NUC** (32). **OCLC** (215).

South American
exploring expedition,
lithograph, sketched
by I. Gibbon

Northwestern Corner of Greenland in 1891

207. Keely, Robert N[eff] (b. 1860).

In Arctic seas: The Voyage of the "Kite" with the Peary Expedition. Together with a Transcript of the Log of the "Kite," by Robert N. Keely and G.G. Davis. *Philadelphia: R.C. Hartranft, 1892. vii, 524 p., frontispiece, illus., maps (1 folding), plates (1 colored), portraits, 23 cm.*

"The work herewith presented to the reader is divided into two separate but closely related parts. The first part, 'The Voyage of the Kite', is the narrative of the expedition sent in 1891 to convey Lieut. Peary to the northwestern corner of Greenland; the second, under the general title of *The Peary Relief Expedition,* is a record of the second voyage of the same vessel in the present year (1892), when she was sent to bring the party home again."—**Publisher's Preface**. "Best edition. Published the same year as the first edition, but with the addition of the log of the 'Kite' on the relief expedition, July 4–September 22, 1892."—**Lefkowicz.**

Lefkowicz (*Catalog Twenty-One*), #172. **USNI Almanac,** 157. **NUC** (16). **OCLC (**102).

First Atlantic Ocean Hydrographic Expedition

208. Lee, Samuel Phillips (1812-1897).

Reports and Charts of the Cruise of the U.S. Brig Dolphin, Made under Direction of the Navy Department, by S.P. Lee. *Washington: B. Tucker, Printer to the Senate, 1854. [1], vii, [1], 331, 2 p., charts (folding), illus., map (folding), tables, 23 cm.*

On October 30, 1852, under command of Lieutenant Samuel P. Lee, USS *Dolphin* departed on an "oceanic research voyage to test the theories of Lt. M.F. Maury, USN, concerning winds, tides, and currents. This was the U.S. Navy's first hydrographic voyage in the Atlantic."—**Cooney.** "In performing this duty he cruised all over the Atlantic. His report was . . . of considerable assistance to Maury in his oceanographic work."—**DAB.**

DAB (6), 129–30. **Cooney,** 69. **Sabin,** #39800. **USNI Almanac,** 154. **Webster,** 234. **NUC** (13). **OCLC** (54).

USS *Pensacola* Eclipse Expedition

209. Loomis, Eben Jenks (1828-1912).

An Eclipse Party in Africa; Chasing Summer across the Equator in the U.S.S. Pensacola, by Eben J. Loomis. *Boston: Robert Brothers, 1896. xii, 218 p., illus., 23 cm.*

David P. Todd of Amherst College Observatory headed this expedition. He notes of it in the introduction: "When, early in September, 1889, I was called by the Secretary of the Navy to the charge of the 'Eclipse Expedition to Africa' authorized by Congress six months previously, it seemed best to organize the Expedition not only with reference to astronomy, but to other branches of scientific investigation as well; for the region to be visited was but imperfectly known. The personnel of the Expedition, therefore, included workers in terrestrial physics, meteorology, natural history, linguistics, and ethnology; and an abundant harvest was garnered, which has from time to time been set forth in technical papers."

NUC (Cleveland Public Library, Library of Congress, Navy Department Library, Princeton University, Smithsonian Institution, University of California at Berkeley, University of North Carolina). **OCLC** (35).

1875 Panama Canal Expedition

10. Lull, Edward P[helps] (1836-1887).

eports of Explorations and Surveys for the Location of nteroceanic Ship-Canals through the Isthmus of Panama nd by the Valley of the River Napipi, by U.S. Naval Expedi- ons. 1875. Commander Edward P. Lull, U.S.N., Commanding anama Expedition. Lieutenant Frederick Collins, U.S.N., ommanding Napipi Expedition. *Washington: Government rinting Office, 1879. 124 p., 3 maps (folding), 10 plans nd profiles (folding), 29 cm.*

ull commanded "the Nicaragua survey expedition in 872–'3, was a member of the interoceanic ship-canal com- iission in 1873–'4, and the following year had charge of a pecial survey of the Panama canal route."—**Appleton.**

.ppleton (4), 53. **DAB** (6), 500–501. **NUC** (12). **OCLC** (54).

Dead Sea 1847–1848 Expedition
Use of Camels in American Southwest

211. Lynch, W[illiam] F[rancis] (1810-1865).

Narrative of the United States' Expedition to the River Jordan and the Dead Sea, by W.F. Lynch, U.S.N., Commander of the Expedition . . . *Philadelphia: Lea and Blanchard, 1849. xx, [13]–509 p., frontispiece, 2 maps (folding), 27 plates, 25 cm.*

"On November 20, 1847, the USS *Supply*, a storeship under the command of Lieutenant William F. Lynch, got underway from the Brooklyn Navy Yard. . . . Lynch's orders were, upon reaching the Mediterranean, to deliver needed provi- sions to the United States Mediterranean Squadron . . . [then] to go to Constantinople and . . . apply to the Ottoman gov- ernment for permission to pass through its territory for the purpose of exploring the River Jordan and the Dead Sea."— **Ponko.** Lynch "landed early in April 1848 at Acre. From there he and his party of 14 men hauled 2 metal boats over- land to the Sea of Galilee, whence they boated down the Jordan River to the Dead Sea. Returning overland through Palestine to the Mediterranean, the party embarked and arrived back in New York in December 1848."—**Webster.** Lynch used camels in Syria on the final segment of his jour- ney. He was "later instrumental in having a group of these beasts shipped to the United States for use in the south- west."—**USNI Almanac.** Major Henry C. Wayne's analysis of military use of camels appeared in *Report of the Secre- tary of War, Communicating, in Compliance with a Resolu- tion of the Senate of February 2, 1857, Information Respect- ing the Purchase of Camels for the Purposes of Military Transportation, 1857.*

Ponko, 33–60. **Sabin,** #42817. **Webster,** 250. **USNI Almanac,** 152. **NUC** (39). **OCLC** (93).

Dead Sea 1847–1848 Expedition

212. Montague, Edward P. (editor).

Narrative of the Late Expedition to the Dead Sea. From a Diary by One of the Party. Ed. by Edward P. Montague. With Incidents and Adventures from the Time of the Sailing of the Expedition in November, 1847, Till the Return of the Same in December, 1848. *Philadelphia: Carey and Hart, 1849. xxiv, 336 p., map (folding), 19 cm.*

"[H]eightened public interest in the expedition."—**Ponko.**

Ponko, 56. **Sabin** (not recorded). **NUC** (13). **OCLC** (44).

1838–1840 Global Circumnavigation

213. Murrell, William Meacham.

Cruise of the Frigate Columbia around the World, under the Command of Commodore George C. Read, in 1838, 1839, and 1840. By William Meacham Murrell. *Boston: B.B. Mussey, 1840. 230, [2] p., 16 cm.*

Columbia departed Hampton Roads, Virginia on May 6, 1838, and returned to the United States with arrival at Boston on June 16, 1840. The vessel's route of circumnavigation was Hampton Roads, Madeira, Rio, Muscat, Bombay, Goa, Columbo, Quallah Battoo, Muckie, Soosoo, Penang, Singapore, Macao, Toonkoo Bay, Oahu, Tahiti, Valparaiso, Callao, Rio, and Boston. *Columbia* entered 18 ports, was 459 days at sea, 313 days in port, and traversed 54,796 knots.

Howes (not recorded). **Sabin,** #51554. **NUC** (American Antiquarian Society, Library of Congress, Longwood Gardens, New York Public Library, University of California at Berkeley, Victoria Provincial Archives). **OCLC** (20).

Alaska Survey of 1885–1887
The Work of a U.S. Navy Commander-Scholar

214. Niblack, Albert P[arker] (1859-1929).

The Coast Indians of Southern Alaska and Northern British Columbia. By Ensign Albert P. Niblack . . . Based on the Collections in the U.S. National Museum, and on the Personal Observation of the Writer in Connection with the Survey of Alaska in the Season of 1885, 1886, and 1887. *[Washington: U.S. Government Printing Office, 1890?]. 225–386 p., illus., maps (folding), 24 cm.*

Niblack is among the group of commander-scholars who found expression in the Navy. A veteran of service in the Spanish-American War and Philippine Insurrection, he commanded the battleship *Michigan* and the 3rd Seaman Regiment during the occupation of Vera Cruz, Mexico in 1914 and several divisions and squadrons of the Atlantic Fleet in World War I. By 1921 he had assumed command of all naval forces in European waters. His writings listed in **Cogar** substantiate the breadth of his experience and thought.

Cogar (2), 201–4. **Howes** (not recorded). **NUC** (22). **OCLC** (60).

South American Expedition Classic

215. Page, Thomas J[efferson] (1808-1899).

La Plata, the Argentine Confederation, and Paraguay. Being Narrative of the Exploration of the Tributaries of the River La Plata and Adjacent Countries during the Years 1853, '54, '55, and '56, under the Orders of the United States Government. By Thomas J. Page, U.S.N., Commander of the Expedition. *London: Trubner & Co., 1859. [1], [ix]–xxii, [1], [25]–632 p., diagrams, illus., map (folding), plates, 24 cm.*

"On January 19, 1853, the USS *Water Witch*, a 150-foot long paddle wheel steamer under the command of Lieutenant Thomas J. Page, left Baltimore . . . to 'explore and survey the river La Plata and its tributaries.' . . . Page in leading two expeditions to explore the La Plata and its tributaries accomplished a feat of reporting on the geographical features and economic resources of the region superior to that of any other nineteenth-century expedition to South America."—**Ponko.** During this exploration, Page charted 3,600 miles of riverbed. "In February 1855, while on the Parana River, the *Water-Witch* was fired on from a Paraguayan fort the vessel suffered considerable damage and one sailor was killed. On his return to the United States in May 1856 Page began agitating for a punitive expedition. Such an expedition of 19 ships was sent out in October 1858 under Commodore William B. Shubrick, with Page . . . as fleet captain and second-in-command. The show of force produced satisfactory diplomatic settlement."—**Webster.**

Larned, #4083. **Ponko,** 108–33. **Sabin,** #58161. **Skallerup,** 192. **USNI Almanac,** 152. **Webster,** 305. **NUC** (25). **OCLC** (10).

South Sea Surveying and Exploring Expedition

216. Reynolds, J[eremiah] N. (1799-1858).

xploring Expedition. Correspondence between J.N. eynolds and the Hon. Mahlon Dickerson, under the espective Signatures of "Citizen" and "Friend to the Navy," ouching the South Sea Surveying and Exploring Expedition. *New York: 1838?]. 151 p., 22 cm.*

Originally published as the 'Correspondence of Citizen and riend to the Navy,' in the *New York Times* and *N.Y. Courier* nd *Enquirer*."—**Sabin.**

Rinderknecht, #52640. **Howes** (not recorded). **Sabin,** 70431. **NUC** (Brown University, Library of Congress, New ork Public Library, Victoria Provincial Archives). **OCLC** (11).

First Treaty with an Oriental Power

217. Roberts, Edmund (1784-1836).

Embassy to the Eastern Courts of Cochin-China, Siam, and Muscat; in the U.S. Sloop-of-War Peacock . . . during the Years 1832-3-4. By Edmund Roberts. *New York: Harper & Brothers, 1837. 432 p., 21 cm.*

On March 20, 1833, Captain Geisinger of USS *Peacock* negotiated and signed the first treaty between the United States and an Asian power. Chapter 20 (pp. 305–18) deal with Siam and the treaty.

Cooney, 53. **Rinderknecht,** #46576. **Sabin,** #71884. **NUC** (17). **OCLC** (62).

1870 Isthmus of Darien Canal Expedition

218. Selfridge, Thomas Oliver (1836-1924).

Reports of Explorations and Surveys to Ascertain the Practicability of a Ship-Canal between the Atlantic and Pacific Oceans by the Way of the Isthmus of Darien. By Thos. Oliver Selfridge, Commander, U.S. Navy. *Washington: Government Printing Office, 1874. 268 p., maps, plates (part folding), 30 cm.*

In 1869, Selfridge was "ordered to conduct a survey of the Isthmus of Darien for an interoceanic canal. He explored all the country south of Panama to the headwaters of the Atrato River in South America. . . . Four years later he was selected to survey the Amazon and Madeira Rivers, and the following year was invited by Ferdinand de Lesseps to attend a congress on interoceanic canals, meeting in Paris."—**DAB.**

Cogar (1), 163–64. **DAB** (8), 568–69. **NUC** (26). **OCLC** (122).

1870–1871 Isthmus of Tehuantepec Canal Expedition

219. Shufeldt, Robert W. (1822-1895).

Reports of Explorations and Surveys, to Ascertain the Practicability of a Ship-Canal Between the Atlantic and Pacific Oceans, by the Way of the Isthmus of Tehuantepec. By Robert W. Shufeldt. Made under the Direction of the Secretary of the Navy. *Washington: Government Printing Office, 1872. 151 p., 20 maps (folding), plates, 31 x 24 cm.*

Shufeldt notes, "A canal through the Isthmus of Tehuantepec is an extension of the Mississippi River to the Pacific Ocean. It converts the Gulf of Mexico into an American lake. In time of war it closes that Gulf to all enemies."

Cogar (1), 166–67. **DAB** (9), 139–40. **USNI Almanac,** 153. **NUC** (19). **OCLC** (117).

1829–1830 South Seas Expedition
First U.S. Navy Warship to Circumnavigate the Globe

220. Stewart, Charles Samuel (1795-1870).

A visit to the South Seas, in the U.S. Ship Vincennes, during the Years 1829 and 1830; with Scenes in Brazil, Peru, Manila, the Cape of Good Hope, and St. Helena. *New York: J.P. Haven, 1831. 2 vols., 357; 360 p., 19 cm.*

On September 3, 1826, USS *Vincennes,* 18 guns, under command of Captain W.B. Finch departed for the Pacific. Returning on June 8, 1830, *Vincennes* had completed the first circumnavigation of the globe by a U.S. warship.

Bruntjen and Bruntjen, #9297. **Cooney,** 51. **Sabin,** #91671. **Sweetman,** 43. **NUC** (25). **OCLC** (89).

Manuscript Log of Frigate *United States,* 1824–1826
Pacific Squadron Service

221. Strong, Augustus R.

Journal of a Cruise from Norfolk, Virginia, to the Pacific Ocean, in the United States Frigate United States, Isaac Hull, Esq'r, Commander. *[1824–1826]. 1 vol. (unnumbered), 30 cm.*

On the cover is "Augustus R. Strong, U.S. Navy" and on the spine is "Journal, 1823–4." Despite the spinal notation, actual coverage is from January 5, 1824 through September 5, 1826. This log is from the period of recommissioning of USS *United States.* She had been "decommissioned on 9 June 1819 and laid up at Norfolk . . . [and] did not sail again until 1824. From 1824 to 1827, she was deployed with the Pacific Squadron under Commodore Isaac Hull and protected American shipping and commercial interests. She put into the Philadelphia Navy Yard in 1828 for extensive repairs and remained there until 1830 when she was placed in ordinary at the New York Navy Yard."—**DANFS.** *See also entry 222.*

DANFS (7), 416. **OCLC** (Navy Department Library).

Journal of a Pacific cruise, 1824-1826 (entries 221 and 222)

Manuscript Log of Schooner
Dolphin, 1825–1826
Searching for Mutineers from Whaleship *Globe*

222. Strong, Augustus R.

Journal of a Cruise from Norfolk, Virginia, to the Pacific Ocean, in the United States Frigate United States, Isaac Hull, Esq'r, Commander. *[1825–1827]. 1 vol. (unnumbered), 1 drawing (pencil with ink notations), 30 cm.*

On the cover is "Augustus R. Strong, U.S. Navy" and on the spine is "Journal, 1825–6." Despite the spinal notation, actual coverage for *United States* is December 16, 1826, through April 18, 1827. Regardless of the entitlement of the printed title page, the majority of this log is for USS *Dolphin* under command of Lieutenant John Percival. Period of coverage for *Dolphin* is August 18, 1825, through August 30, 1826. "The second *Dolphin,* a schooner, was launched 23 June 1821 by Philadelphia Navy Yard and sent to New York to be readied for sea . . . cruised on the coasts of Ecuador, Peru, and Chile to protect American commerce and the whaling industry. Between 18 August 1825 and 24 August 1826 she cruised to search for mutineers of the American whaler *Globe,* returning to Callao, Peru, with the two surviving members of the mutiny."—**DANFS.** *See also entry 221.*

DANFS (2), 284. **OCLC** (Navy Department Library).

Tao-Kuang, Emperor of China (entry 223)

Circumnavigation of
USS *Columbia*

223. Taylor, Fitch W[aterman] (1803–1865).

The Flag-Ship: or, A Voyage around the World in the United States Frigate Columbia; Attended by Her Consort the Sloop of War John Adams and Bearing the Broad Pennant of Commodore George Read. By Fitch W. Taylor. *New York: D. Appleton & Co., 1840. 2 vols., frontispiece, 20 cm.*

"The first *Columbia,* a ship-rigged sailing frigate, was built at the Washington Navy Yard . . . but she was not launched until 9 March 1836. On her first cruise from May 1838 to June 1840 . . . one of the first U.S. naval ships to circumnavigate the globe."—**DANFS.**

DANFS (2), 146. **Rinderknecht and Bruntjen,** #40-6444. **Sabin,** #94456. **NUC** (13). **OCLC** (39).

Fiji Islands Intervention
First United States Scientific Expedition by Sea

224. Wilkes, Charles (1798–1877).

Narrative of the United States Exploring Expedition during the Years 1838, 1840, 1841, and 1842. By Charles Wilkes. *Philadelphia: Lea and Blanchard, 1845. 5 vols., illus., 14 maps (some folding), plates (64 leaves), 28 cm.*

"The first United States scientific expedition by sea. Wilkes sailed along and surveyed the whole Northwest coast. . . . The official edition of the Narrative was followed, 1846–1858, by volumes giving scientific data; these were numbered 6 to 17, 20 and 23 [volumes 18, 19, 21, 22 and 24 never issued]."—**Howes.** During this expedition, naval forces intervened in the Fiji Islands in retaliation for the murders of Lieutenant Underwood and Midshipman Henry during their exploration of the island. Lieutenant Charles Wilkes commanded the retaliatory force that reduced the town at Saulih Bay, Fiji Islands, on July 12, 1840. On July 26, 1840, Lieutenant Cadwallader Ringgold commanded a punitive force of 70 men in the destruction of the town of Arro Saulih. The force was landed from USS *Vincennes*, part of the Wilkes Exploring Expedition, and was in retaliation for the massacre of an American shore party.

Cooney, 57. **Howes,** W414. **Sabin,** #103994. **NUC** (not recorded). **OCLC** (19).

Asiatic Fleet Flagship, 1875–1878
With a Collection of Poems and
Songs Written On Board

225. Willis, Geo[rge] R. (d. 1884).

Lights and Shadows of Our Cruise in the U.S. Frigate "Tennessee," Flagship of the Asiatic Fleet, 1875, '76, '77, '78, By Geo. R. Willis. *New York: Published by the Crew, 1878. 134 p., illus., 19 cm.*

USS *Tennessee* covered approximately 45,000 miles on this cruise. She sailed from New York to Gibraltar, Palermo, Port Said, through the Suez Canal to Suez, Aden, Bombay, Colombo (Ceylon), Penang (Malacca), Singapore, Manilla, Amoy (China), Woosung Bar, Nagasaki, Shanghai, Yokohama, Yokoska, Yokohama, Hiogo, Shiminoseki, Nagasaki, Chefoo (China), Newchwang, Taku, Chefoo, Hiogo (Japan), Yokohama, Hong Kong, Bankok, Singapore, Victoria (Labuan), Manilla, Hong Kong, Yokohama, Hakodate, Hiogo, Nagasaki, Shanghai, Amoy, Hong Kong, Singapore, Penang, Colombo (Ceylon), Aden, Suez, through Suez Canal, Port Said, Alexandria, Naples, Villefranche (France), Gibraltar, Funchal (Madeira), and New York. Pages 109–23 carry poems and songs written on board during the voyage.

NUC (Brown University, Navy Department Library, New York Public Library). **OCLC** (American Antiquarian Society Library, Brown University, Mariner's Musuem, Navy Department Library, Rutherdord B. Hayes Presidential Center Library).

Firsthand Account from 1836 to 1878

226. Ammen, Daniel (1820-1898).

The Old Navy and the New: Memoirs of Rear-Admiral Daniel Ammen, U.S.N., for More Than Half a Century Ashore and Afloat . . . With an Appendix of Personal Letters from General Grant. *Philadelphia: J.B. Lippincott Company, 1891. xvi, [15]–553 p., facsimiles, frontispiece, portrait, 23 cm.*

Ammen, joining the Navy as a midshipman in 1836, achieved the rank of rear admiral. "The first chapters of the book, devoted to the early naval life of the Admiral as midshipman and lieutenant, have a decided sea flavor . . . and often seem to have been written for the benefit of the younger officers of the service."—**Larned.** "During the more than a half a century covered by this chronicle, so marvelous have been the changes in naval architecture and armament, in the development of means of locomotion both on shore and afloat, and in the establishment of rapid communication over the inhabited globe, that the intelligent reader can hardly realize that they have occurred within so brief an historical period of time. A principal object of these memoirs has been to note these mutations in their order, and to present a picture of naval life as affected by them."—**Preface.**

Cogar (1), 5–6. **Larned,** #2485. **NUC** (28). **OCLC** (113).

Rise and Progress as Viewed in 1828

227. Anonymous.

A General View of the Rise, Progress, and Brilliant Achievements of the American Navy, Down to the Present Time. Illustrated by Biographical Sketches, Official Reports, and Interesting Views of American Commerce. To Which Is Affixed a Succinct Account of the Origin and Progress of the Greek Revolution. Terminating with the Glorious Victory of Navarino, October 20, 1827. *Brooklyn, N.Y.: 1828. [8], [13]–484 p., 19 cm.*

The author begins with some minor discussion of naval activities in the colonial period and progresses through the War of 1812—the point of emphasis. Biographies are interjected (Nicholas Biddle, John Paul Jones, and Thomas Truxtun).

Harbeck, 5. **Howes,** G98. **Sabin,** #26917. **Shoemaker,** #33335. **NUC** (13). **OCLC** (30).

First History of the American Navy

228. Clark, Thomas (1787-1860).

Sketches of the Naval History of the United States; from the Commencement of the Revolutionary War, to the Present Time . . . Likewise an Appendix, Wherein the Chief Part of the Important Documents Concerning the Navy Are Collected. By Thomas Clark . . . *Philadelphia: M. Carey, 1813. xiv, [13]–177 p., 1 l., cxxxix p., frontispiece, 20 cm.*

"The first attempt to write a history of the American Navy . . . is virtually a primary source work for the Revolutionary era."—**Coletta**. "The author, a contemporary of the events about which he writes, relies heavily on personal communication with some of the major participants, including John Adams and Commodore Thomas Truxtun."—**Lynch**. This entry is the first edition.

Coletta, #691. **Howes,** C446. **Lynch,** 3. **Sabin,** #13377. **Shaw and Shoemaker,** #28151. **NUC** (14). **OCLC** (24).

Literary Figure and Former Naval Officer

229. Cooper, James Fenimore (1789-1851).

The History of the Navy of the United States of America. By J. Fenimore Cooper. *Philadelphia: Lea & Blanchard, 1839. 2 vols., 394; 282 p., map, plan, 25 cm.*

With regard to the Barbary Wars and the Quasi-War with France, **Smelser** notes Cooper as "more detached and critical." "Excellent account of battles by a former naval person."—**Coletta**.

Coletta, #949. **DAB** (2), 400–406. **Howes,** C748. **Larned,** #2510. **Rinderknecht,** #55148. **Sabin,** #16442. **Smelser,** 216. **NUC** (46). **OCLC** (144).

Pioneer in Documenting American Warships

230. Emmons, George F[oster] (1811-1884).

The Navy of the United States, from the Commencement, 1775-1853; with a Brief History of Each Vessel's Service and Fate . . . Comp. by Lieut. George F. Emmons . . . Under the Authority of the Navy Dept. To Which Is Added a List of Private Armed Vessels, Fitted Out under the American Flag, Previous and Subsequent to the Revolutionary War, with Their Services and Fate; Also a List of the Revenue and Coast Survey Vessels, and Principal Ocean Steamers, Belonging to Citizens of the United States in 1850. *Washington: Printed by Gideon & Co., 1853. [6], 208, [1] p., 30 x 25 cm.*

"Presents the most useful statistical ships' histories prior to the Naval History Division's *Dictionary of American Naval Fighting Ships*."—**Lefkowicz**. As a compilation of data on vessels, rather than a narrative history of the Navy, the work is a pioneer in documenting the American naval vessel. Emmons achieved the rank of rear admiral. "In 1837, [he] escorted General Santa Anna back to Mexico after his defeat in Texas."—**Cogar**.

Cogar (1), 52. **Howes,** E144. **Lefkowicz** (*Catalog Twenty-One*), #98. **Sabin,** #22519. **Young,** 38–39. **NUC** (24). **OCLC** (68).

Most Important Battles, 1775–1846

231. Harrison, Henry William.

Battle-Fields and Naval Exploits of the United States, from Lexington to the City of Mexico, by Henry W. Harrison. Illustrated with One Hundred and Fifty Engravings. *Philadelphia: H.C. Peck & T. Bliss, 1858. 448 p., illus., plates, 24 cm.*

"This work is designed to present a coup-d'oeil of American military history by means of lively sketches of the most important battles fought since the commencement of the Revolutionary War, by troops and naval forces of the United States."—**Preface**.

Sabin, #30559. **Howes** (not recorded). **NUC** (Haverford College, Kansas State University, New York Public Library, University of Alabama, University of Southern Illinois, Western Reserve Historical Society). **OCLC** (14).

Constitution sea battle, woodcut

"The Pulse of the Commander Is Felt"

232. Anonymous.

[A Plea in Favor of Maintaining Flogging in the Navy]. *[United States: c1848]. [1], 2–14 p., 21 cm.*

"As at the present time a great effort is being made to abolish the law which authorizes flogging in the Navy . . . a member of that service desires to express his views upon the subject. The Navy is the armed police of the country upon the oceans; its purposes are warlike, and its service is that of emergencies, whilst its duties are always rendered precarious by the nature of the element upon which it exists. . . . The crew of our vessels of war, comprise men of all nations and almost every variety of character.—Among them are many who are respectable in their demeanor, capable, tractable and industrious; there are many others who are insolent, ignorant, quarrelsome, lazy and mischievous. And there is always, in every ship, a knot of abandoned and incorrigible vagabonds, sweepings of the jails and streets, the outcasts of the shore, who herd with the vicious portion of the seamen, and form a turbulent and unruly gang. . . . The laws for the government of men thus banded together for the purposes of war, are necessarily arbitrary and severe. Death is prescribed as the penalty for offences, which, in shore communities, would be deemed trivial, as well as for the higher crimes. . . . How is her nondescript community to be governed? . . . Not like a town, where the inhabitants are born, grow up, feel local attachments, have centered their families, property and business, and therefore feel a strong and lasting interest in its prosperity. . . . There can be no rational hope, that a better class of men than such as ships now get, will speedily, if ever, be furnished our vessels of war. The inducements offered by a sea-life are not of the kind to attract quiet people afloat. . . . It is not contended that flogging on the bare back, with the cat-o'-nine tails, should be the sole and universal method of punishment on ship board: far from it. An infinite variety of milder forms answers perfectly for the generality of offenders. . . . [T]ere are, and ever will be, cases that nothing but the lash will reach, and occasionally, some hardened reprobates who care not for the pain and degradation of the lash, until its repetition, combined with other extremes, brings even them into subjection. Lenient schemes are of no avail with such characters. . . . Solitary confinement is not practicable on board ship, for the want of room. . . . Bread and water diet has been tried, but does not succeed well, owing to the many opportunities for contraband supplies . . . . The offenses commonly committed on board ship, are such as these: disobeying and thwarting the rules for the preservation of cleanliness, system and order; defacing the ship's furniture, and throwing parts of it overboard; stealing; smuggling liquor on board, and getting drunk thereon; . . . inciting quarrels at meal times; getting up fights; receiving orders with contempt, obeying them with sullen murmurs or neglecting to obey them at all; . . . contriving all kinds of malicious and outrageous acts to throw discredit upon the ship generally . . . ; getting up insubordinate plots; . . . refusing flatly to obey orders; uttering mutinous language. . . . These things commence at the beginning of a cruise; the pulse of the commander is felt, as it were, and as he is either resolute or weak in the exercise of his authority, so follows either the good or bad condition of his ship. . . . And when that day comes, perhaps the nations will at last be at peace, and men will no longer be trained for the purposes of war. . . . [W]hile maintaining them [forces], in an unnatural state of association for such bloody ends, it is found necessary to govern them with the laws of Draco, taking life for crimes that would be but venal offenses in peaceable communities on the land."

Sabin (not recorded). **NUC** (Navy Department Library). **OCLC** (Navy Department Library).

First Chief of Bureau of Medicine and Surgery

233. Barton, William P[aul] C[rillon] (1786-1856).

Hints for Naval Officers Cruising in the West Indies. By William P.C. Barton, M.D. *Philadelphia: E. Littel; Boston: Carter & Hendee, 1830. 222 p., 15 cm.*

Barton entered naval service during 1809, "serving on active duty with the frigates *United States, Essex, Brandywine* and in the naval hospitals, then called marine hospitals, at Philadelphia, Norfolk, and Pensacola."—**DAB.** In 1842 he became the first chief of the Bureau of Medicine and Surgery. The *Dictionary of American Biography* notes that Barton's *Hints for Naval Officers* "contains many literary references and moral admonitions, with remarks on gambling and temperance. Nevertheless, this book and his report on marine hospitals, were according to [Frank Lester] Pleadwell, the first signs of a modern medical view of sanitation and provision for the sick in the history of the navy."

Cooper, #394. **DAB** (1), 25–26. **Howes** (not recorded). **Sabin,** #3860. **NUC** (10). **OCLC** (15).

1814 Plan for Marine Hospitals
First Modern Naval View of Sanitation and Hospitals

234. Barton, William Paul Crillon (1786-1856).

A Treatise Containing a Plan for the Internal Organization and Government of Marine Hospitals in the United States: Together with a Scheme for Amending and Systematizing the Medical Department of the Navy, by William P.C. Barton, A.M., M.D., Member of the American Philosophical Society, and a Surgeon in the Navy of the United States. *Philadelphia: Printed for the author. Sold by Edward Parker, no. 178, Market-street, and Philip H. Nicklin, no. 51, Chestnut street, 1814. xxv, [1], 1 l., 244 p., plate, 22.5 cm.*

The *Dictionary of American Biography* cites this treatise together with Barton's *Hints* as "the first signs of a modern medical view of sanitation and provision for the sick in the history of the navy." Organized into two parts, the second is *A Scheme for Amending and Systematizing the Medical Department of the Navy of the United States.* It includes such topics as "Of the introduction of the lemon-acid into the Navy"; "Of the mode of furnishing the medicine and store chests, the mode of furnishing surgical Instruments to the Navy"; "Of the duties of a surgeon and surgeon's-mate in the Navy, on ship-board"; and "Detail of the duties and offices of a surgeon's mate of the Navy, and of the expediency of altering the present ration." Pages 186–88 list instruments provided by a surgeon and a surgeon's mate. Pages 168–83 list by rate of ship the bedding, fumigating articles, lemon juice, medicines, and utensils required.

DAB (1), 25–26. **Howes** (not recorded). **Sabin,** #3862. **Shaw and Shoemaker,** #30809. **NUC** (13). **OCLC** (25).

SCHEME OF DIET

FOR THE U. S. MARINE HOSPITALS.

Full Diet.

A pint of tea in the morning for breakfast, and a like quantity in the evening; sixteen ounces of bread; sixteen ounces of beef or mutton; one pint of broth; sixteen ounces of greens, or good sound potatoes, and two quarts of small beer.

Half Diet.

Tea morning and evening as above; sixteen ounces of bread; eight ounces of beef or mutton; eight ounces of greens or good sound potatoes; one pint of broth; and three pints of small beer.

Low Diet.

Tea morning and evening as above; eight ounces of bread; two ounces of butter, or in lieu of butter, one pint of milk; half a pint of broth, or such an additional quantity thereof as the physician or the surgeon shall judge proper.

Casualty Diet for men received.

The physicians and surgeons are to prescribe half-diet, or low-diet, for such patients, according to the state of their health when they are received; and the proportions of each species of provisions to be issued by the steward, is the same as to the other patients on half and low-diet.

Hospital diets

Established proportion of Instruments, &c. to be provided by a Surgeon.

Established proportion of Instruments, &c. to be provided by a Surgeon.	State of those in possession of the Surgeon of the Ship.			Deficient of the established proportion.
	In good order.	Requiring repair.	Unserviceable.	
Three Amputating Knives.				
One Ditto Saw with spare Blade.				
One Metacarpal ditto with ditto.				
Two Catlins.				
Pair of Artery Forceps.				
Two dozen curved Needles.				
Two Tenaculums.				
Six Pettit's Screw Tourniquets.				
Pair of Bone-Nippers and Turnscrew.				
Three Trephines.				
Saw for the Head.				
Lenticular and Rugine.				
Pair of Forceps.				
Elevator.				
Brush.				
Two Trocars.				
Two Silver Catheters				
Two Gum Elastic ditto				
Six Scalpels.				
Small Razor.				
Key Tooth Instrument.				
Gum Lancet.				
Two pairs of Tooth-Forceps.				
Punch.				
Two Seton Needles.				
Pair of strong Probe Scissars.				
Curved Bistory with a Button.				
Long Probe.				
Pair of Bullet-Forceps.				
Scoop for extracting Balls.				

Evaluation form for surgical instruments (entry 234)

Established proportion of Instruments, &c. to be provided by a Surgeon. (Continued.)

Established proportion of Instruments, &c. to be provided by a Surgeon.	State of those in possession of the Surgeon of the Ship.			Deficient of the established proportion.
	In good order.	Requiring repair.	Unserviceable.	
Two Probangs.				
Half a Pound of Ligature Thread				
One Paper of Needles.				
Case with Lift-out				
Apparatus for restoring suspended animation.				
Set of Pocket Instruments.				
Six Lancets, in a Case.				
Two dozen Bougies, in a Case.				
Two Pint Pewter Clyster Syringes.				
Six small Pewter Syringes.				
Two sets or bundles of common Splints.				
Set of japanned Iron ditto for Legs.				
Twelve Flannel or Linen Rollers.				
Two 18 tailed bandages.				
Twenty yards of Web for Tourniquets.				
Sixty yards of Tape, different Breadths				
A Cupping Apparatus, consisting of one Scarificator and six Glasses.				

U. S. Marine Hospital, at

I do hereby certify, that in pursuance of the direction of the Board of Medical Commissioners for conducting the Hospital Department of the U. S. naval service, and for providing for sick, hurt, and disabled seamen: I have this day examined the instruments belonging to   surgeon of the and find their state to be as above expressed.

         Surgeon of   *Hospital.*

Shipboard Social Reformer

235. Bates, Joseph (1792-1872).

The Autobiography of Elder Joseph Bates; Embracing a Long Life on Shipboard, with Sketches of Voyages on the Atlantic and Pacific Oceans, the Baltic and Mediterranean Seas; Also Impressment and Service On Board British War Ships, Long Confinement in Dartmoor Prison, Early Experience in Reformatory Movements; Travels in Various Parts of the World and a Brief Account of the Great Advent Movement of 1840-44. *Battle Creek, Mich.: Steam Press of the Seventh-day Adventist Publishing Association, 1868. 318 p., port., 18 cm.*

A native of Massachusetts, Bates began his seafaring life in June 1807 as a cabin boy. By April 27, 1810, his taking to the sea had resulted in impressment in the Royal Navy. With the outbreak of war in 1812, he became a prisoner of war on board *"Crown Princen*, formerly a Danish 74-gun ship, a few miles below Chatham dock-yard, and seventy miles from London. . . . Here about seven hundred prisoners were crowded between decks, and locked up every night, on a scanty allowance of food, and in crowded quarters." Bates' account presents some excellent detail on both his impressment and his experience as a prisoner of war during the War of 1812. His work as a whole is interesting for its view of extensive naval and maritime service as seen by a man who found his calling in the church.

Portrait of Elder Joseph Bates, lithograph

Howes (not recorded). **NUC** (9). **OCLC** (23).

Irish Famine
United States Warship as an Agent of Mercy

236. [Forbes, Robert Bennet] (1804-1889).

The Voyage of the Jamestown on Her Errand of Mercy. *Boston: Eastburn Press, 1847. xi, [7]–27, [2], [i]cliv p., plate, 23 cm.*

The frontispiece is a handsome lithograph after Fitz Hugh Lane's painting of USS *Jamestown*. It depicts *Jamestown* at Boston on March 28, 1847, under command of Commander R.B. Forbes, as she departed for Cork, Ireland. "Another New England luminist of this generation was Fitz Hugh Lane (1804–1865) of Gloucester. . . . He returned to Gloucester after 1847 and devoted himself to marine painting . . . [his] spider-web precision of drawing and delicacy of tone . . . shows a sensitive natural artistry."—**Richardson.** Prior to 1847, Lane did not chronicle the marine world. This is an early example of his change to that genre. *Jamestown* and *Macedonian* had been authorized by Congress to carry relief to Ireland during the famine of 1847. This is the account of Robert Bennet Forbes who was the commander of the American relief expedition. Forbes (1804–1889) was a noted mariner and American China merchant. "He invented the 'Forbes rig' for sailing vessels . . . [and] was among the first to have faith in the screw propeller and iron hulls. . . . He sent small iron steamers to China, California and South America on the decks of sailing vessels, an idea as ingenious as his earlier sending of ice to the Orient. He was also interested in humanitarian work. In 1847, he commanded the USS *Jamestown*, loaned to carry contributions from Boston to Irish famine sufferers."—**DAB.**

DAB (3), 509. **Richardson,** 171. **Sabin,** #25051. **NUC** (15). **OCLC** (23).

Pioneer Work on Naval Hygiene
Medical Examination of the
Naval Recruit in 1871

237. Gihon, Albert Leary (1833-1901).

Practical Suggestions in Naval Hygiene by Albert Leary Gihon. *Washington: Government Printing Office, 1871. 151 p., 20 cm.*

Gihon wrote on October 1, 1871, to William Maxwell Wood, surgeon general of the Navy, putting forth this work as a possible "code of sanitary regulations for the Navy of the United States." Noting his work as an attempt to "plow up a field hitherto so neglected," he is supported by naval doctor W.S.W. Ruschenberger in an October 2, 1871 letter from the U.S. Naval Hospital at Philadelphia: "You will not expect to see your suggestions adopted at once. But you may reasonably hope that, by the time those young aspirants for renown in the Navy, who are now just entering the Naval Academy, are captains and commodores, the truths which you set forth so well will come to be considered worthy of attention." Gihon gives considerable attention to "The Examination of Recruits "(pp. 12–27). Other sections of his work include "The Receiving Ship," "Navy Yards," "Ventillation," "Clothing," "Food," "Sleep," "Exercise," "The Sick-Bay," and "Sanitary Regulations for Transports."

NUC (Academy of Natural Sciences in Philadelphia, College of Physicians in Philadelphia, Library of Congress, New York Public Library, Oberlin College, U.S. National Library of Medicine). **OCLC** (9).

Dueling in the Navy

238. Henderson, Thomas (1789-1854).

Duels and Duelling in the Naval Service of the United States: A Series of Letters in the National Intelligencer, Addressed to the Secretary of the Navy in May and June 1845, Urging the Establishment of a Naval Academy by Thomas Henderson. *[1845]. 27 leaves, facsimiles, 26 cm.*

"The following observations . . . appeared in the form of letters contributed to the *National Intelligencer*, of Washington, in April (26th) and May (8th and 22nd), 1845. They were addressed to George Bancroft, then Secretary of the Navy, and bore the signature of 'Washington.' Their purpose, beside that of discouraging the practice of duelling in the Navy, was to call public attention to the need of opening and maintaining a school for the training of Naval Cadets, similar to the Military Academy at West Point. The writer was Doctor Thomas Henderson, a Surgeon in the Army, who had served for many years at West Point."—**Prefatory Note.**

Sabin (not recorded). **NUC** (not recorded). **OCLC** (Navy Department Library).

Forerunner of United States Naval Academy
Original and Unpublished Manuscript

239. Hooker, Edward (1822-1903).

The U.S. Naval Asylum. A Sketch of Its Origin and History and a Record of Useful Information Regarding It Prepared by Edward Hooker, Lieut. Comdr. U.S.N. Under the Direction of J.R.M. Mullany, Rear Admiral U.S.N., Governor. *[Philadelphia]: 1878. [54 lined pages with some manuscript entries], [3 manuscript pages], 261 numbered ledger pages in manuscript, 262–404 numbered ledger pages without entry, maps, 33 cm.*

"This school soon eclipsed the others in importance and in doing so, prepared the way for the establishment of the long-awaited single permanent naval academy."—**Skallerup.** "The origin of the Naval Asylum dates from 1799 when an act of Congress provided a hospital fund to which all seamen, government and merchant, were required to contribute twenty cents monthly out of their pay. In 1811 an act directed this money be turned over to a board of commissioners of Navy hospitals. The War of 1812 intervened and it was not until 1826 that the commissioners recommended that a naval asylum be established. Dr. Thomas Harris, a distinguished naval surgeon, and William Strickland, the eminent architect, selected a site in Philadelphia. The cornerstone of the building was laid in 1827. The asylum was opened in 1831 with four inmates."—**Gleaves.** During the late 1830s the asylum was also used to house a naval school for the instruction of midshipmen who were being trained on receiving ships at Boston, New York, and Norfolk. This copy is the original manuscript for the title in the main entry above. It was never published, but microfilm copies exist.

Gleaves, 473–74. **Skallerup**, 160. **OCLC** (Navy Department Library).

Ranked with Herman Melville
as Agent of Reform

240. [Jones, George] (1800-1870).

Sketches of Naval Life with Notices of Men, Manners and Scenery on the Shores of the Mediterranean in a Series of Letters from the Brandywine and Constitution Frigates. By a "Civilian." *New-Haven: H. Howe, 1829. 2 vols., vii, 286, [1]; viii, 284 p., frontispiece (folding), maps, plans, plates, 19 cm.*

George Jones, valedictorian of the Yale class of 1823, served on board as schoolmaster from 1825 to 1828. "During this period he frequently acted as chaplain. . . . The writings of Chaplain George Jones, Chaplain Walter Colton and Herman Melville, combined with the personal influence of the first two mentioned, were largely instrumental in securing the abolition of flogging in the Navy, and had much to do with the suppression of the rum issue."—**Edel.**

Edel, 883–84. **Shoemaker and Cooper,** #39158. **Young,** 87–88. **Skallerup,** 37. **Sabin** (not recorded). **NUC** (14). **OCLC** (35).

First Navy Promulgation of Emancipation Proclamation

241. Lincoln, Abraham. (1809-1865).

General Order, No. 4. The Following Proclamation of the President Is Published for the Information and Government of the Officers and Others of the Naval Service. GIDEON WELLES, Secretary of the Navy. *[Washington]: Navy Department, January 14, 1863. [2] p., 18 cm.*

This first official Navy promulgation of President Abraham Lincoln's Emancipation Proclamation not only freed African Americans within designated areas of the United States but also marked the official beginning of Washington support for participation of African Americans in the armed forces of the Union. Although the War Department printing is frequently seen, this Navy Department printing is rarely seen.

Moebs (*Black Soldiers*), #6-7. **OCLC** (Navy Department Library).

"Like Molten Lead on the Bare Back"

242. [Lockwood, John A.].

An Essay on Flogging in the Navy: Containing Strictures upon Existing Naval Laws, and Suggesting Substitutes for the Discipline of the Lash. *New York: Pudney & Russell, Printers, 1849. [4], 56 p., 23 cm.*

"Some men were known to have taken 12 lashes without uttering a sound. It was said that old seamen became hardened to it. Others, particularly first offenders, suffered horribly. The lash was said to feel like molten lead on the bare back. . . . The surgeon stood by during all the floggings. . . . If the surgeon believed that a man could stand only a part of his punishment, the prisoner was cut down and made to stand the rest of his lashes at a time when his back was healed."—**Langley.** On September 28, 1850, flogging was outlawed in the Navy. The author of this tract was a naval surgeon. This copy, belonging to Rear Admiral George Henry Preble, bears his signature on the title page.

Carruth, 242. **Howes** (not recorded). **Langley,** 179. **Sabin** (not recorded). **Skallerup,** 110. **NUC** (Boston Public Library, Brown University, Harvard University Library, Library of Congress, Newberry Library, Pennsylvania Historical Society, Yale University). **OCLC** (Boston Athenaeum, Brown University, Dartmouth College, Navy Department Library).

Sea Sermons for the Sailor of the 1850s

243. Lorrain, Alfred M.

The Square-rigged Cruiser; or, Lorrain's Sea-Sermons Dedicated to the United States Navy, Officers and Seamen of American Merchantmen . . . By Alfred M. Lorrain . . . *Cincinnati: Swormstedt & Poe, 1855. 252 p., 17 cm.*

Lorrain's work contains ten sermons tailored in content for the seaman of the 1850s. The author had served both as a sailor and an officer at sea. In the Introduction, Lorrain notes that he had "spent the morning of his life at sea, both afore and abaft the mast. . . . The most vivid and lifelike dreams, that come over him in the slumbers of the night are dressed in marine scenery . . . the motion of the ship, the peculiar odor of the rigging, the saline savor of the Atlantic atmosphere." Thus, expressing his attachment to the men who lead the seafaring life, he offers his book "as a pocket-companion for the sailor" realizing, "We can hardly look forward to any time, when every vessel can be supplied with a living minister." These sermons yield a glimpse of religious and moral issues and the American seaman in the middle of the 19th century.

Howes (not recorded). **Sabin** (not recorded). **NUC** (Andover-Harvard Theological Library, Duke University, Emory University, Harvard University Library, Navy Department Library, Ohio State University, Ohio Wesleyan University). **OCLC** (Emory University, Harvard University Library, Navy Department Library, Ohio State University Library, Ohio Wesleyan University, Pittsburgh Theological Library).

Gunner's Recommendation for Reforms

244. McNally, William.

vils and Abuses in the Naval and Merchant Service, xposed; with Proposals for Their Remedy and Redress by illiam McNally. *Boston: Cassady and March, 1839. viii, 01 p., 18 cm.*

ne of the proposals of McNally, a naval gunner, was "to et the navy to furnish books to seamen."—**Skallerup.**

inderknecht, #56989. **Sabin,** #43592. **Skallerup,** 87. oung, 104–5. **Howes** (not recorded). **NUC** (American niversity, Library of Congress, Navy Department Library, eabody Institute in Baltimore). **OCLC** (19).

Drunken Conduct of Sailors in the 1840s

245. Rockwell, Charles (1806-1882).

Sketches of Foreign Travel, and Life at Sea: Including a Cruise On Board a Man-of-War, As Also a Visit to Spain, Portugal, the South of France, Italy, Sicily, Malta, the Ionian Islands, Continental Greece, Liberia, and Brazil: and a Treatise on the Navy of the United States by the Rev. Charles Rockwell. *Boston: Tappan and Dennet; New York: D. Appleton, 1842. 2 vols., xviii, 1 blank leaf, 404; viii, 437 p., frontispiece, 22 cm.*

Charles Rockwell, a Navy chaplain, provided "Fresh evidence of the conditions of the Navy . . . [to] the reading public in 1842. . . . He lamented the shameful drunken conduct of our sailors in foreign ports and reported that the balance of punishments on shipboard for drunkenness and other crimes were seven to one against whiskey drinkers. Many others who were never drunk were made irritable, silly, disobedient, or reckless by the Navy spirit ration. Because men on the sick list did not draw their grog, many neglected to report themselves when sick. Many forfeited their lives for this neglect."—**Langley.**

Langley, 237. **Rinderknecht and Bruntjen,** #42-4315. **Sabin,** #72420. **NUC** (15). **OCLC** (46).

Grog Ration a Market for the Surplus Grain of the West

246. Rockwell, John A[rnold] (1803-1861).

Speech of Mr. Jno. A. Rockwell, of Ct., in Favor of Abolishing the Spirit Rations in the Navy: Delivered in the House of Representatives of the U.S., Jan., 27, 1847. *Washington, D.C.: J. & G.S. Gideon, printers, 1847. 16 p., 23 cm.*

Langley comments, "Congress gave the men of the Navy a spirit ration to furnish a market for the surplus grain of the West," and quotes from Navy chaplain Charles Rockwell, "Representatives in Congress are not ashamed to argue in favor of this evil, because their constituents are whiskey makers." In his January 1847 speech, John A. Rockwell "introduced an amendment to the naval appropriation bill abolishing the spirit ration and providing for the payment of six cents a day in lieu thereof. . . . Rockwell's amendment was stricken out. . . . [His] interest in temperance in the Navy did not end with the rejection of his amendment. Instead, it deepened. As chairman of the naval committee of the House he had already collected facts on the subject and had presented them to Congress."

Langley, 237, 250. **Sabin,** #72437. **NUC** (Harvard University Library, Library of Congress, New York Public Library, University of Delaware). **OCLC** (Boston Athenaeum, Grinnell College Library, Harvard University Library, Navy Department Library, New York Public Library, Oskar Diethelm Library, University of Delaware).

"Stirring Speech"
Stopped Restoration of Flogging in the Navy

247. Stockton, [Robert Field] (1795-1866).

Speech of Mr. Stockton, of New Jersey, on Flogging in the Navy. Delivered in the Senate of the United States, January 7, 1852. *[Washington: L. Tower, printer, 1852]. 16 p., 22 cm.*

"Stockton served a brief term in the U.S. Senate during which he urged improved harbor defenses and the abolition of flogging in the navy."—**Webster.** That congressional service followed on active service as a naval officer which cut across the period 1811–1850, several separations included, and saw his rise to commodore. "Flogging finally was abolished [September 28, 1850]. . . . There is some reason for believing that the abolition was approved by some with the idea that within a short time the measure would be repealed as a result of the deterioration of discipline. . . . But the proflogging faction underestimated their opposition. When Congress received mixed reports on the results of the experiment, an attempt to restore the lash was abruptly stopped. The man who won that battle was Robert F. Stockton, the naval officer turned senator. Senator Mallory and other members of the Senate Committee on Naval Affairs, who hoped to restore flogging, were checkmated by Stockton's stirring appeal to the Senate."—**Langley.**

DAB (9), 48–49. **Howes** (not recorded). **Langley,** 278. **Sabin,** #91911. **Webster,** 415. **NUC** (Library Company of Philadelphia, Library of Congress, Navy Department Library, Pennsylvania Historical Society, Princeton University, Rutgers University, University of Virginia). **OCLC** (9).

Second American Naval Medical Officer Handbook

248. United States. Bureau of Medicine and Surgery.

Instructions for the Government of the Medical Officers of the Navy of the United States. *Washington: R. Armstrong, printer, 1853. 39 p., 18 cm.*

This is apparently the second publication of U.S. Navy instructions for the government of medical officers. The earliest cited by the **NUC** (U.S. National Library of Medicine) is dated 1844. The 1853 printing in the main entry above and a printing for 1857, 1867, 1873, 1878, and 1881 are credited by the **NUC** to the Navy Department Library. Of particular interest are pages 28–30, which define the 12 classes under which surgeons are to classify injury or disease. 17

NUC (Navy Department Library). **OCLC** (Navy Department Library).

1819 Report on Hospital Accommodations for Seamen

249. United States. Navy Department. Secretary.

Letter from the Secretary of the Navy Transmitting Sundr[y] Statement[s] and Papers Showing the Provisions Which Hav[e] Been Made for the Accommodation of Seamen; the Numbe[r] of Persons Accommodated, and the Expense Attending th[e] Same. Prepared in Obedience to a Resolution of the House o[f] Representatives of April 17, 1818. *Washington: Printed by [?] de Krafft, 1819. 23 p., 3 folded leaves, 23 cm.*

This report is an early source on naval hospitals.

Shaw and Shoemaker, #49820. **NUC** (Countway Library o[f] Medicine at Harvard University, Library of Congress, U.[S.] National Library of Medicine).

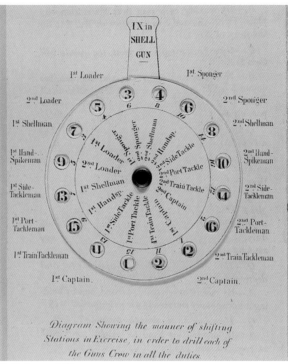

Guide to gun drills

Gunnery Catechism

250. Brandt, John D.

Gunnery Catechism, As Applied to the Service of Naval Ordnance: Adapted to the Latest Official Regulations, and Approved by the Bureau of Ordnance, Navy Department by J.D. Brandt. *New York: D. Van Nostrand, 1865. 204 p., illus, plates, 16 cm.*

The author had formerly served as a gunner in the United States Navy. He presents this gunnery catechism in a question and answer format. First approved by the Bureau of Ordnance on July 30, 1864, this 1865 printing is a revised edition. The work includes among its illustrations a moveable diagram "showing the manner of shifting stations in exercise, in order to drill each of the guns crew in all the duties." Contents include broadside guns, exercise of pivot guns, quick firing with broadside guns, shifting breeches in action, rifled cannon and projectiles, passing powder, shell rooms, 15-inch guns, mortars, and mortar practice, and general precautions to be observed in times of war.

Howes (not recorded). **Sabin** (not recorded). **Young,** 16–17. **NUC** (Boston Public Library, Free Library of Philadelphia, Harvard University Library, Library of Congress, Navy Department Library, University of Virginia Library). **OCLC** (Kentucky Historical Society, Naval Postgraduate School, Navy Department Library, South Street Seaport Musuem).

James Fenimore Cooper Reviews the *Somers* Mutiny

251. [Cooper, James Fenimore] (1789–1851).

Proceedings of the Naval Court Martial in the Case of Alexander Slidell Mackenzie, a Commander in the Navy of the United States, &c.: Including the Charges and Specifications of Charges, Preferred Against Him by the Secretary of the Navy. To Which Is Annexed, an Elaborate Review, by James Fennimore [sic] Cooper. *New York: Henry G. Langley, 1844. 344, 12 p., 24 cm.*

The *Somers* episode is the only case of a mutiny on board an American warship. In May 1864, 220 naval recruits, at sea between New York and Panama and in the charge of future admiral Daniel Ammen, mutinied. Ammen put down the revolt by shooting two of the ringleaders. The episode, however, occurred on the merchant vessel *Ocean Queen*. The mutiny on board the warship *Somers* was put down by the vessel's commander, Alexander Slidell Mackenzie, who executed, by hanging at sea, the three leaders. One of them, Spencer, was the son of the Secretary of War. "The ringleader, Midshipman Spencer, planned to murder the officers, take over the ship, and become a pirate."—**USNI Almanac.** "When the brig reached the United States this extreme act of discipline caused much public excitement, and in circles friendly to Spencer, who was a notorious scapegrace but a son of the secretary of war, the feeling against Mackenzie was bitter. . . . The court martial . . . exonerated him, and all attempts to indict him in civil courts failed."—**DAB.** *See also entry 267.*

DAB (6) 90–91. **Rinderknecht and Bruntjen,** #44-3961. **Sabin,** #43426. **USNI Almanac,** 194. **NUC** (20). **OCLC** (38).

1872 Broadsword Manual

252. Corbesier, Antoine J. (b. 1837).

Principles of Squad Instruction for the Broadsword by A.J. Corbesier. *Philadelphia: J.B. Lippincott & Co., 1872. x, 11–47 p., 10 plates, 18 cm.*

The author was sword-master of the United States Naval Academy. Eight of the plates illustrate swordplay.

Young, 26–27. **NUC** (Navy Department Library, University of Virginia). **OCLC** (Babson College, Kent State University, Navy Department Library, Springfield College, United States Military Academy).

1873 Sword-Master of Annapolis

253. Corbesier, Antoine J. (b. 1837).

Theory of Fencing; with the Small-Sword Exercise. By A.J. Corbesier, Sword-Master of the U.S. Naval Academy, Annapolis, Md. *Washington: Government Printing Office, 1873. [5], 6–36 p., 23 plates, 24 cm.*

Issued only in this printing, it is well illustrated.

Young, 26–27. **NUC** (Harvard University Library, Library of Congress, Navy Department Library, University of Illinois). **OCLC** (16).

Position Nº 6   The Straight thrust in high Tierce.

Fencing instruction

Rare Man-of War Manual by
First Jewish Captain
Presentation Copy to Secretary of the Navy

254. [Levy, Uriah Phillips] (1792?-1862).

Manual of Rules for Men-of-War. New York: Appleton & Co.'s, between 1853 and 1857]. 24 p., 17 cm.

The manual covers "Naval Rules," "Duties of the First Lieutenant," "Duties of the Master," "Orders for the Officer of the Watch," "Orders for the Magazine," "Orders for the Gunner," "General Orders in Case of Fire," "Orders for Surgeon," and "Orders for the Purser." The author presented his copy to Secretary of the Navy James Dobbin. One of the interesting sidelights of this naval officer, whose career was shrouded in controversy and several duels, is a connection with Thomas Jefferson, which is recounted by **Webster:** "Before his death in New York City on March 22, 1862, he had, because of his intense admiration for Thomas Jefferson, purchased Monticello, Jefferson's home near Charlottesville, Virginia. The property had fallen into disrepair, and Levy evidently hoped to restore it and offer it to the nation as a public shrine. He willed Monticello to the United States at his death, but litigation among his heirs kept the estate in private hands until 1923, when it was bought by subscription and opened to the public after restoration had been completed."

Sabin, #40765. **Webster,** 237. **Young,** 92–93. **NUC** (Library of Congress, New York Public Library, University of Michigan). **OCLC** (Library of Congress, Navy Department Library).

1822 Norfolk, Virginia Printed
Gunnery Manual

255. Marshall, George (d. 1855).

Marshall's Practical Marine Gunnery: Containing a View of the Magnitude, Weight, Description & Use, of Every Article Used in the Sea Gunner's Department, in the Navy of the United States. Norfolk: Printed by T.G. Broughton and published by C. Hall, 1822. 136 p., table (folding), 22 cm.

"This book has been strictly examined by some of the most experienced officers in the United States' Navy, particularly by Captains Arthur Sinclair, Lewis Warrington and William M. Crane, and they have authorized me to say that they consider it a useful work for all classes of officers, but more particularly for the junior class."—**Advertisement.** The author identifies himself as a Navy gunner of 12 years' experience. Pages 13–26 are "A List of Sea Stores and Outfits Required to Equip a Man of War for a Cruize [*sic*]." This copy is the only printing recorded in the **NUC.**

Sabin, #44772. **NUC** (Duke University, Library of Congress, Navy Department Library, Yale University). **OCLC** (10).

"Most Important Branch of
Naval Service"
1848 Cannon Pointing Instructions
for Young Sea Officers

256. Officer of the U.S. Navy.

Instruction upon the Art of Pointing Cannon: For the Use of Young Sea Officers. Translated from the French, by an Officer of the U.S. Navy. Washington: J. and G.S. Gideon, 1848. 23 p., illus., 23 cm.

"The following translation of a French tract, published in 1841, is offered to the young officers of the Navy by one of their brethren, in the humble hope that it may contribute, even a little, toward their instruction in the most important branch of naval service.... The progress made in naval gunnery, by the maritime nations of Europe, leaves it no longer a question with the sea officer of our country, whether he shall study the subject."—**Preface.**

Sabin (not recorded). **NUC** (Coast Guard Academy Library, Library of Congress, New York Public Library, Yale University). **OCLC** (Christopher Newport University, Harvard University Library, Independence Seaport Museum, Mariner's Museum, Navy Department Library, United States Naval Academy).

Fleet Tactics under Steam in 1870
**Based on Two Years' Command of
the Potomac Flotilla**

257. Parker, Foxhall A[lexander] (1821-1879).

Fleet Tactics under Steam. By Foxhall A. Parker. *New York: D. Van Nostrand, 1870. 250 p., diagrams, 16 cm.*

This work "attracted attention at home and abroad for its advocacy of 'obliquing into line' to avoid exposure of broadsides and facilitate use of the ram."—**DAB.** In his preface to "Squadron Tactics under Steam," published early in 1864, the author remarked, "the 'Naval Warfare' of Sir Howard Douglas, and the 'Tactique Navale' of the French, are, at present, the only works on *steam* tactics deserving consideration. To these must now be added 'Nouvelles Bases de Tactique Navale,' by Rear-Admiral Gregoire Boutakov, of the Russian Navy, a book of far greater scientific merit than anything that has preceded it. Believing, however, that a plain, practical work on this subject is still needed, the author has been encouraged to publish this volume, which is simply an adaptation of military to naval tactics, *as put to the practical test* during the two years that he commanded the Potomac flotilla."—**Preface.**

DAB (6), 220–21. **Webster,** 306–7. **Young,** 114–15. **NUC** (Boston Public Library, John Crerar Research Library, Library of Congress, Naval Observatory, Navy Department Library, New York Public Library, University of Michigan). **OCLC** (9).

Squadron Tactics under Steam
1864 Adaptation of Military Tactics to Naval Tactics

258. Parker, Foxhall Alexander (1821-1879).

Squadron Tactics under Steam. By Foxhall A. Parker. *New York: D. Van Nostrand, 1864. 172 p., frontispiece (folding), 77 plates (2 folding), 24 cm.*

During 1863, Parker "was on special duty in Washington, and at work on tactical problems, first set forth in his *Squadron Tactics under Steam.*"—**DAB.** "Intending to treat fully, in a forthcoming book on Fleet Tactics under Steam, of the whole subject of Naval Warfare, the author would simply remark here, that the present work is the result of much labor in the adaptation of military to naval tactics. He contends that the winds, waves, currents, and tides of the ocean present no more serious obstacle to the movements and manoeuvres of a steam-fleet than the inequalities of the surface of the earth present to the movements and manoeuvres of an army. He therefore regards a fleet as an army, whose divisions, brigades, regiments, and companies, as will hereafter be shown, have each their appropriate representatives afloat."—**Preface.** Parker has meticulously illustrated his work with 76 plates.

DAB (7), 220–21. **Howes** (not recorded). **Sabin,** #58665. **Webster,** 306–7. **Young,** 114–15. **NUC** (8). **OCLC** (25).

First American Naval Militia Handbook
**Includes Discussion of Suppression of
Waterfront Riots**

259. Stayton, William H.

Naval Militiaman's Handbook by Lieut. William H. Stayton. *New York: A.R. Pope, 1895. 3–165, iv p., 15 cm.*

This entry is the only printing of what appears to be the first American naval militiaman's handbook. In a prefatory Stayton notes that this handbook "has been written merely that a beginning might be made" and hopes that "some naval militiaman will be induced to revise and perfect it . . . to produce a proper handbook." Contents include artillery drill, coast defense work, cutlasses, duties of naval militiamen, gatling guns, Hotchkiss gun, mines, naval academy, revolver drill, torpedo boats, waterfront riots, and wig-wag codes. Pages 12–14 discuss waterfront riots.

NUC (Boston Public Library, Library of Congress). **OCLC** (Cleveland Public Library, Navy Department Library, University of Michigan).

1896 General Quarters Instructions

260. United States. Bureau of Navigation (Navy Department).

General Instructions, Clearing Ship for Action. Bureau of Navigation, Navy Department. *Washington, D.C.: Government Printing Office, 1896. 13 p., 13 cm.*

This entry is the only printing of a rare set of Spanish-American War period instructions for preparing warships for battle. The instructions number 53 and include the following: "Modern vessels are expected to fight under way. These instruction, therefore, apply to that condition alone. Should a ship fight at anchor, it would be under very exceptional circumstances. . . . Splinters are as much to be guarded against in the powder division as in the battery. . . . For actual battle release all prisoners. . . . In square-rigged vessels bend topsails, courses, jib. . . . Send below the protective deck all compasses and their binnacles except one. . . . For night action if desirable whitewash the deck of the battery below the spar deck. . . . Place signal books in weighted covers ready to be thrown overboard if so ordered."

NUC (New York Public Library). **OCLC** (Navy Department Library, United States Naval Academy).

1874 Naval Brigade Landing Drill

261. United States. Bureau of Ordnance (Navy Department).

Landing Drill of Naval Brigade at Key West, March 23, 1874. *[United States: 1874?]. 18 p., 3 plates (folding), 22 cm.*

This tract describes in detail the organization and the landing and operations of a naval brigade of approximately 2,700 men. One of the folding plates depicts the naval brigade, formed on land, with supporting warships in the background and landing craft just off the beachhead.

NUC (Boston Public Library, Duke University, John Crerar Library, Navy Department Library, New York Public Library, New York State Library). **OCLC** (9).

1873 Gatling Gun Drill
"No Practical Experience with This Gun On Board Ship"

262. United States. Bureau of Ordnance (Navy Department).

Provisional Drill of Gatling Gun. *[United States]: Bureau of Ordnance, Navy Department, 1873, 16 p., photographic frontispiece, 13 cm.*

The verso of the title page carries a May 1, 1873 letter from the Bureau of Ordnance stating, "As there has been no practical experience with this gun on board ship, the following 'Provisional Drill' has been adopted. The Bureau desires officers to test it, and forward any suggestions for modification." The frontispiece is an original tipped in photograph that depicts the Gatling gun for which this drill applies. The instructions are in the original red leather limp binding with bold gilt embellishment of the crossed cannon and anchor seal of the Bureau of Ordnance.

NUC (Harvard University Library, Navy Department Library, New York Public Library). **OCLC** (Harvard University Library, Navy Department Library, New York Public Library, Princeton University).

1876 Instructions for Spar and Towed Torpedoes

263. United States. Naval Underwater Ordnance Station, Newport.

Torpedo Instructions: Arranged in Two Parts. Part I. Spar Torpedo. Part II. Towing Torpedo. Prepared at the Torpedo Station. *[Washington, D.C.]: Bureau of Ordnance, 1876. 83 p., [22] leaves of plates, illus., 14 cm.*

Issued in gilt decorated and entitled red leather, the instructions are well illustrated. This copy is of comparative interest because it has been corrected to September 1883.

NUC (Harvard University Library, John Crerar Research Library, Navy Department Library, New York Public Library). **OCLC** (Mariner's Museum, Navy Department Library, New York Public Library).

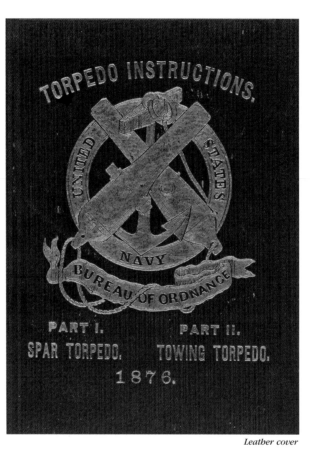

Leather cover

Eleven Superbly Colored Uniform Plates

264. United States. Navy Department.

Regulations for the Uniform & Dress of the Navy and Marine Corps of the United States. From the Original Text and Drawings in the Navy Department. *Philadelphia: Printed for the Navy Department, by T.K. and P.G. Collins, 1852. [4], [5]–15, [1] p., 12 plates (11 colored), 36 x 29 cm.*

This copy is the first American book of color plates on Navy uniform regulations. Illustrated with 13 large plates, 11 of which are in superb colors, the first four plates are colored and depict in full figure an officer wearing the designated uniform. The first four plates are Full Dress (Chief Engineer, Purser, Surgeon, Captain), Full Dress (Master, Passed Midshipman, Midshipman, Lieutenant), Service Dress (Captain, Midshipman, Surgeon, Purser), and Service Dress (Commander, Passed Midshipman, Chief Engineer, Master). There follow two colored plates of collar and cuff insignia, three colored plates of epaulets, one colored plate of headgear, and two black and white plates of headgear. Also in the rare book holdings of the Navy Department Library there is a second and partial copy of this work that is remarkable. The second copy has within it original drawings for uniforms and insignia, pasteup changes, printed ephemeral uniform regulations, and manuscript correspondence in regard to uniform regulations from naval officers who include Admiral David Dixon Porter. There are also uniform illustrations bearing manuscript approval in 1863 by Gideon Welles, Secretary of the Navy. This second copy is apparently a working dummy for a redo of the 1852 uniform regulations planned for issue after 1866 or later.

Bennett (not recorded). **Howes,** R158 (calling for 15 plates with 13 colored). **Sabin,** #68960 (without pagination). **NUC** (Buffalo and Erie County Public Library). **OCLC** (11).

SERVICE DRESS.

Commander.   Passed Midshipman.   Chief Engineer.   Master.

Service dress uniforms, drawn by J. Goldsborough Bruff (entry 264)

1852 Marine Corps Uniform Regulations

265. United States. Navy Department.

Regulations for the Uniform and Dress of the Navy and Marine Corps of the United States, March 1852 from the Original Text and Drawings in the Navy Department. *Washington: C. Alexander, Printer, 1852. 38 p., 19 cm.*

Pages 25–38 are "Dress of the Officers," "Non-Commissioned Officers," and "Musicians and Privates, of the Marine Corps of the United States."

NUC (Cornell University, Library of Congress, New York Public Library). **OCLC** (Brown University Library, College of William and Mary Library, Library of Congress, Navy Department Library, Smithsonian, United States Naval Academy).

Take this eagle, as to the body, the others are too fat.

Pencil sketch for insignia (entry 264)

Large 1869 Colored Plates of
Uniform Insignia

266. United States. Navy Department.

Uniform for the United States Navy, Prepared under Direction of the Secretary of the Navy. *Washington: Government Printing Office, 1869. [4], [5]–12 p., 9 leaves of plates (8 colored), 39.5 cm.*

The plates, of which eight are in fine colors, are limited to insignia, sword belt, sling, shoulder loops, shoulder straps, and cap cord.

Bennett, 82. **Howes,** U14. **NUC** (Library of Congress, Smithsonian Institution, War Library and Museum of the Military Order of the Loyal Legion of the United States in Philadelphia). **OCLC** (10).

Only United States Navy
Warship Mutiny

267. United States. Navy Department.
Court of Inquiry.

Proceedings of the Court of Inquiry Appointed to Inquire into the Intended Mutiny On Board the United States Brig of War Somers, on the High Seas: Held On Board the United States Ship North Carolina Lying at the Navy Yard, New-York; with a Full Account of the Execution of Spencer, Cromwell and Small, On Board Said Vessel. Reported for "The New-York Tribune." *New York: Greeley & McElrath, 1843. 48 p., illus., 21 cm.*

The *Somers* episode is the only case of a mutiny on board an American warship. In May 1864, 220 naval recruits, at sea between New York and Panama and in the charge of future admiral Daniel Ammen, mutinied. Ammen put down the revolt by shooting two of the ringleaders. The episode, however, occurred on the merchant vessel *Ocean Queen.* The mutiny on board the warship *Somers* was put down by the vessel's commander, Alexander Slidell Mackenzie, who executed, by hanging at sea, the three leaders. One of them, Spencer, was the son of the Secretary of War. "The ringleader, Midshipman Spencer, planned to murder the officers, take over the ship, and become a pirate."—**USNI Almanac.** When the ship reached the United States, a court of inquiry was held, leading to the court-martial of Commander Mackenzie. *See also entry 251.*

Howes (not recorded). **Rinderknecht and Bruntjen,** #43-4686. **Sabin,** #86804. **USNI Almanac,** 194. **NUC** (11). **OCLC** (11).

Monthly Magazine and Annual Report for Sailors

268. American Seamen's Friend Society.

Sailor's Magazine and Naval Journal. *New York: American Seamen's Friend Society, 1830–1863. 36 vols., illus., 23 cm.*

Publication began during September 1828, issues appearing monthly. The Navy Department Library has 21 of 36 volumes. In 1857 the name was changed to *Sailor's Magazine*.

Sabin, #74975. **Unsworth** (not recorded). **NUC** (19). **OCLC** (10).

Cabin boys' locker, woodcut

"First Stirrings of American Military Professionalism"

269. Homans, Benjamin (publisher).

Army and Navy Chronicle. *Washington, D.C.: Benjamin Homans, 1835–1842. 13 vols., illus., 28 cm.*

"This offspring of editor Benjamin Homans charted the course of the armed forces during a period that saw the first stirrings of American military professionalism . . . provided news on military topics and events such as the Second Seminole War (1835–1842), the war scare with France in 1835–1836, and Texas' rebellion against Mexico in 1836 . . . [and] furnished a forum for those officers who desired to advance their views about problems in the services."—**Unsworth.** The editor had been a long serving senior clerk in the Navy Department. His publication appeared on a weekly basis from January 3, 1835, through December 30, 1841. It was issued biweekly from January 22, 1842, through May 21, 1842.

Rinderknecht, #30118. **Sabin,** #2043. **Unsworth,** 57–59, 130–31. **NUC** (21). **OCLC** (74).

"Much Attention Was Given to Steam Vessels."

270. Force, William Q. (editor).

Army and Navy Chronicle, and Scientific Repository. *Washington, D.C.: [Wm. Q. Force], 1843–1844. 3 vols., illus, 26 cm.*

"This successor to Benjamin Homans' *Army and Navy Chronicle* continued much of its predecessor's features, but expanded the coverage of scientific news as indicated in the title. . . . Much attention was given to steam vessels."—**Unsworth.** The publication appeared on a weekly basis from January 12, 1843, through June 22, 1844.

Rinderknecht and Bruntjen, #43–227. **Sabin,** #2042. **Unsworth,** 58–60. **NUC** (Library of Congress, Oregon State University at Corvallis). **OCLC** (45).

1823 Newspaper and Periodical Subscriptions

271. United States. Navy Dept.

Letter from the Secretary of the Navy Transmitting a List of Newspapers and Periodical Works, with a Catalogue of the Books Purchased for the Use of the Navy Department, for the Last Six Years; and a Similar List and Catalogue for the Office of the Commissioners of the Navy. *Washington: Printed by Gales & Seaton, 1823. 1 leaf, 5–14 p., 24 cm.*

This document lists domestic and foreign newspaper and journal subscriptions as well as maps, charts, prints, and books received between 1817 and 1822 by the Navy and the office of the Commissioners of the Navy. The materials indicate wide-ranging interest in naval and military science, history, politics, law, mathematics, chemistry, philosophy, architecture, geography, and exploration. Regions covered include the United States, Mexico, West Indies, Brazil, Falkland Islands, Africa, Patagonia, Kamchatka, New Guinea, Australia, Russia, Persia, and the Arctic. The purchase price of individual books is also noted.

Shoemaker, #14569. **NUC** (Library of Congress). **OCLC** (Navy Department Library).

"Most Successful Effort in Antebellum Military Journalism"

272. Thompson and Homans (publishers).

The Military and Naval Magazine of the United States. *Washington, D.C.: Thompson and Homans, 1833–1836. 6 vols., 384; [4], 392; 480; [4], 480; [4], 480; 444 p., 21 cm.*

"Benjamin Homans launched the most successful effort in antebellum military journalism with the establishment of *Military and Naval Magazine of the United States* in 1833. . . . The virtues of American-born as opposed to foreign-born seamen were debated. The need for naval reorganization was promoted as well as rationalization of naval ranks (the sea service lacked a grade higher than Captain). Articles on seamanship and ship construction were numerous."—**Unsworth.** This periodical appeared on a monthly basis from March 1833 through February 1836. In February of 1836 it merged into the *Army and Navy Chronicle* (1835–1842) and "had a rebirth as the *Army and Navy Chronicle and Scientific Repository* (1843–1844)."—**Skallerup.**

Rinderknecht and Bruntjen, #20142. **Sabin,** #48953. **Skallerup,** 213. **Unsworth,** 130–31. **NUC** (8). **OCLC** (60).

"High Rank" among World Professional Journals

273. United States Naval Institute.

Proceedings of the United States Naval Institute. *[Annapolis, Md., etc.]: United States Naval Institute, 1874–. vols., charts, facsimiles, illus., maps, plans, plates, portraits, 26 cm.*

First issued as *Papers and Proceedings of the United States Naval Institute* and continued as *Proceedings*, this journal "quickly gained a high rank among other professional journals of the world."—**Skallerup.** Within its more than 1,500 issues is found a wealth of policy and strategy analyses, battle narrative, history, and weapons development, much of it written by participants and key players in the episodes and developments recounted.

Skallerup, 183–84. **Unsworth,** 224–27. **OCLC** (618).

Early Naval Officer Writings

274. United States Naval Lyceum.

The Naval Magazine. *New York, N.Y.: United States Naval Lyceum, 1836–1837. 2 vols., 615, [1], [2], [3]–71, [2], [1]–612, [1], 87 p., illus., 22 cm.*

"This bimonthly publication, edited by Chaplain Charles S. Stewart, was launched with hopes for its self-supporting success in 1836. But even with a boost from the Navy Department in the form of a pledge for thirty-two subscriptions, it survived only two years. The magazine contained general naval intelligence, articles on professional subjects, fiction, travel sketches, and other miscellaneous pieces. Among its contributors were James Fenimore Cooper, Alexander Slidell Mackenzie, and well-known naval officers of the day, many writing under noms de plume. On the whole, the *Naval Magazine* was one of quality in content."—**Skallerup.** "The articles on naval developments do cover the concerns of the Navy: creation of the rank of admiral, establishment of a formal training school for naval officers, use of steamships for naval operations, size of the fleet, and various personnel matters. Despite its short run, the *Naval Magazine* provides an interesting glimpse of the U.S. Navy during a long peacetime hiatus."—**Unsworth.** This periodical appeared on a bimonthly basis from January 1836 through November 1837.

Rinderknecht, #39142. **Sabin,** #52079. **Skallerup,** 174–75. **Unsworth,** 168–69. **NUC** (Boston Public Library, Coast Guard Academy, Library of Congress, Pennsylvania Historical Society, Princeton University, United States National War College, University of Minnesota). **OCLC** (51).

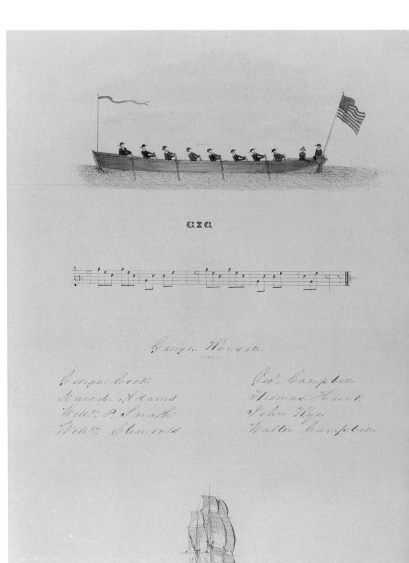

U.S. brig Somers *(entry 289)*

Captain's gig and roster (entry 289)

1813 Naval Tactics and Signals

275. Blunt, Edmund March (1770-1862).

Seamanship, Both in Theory and Practice. To Which Is Annexed, an Essay on Naval Tactics and Signals. Also, Regulations for the Government of the Navy of the United States of America, with Observations and Instructions for the Use of the Commissioned, the Junior, and Other Naval Officers, on All the Material Points of Professional Duty: Including Also, Forms of General and Particular Orders for the Better Government and Discipline of Armed Ships: Together with a Variety of New and Useful Tables . . . With a System of Naval Discipline, and the Acts Concerning Letters of Marque, Reprisals, Their Officers and Men . . . Illustrated with Engravings and Cuts. *New-York: Printed and sold by Edmund M. Blunt . . . 1813. 285 p., illustrated diagrams (part folding), plates, tables, 22 cm.*

This work first appeared in 1811 and was followed by printings in 1812 and 1813. Each printing is rare. The **NUC** locates two copies of the 1811 printing (Coast Guard Academy and Philadelphia Union Catalog) and three copies of the 1812 printing (American Antiquarian Society, New York Public Library, and U.S. Office Naval Records and Library).

Howes (not recorded). **Sabin** (not recorded). **Shaw and Shoemaker,** #27969. **NUC** (New York Public Library). **OCLC** (Navy Department Library).

"DON'T GIVE UP THE SHIP."

"Ships our cradles, decks our pillows,
   Lulled by winds and rocked by billows;
Gaily bound we o'er the tide,
   Hope our anchor, Heaven our guide."

*Engraving by author and
artist William N. Brady
(entry 276)*

1864 Young Sailors' Assistant

276. Brady, William N.

The Kedge-Anchor; or, Young Sailors' Assistant. Appertaining to the Practical Evolutions of Modern Seamanship, Rigging, Knotting . . . and Other Miscellaneous Matters, Applicable to Ships of War and Others. Illustrated with Seventy Engravings. Also Tables of Rigging Spars, Sails . . . etc. Relative to Every Class of Vessel. By William N. Brady. *New York: The Author; London: Sampson, Low, Son & Co., 1864. 400 p., illus., plates, 24 cm.*

"[W]ritten for the use of the Naval and Merchant Service of the United States, as a ready means of introducing Young Sailors to the theory of that art by which they must expect to advance in the profession they have chosen."—**Preface.** First issued during 1841. William N. Brady was a boatswain in the U.S. Navy.

Howes, B715. **Sabin,** #7316 (1857 printing). **Young,** 16–17. **NUC** (Columbia University, Franklin Institute, Free Library of Philadelphia, New York Public Library, University of Texas at Austin). **OCLC** (Aurora University Library, Navy Department Library, New York Public Library, Virginia Tech Library).

1799 Seamanship and Naval Tactics Manual

277. Dobson, Thomas (1751–1823).

A System of Seamanship and Naval Tactics. Extracted from the Encyclopedia. Published by Thomas Dobson. Illustrated with Copper-Plates. *Philadelphia: Printed for Thomas Dobson at the Stone-House, 1799. 192 p., 8 plates (folding), 22 cm.*

This is the first treatise on naval tactics published in America. Seven of the plates describe tactical formations. "Naval Tactics; or, The Military Operations of Fleets" occupies pages 85–192. "A System of Seamanship" occupies pages 3–84. **Evans** cites author as John Clerk (1728–1812).

Evans, #36393. **Lefkowicz** (*Catalog Twenty-One*), #57 (1804 British printing). **Sabin** (not recorded). **NUC** (Boston Public Library, Coast Guard Academy). **OCLC** (Auburn University, Navy Department Library).

1800 American Coastal Pilot

278. [Furlong, Lawrence] (1734–1806).

The American Coast Pilot, Containing the Courses and Distances between the Principal Harbours, Capes and Headlands, from Passamaquoddy through the Gulf of Florida . . . Together with the Courses and Distances from Cape-Cod and Cape-Ann to Georges-Bank . . . With the Latitudes and Longitudes of the Principal Harbours on the Coast. Together with a Tide Table. By Capt. Lawrence Furlong. Corrected and Improved by the Most Experienced Pilots in the United States . . . *Newburyport, Mass.: Printed by Edmund M. Blunt, (proprietor), 1800. xvi, [17]–251 p., 22 cm.*

Originally printed during 1796. Of the 1800 printing, "There are two issues, one with the advertisement on the last page dated Sept. 18, 1800, and the other with a different advertisement dated Nov. 26, 1800."—**Evans.** "The last edition of the *Pilot* published without charts. Appended to the sailing directions are notes on laws relating to seamen, laws against carrying away soldiers or sailors of the U.S., custom laws, and the like."—**Lefkowicz.**

Campbell, #3. **Evans,** #37483. **Howes,** F421. **Lefkowicz** (*Catalog Twenty-One*), #117. **Sabin,** #26219. **NUC** (American Antiquarian Society, Boston Public Library, John Carter Brown Library, Library of Congress, New York Public Library, Ohio State University, Philadelphia Union Library Catalog). **OCLC** (9).

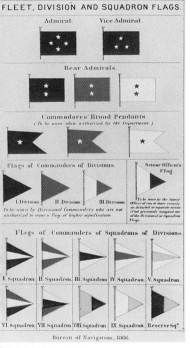

Fleet, division and squadron flags

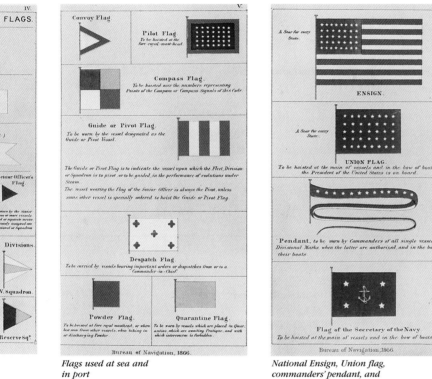

Flags used at sea and in port

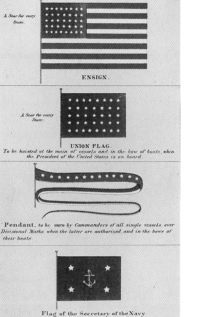

National Ensign, Union flag, commanders' pendant, and flag of the Secretary of the Navy

Presentation Copy from Commodore Jenkins

279. Jenkins, Thornton A. (1811-1893).

The United States Naval Signal Code. Prepared by Authority of the Hon. Gideon Welles, Secretary of the Navy, by Thornton A. Jenkins. *Washington: Government Printing Office, 1867. 69 p., illus., plates (some colored), 24 cm.*

The illustrations in this signal code are extensive. Plates III–XVIII are colored and cover "Fleet, Division and Squadron Flags," "Day Distinguishing Pendants," and "Night Distinguishing Lights." The colored plates are followed by Plates XIX–XLIII and a–d that present "Army Signals." The other Roman numeral plates deal with the order of sailing, steaming, and retreat. The Navy Department Library copy is inscribed: "Commodore Lanman from Commodore Jenkins—20th September 1867."

Howes (not recorded). **Sabin** (not recorded). **NUC** (Coast Guard Academy, Naval Observatory Library, Navy Department Library, Smithsonian Institution). **OCLC** (8).

First American Printing

280. Lever, Darcy (1760?–1837).

The Young Sea Officer's Sheet Anchor; or, A Key to the Leading of Rigging, and to Practical Seamanship, by Darcy Lever. *Philadelphia: M. Carey, [1819]. xii, [2], 120 p., illus., 28 cm.*

More than 600 illustrations of rigging, anchoring, etc. are found in this first American printing, which is based on the second London edition.

Shaw and Shoemaker, #48484. **Howes** (not recorded). **Sabin** (not recorded). **NUC** (13). **OCLC** (8).

"World's First Authoritative Work on Sailing Directions"

281. Maury, Matthew Fontaine (1806–1873).

Explanations and Sailing Directions to Accompany the Wind and Current Charts. Approved by Lewis Warrington, and Published by Authority of William A. Graham, by M.F. Maury, Superintendent of the National Observatory. *Washington: C. Alexander, Printer, 1851. 315, [2] p., illus., 12 plates (including charts), 28 x 23 cm.*

Citing him as the first oceanographer to chart seas for ocean travel, the **USNI Almanac** comments that Maury "wrote world's first authoritative work on Sailing Directions in 1851, [and] was first to advocate sailing along great circle routes, [as] the shortest distance between any two points on globe."

Sabin, #46963. **USNI Almanac,** 196. **NUC** (Library of Congress, New York Public Library, Oberlin College Library, U.S. Department of Environmental Science Services Administration, University of Michigan Library, University of Virginia Library). **OCLC** (Brooklyn Public Library, Dartmouth College Library, Mariner's Museum Library, Navy Department Library, Oberlin College Library, Naval Observatory Library, University of Virginia Library).

"First Work of Modern Oceanography"

282. Maury, M[atthew] F[ontaine] (1806–1873).

The Physical Geography of the Sea by M.F. Maury. *New York: Harper & brothers, 1855. xxiv, [25]–287 p., illus., 8 plates (folding), 24 cm.*

This book by Maury is "considered the first work of modern oceanography."—**Webster.** "The sea, for the first time, was here viewed as the subject matter of a distinct branch of science with problems of its own. The importance of these problems Maury discussed in engaging and stimulating fashion." Appearing the same year as the first edition, this is the second edition, "enlarged and improved." The first edition is also in the Navy Department Library's holdings.

DAB (6), 428–31. **Sabin,** #46969. **Webster,** 274–75. **NUC** (27). **OCLC** (58).

First Naval Observatory Nautical Monograph

283. Maury, Matthew Fontaine (1806-1873).

The Winds at Sea; Their Mean Direction and Annual Average Duration from Each of the Four Quarters. *[Washington: 1859]. 8 p., iv plates (3 colored, 2 double), 29 x 24 cm.*

Maury began his research on winds and currents in 1845. This document was issued during October 1859 as Nautical Monographs No.1 of the Naval Observatory in Washington, D.C.

DAB (6), 428–31. **Sabin** (not recorded). **NUC** (John Crerar Research Library, Library of Congress, Navy Department Library). **OCLC** (12).

Unique 1809 Manuscript Signals Book For New Orleans Station

284. Porter, David (1780-1843).

A Code of Signals, by David Porter, Commanding Officer, New Orleans Station, Adopted There by Authority of the Navy Department in 1809. *[New Orleans]: 1809. Unpaged, illus. (some colored), 20 cm.*

Contained in the original binding, the title, as in the main entry above, appears in manuscript on the front inside cover. There follow four pages of hand-drawn and hand-colored signal flags, 31 manuscript pages of numbers corresponding to signals, 8 blank pages, 14 manuscript pages explanatory of signals and including 11 hand-drawn and hand-colored signal illustrations, 2 pages of hand-drawn sailing formations, 43 manuscript pages explaining sailing formations, 4 manuscript pages describing night signals, 7 blank pages, 3 manuscript pages describing fog and distant signals, and 44 blank pages. The illustrations and cursive handwriting are of high quality.

DAB (8), 83–85. **OCLC** (Navy Department Library).

Civil War Signals and Code Book with Lead Sinking Plates

285. United States. Bureau of Ordnance (Navy Department).

Code of Flotilla and Boat Squadron Signals for the United States Navy. Prepared by Thornton A. Jenkins. [Under Instructions of the Bureau of Ordnance and Hydrography.] By Order of the Hon. Gideon Welles. *Washington: Government Printing Office, 1861. xiv, 191 p., illus. (some colored), 16 cm.*

The Navy Department's copy has bound in material not shown in the pagination. At the front are two lined leaves, each carrying hand-drawn and hand-colored signal flags, 26 in number. Signal flags identify the vessels, including *Ariel, De Soto, Fort Henry, Gem of the Sea, Honduras, Pursuit, Restless, Sagamore, San Jacinto, Stars & Stripes*, and *Wanderer*. These signal flags are followed by a list of 512 United States vessels. The "List of the United States Navy" provides an identification number for each vessel. The body of the code book includes commands, geographical locations, and vocabulary that are assigned a one to four digit number, which can be signaled by the numbered flags. This copy has riveted to the exterior of each board a lead plate to ensure rapid sinking of the code and signals in the event of pending capture of the warship. Thornton A. Jenkins, an American naval officer who attained the rank of rear admiral, was the author of this book. During the Civil War, Jenkins served as fleet captain and chief of staff to Admiral Farragut. The **DAB** specifically cites this code and signals book as by Jenkins and as one of a "number of government publications in his special field of navigation."

Cogar (1), 85–86. **DAB** (5), 50–51. **NUC** (Duke University, Library of Congress, Navy Department Library). **OCLC** (9).

Printed On Board USS *Hartford* on Asiatic Station

286. United States. Navy. Naval Force on Asiatic Station.

Tactics for Boats Exercising under Oars: For the Use of the Vessels on the Asiatic Station U.S. Flag Ship "Hartford." *[USS Hartford Flagship Print?], 1873. 23 p., illus., 14 cm.*

It is quite probable that this publication was printed on board USS *Hartford* while steaming on the Asiatic Station. The imprint on the title page is: "U.S. Flag Ship 'Hartford.' 1873." The verso of the title page bears the authentication: "Thornton A. Jenkins, Rear Admiral Comdg. U.S. Naval Forces on the Asiatic Station." The field of 19th-century publications printed on board ships is a fascinating one, which deserves much investigation. This particular example is not recorded by the **NUC**, although that catalog does cite, under "U.S. Bureau of Naval Personnel," the Navy Department Library as sole holder of a publication entitled *Tactics for Boats under Bars* [*sic*], by Rear Admiral A. Jenkins, Washington, [n.d.]. This pocket-sized publication is illustrated with three plates in color. One depicts the signal flags for numbers 1 through 9, and 0. The back of the publication lists 332 command lines, some blank, which correlate to one- to three-digit numbers signaled by the flags for 1 through 9, and 0.

NUC (not recorded). **OCLC** (Navy Department Library).

1807 Gunboat Signals Book with Hand-Colored Flags

287. United States. Navy. Signals Book.

Signals to Be Used by the Squadron under Command of . . . *Brooklyn (L.I.): Printed By Robinson & Little, 1807. [2] p., 1 leaf with manuscript entries on recto and hand-colored signal flags on verso, [3]–44 p., 3 pages of manuscript, 18.5 cm.*

Commodore John Rodgers issued this signals book. His signature appears in print on page 44 as the issuing authority. In all cases, the number corresponding to the signal has been left out by the printer and subsequently entered in manuscript by a user. There is a special section on "Night Signals." This copy has many manuscript entries. On the verso of the leaf following [2] is a set of hand-drawn and hand-colored number signal flags for 1 through 9, and 0.

Shaw and Shoemaker, #14091. **OCLC** (John Hopkins University, Navy Department Library, New York Public Library).

War of 1812 Signals Book Issued by Commodore Rodgers

288. United States. Navy. Signals Book.

Signals to Be Used by the Squadron under Command of . . . *Brooklyn, L.I.: Printed by Thomas Kirk, 1812. [3], 4–47 p., 18 cm.*

Commodore John Rodgers issued this signals book for his New York-based gunboats. The *American Imprints Inventory* for 1801–1820 cites just three signals books. The earliest is *Signals to Be Used by the Squadron . . .* (see entry 287). The second is described as *Signals to Be Used by the Squadron under Command of Com. John Rogers* [*sic*] Brooklyn, 1812, 47 p. This signals book is apparently the second signals book described by **Shaw and Shoemaker** who have added "John Rogers" to the title. In fact John Rogers is a mistake for John Rodgers, his name appearing in print on page 47 as the issuing authority. Neither of these two signals books is described in the **NUC** under title "United States. Navy" or "United States. Navy Department." The **NUC** does describe an 1813 signals book, *Signals for the Use of the U.S. Navy As Adopted by Order of the Navy Department, August, 1813,* 163 p.

NUC (not recorded). **Shaw and Shoemaker,** #26647. **OCLC** (Brooklyn Historical Society Library, Navy Department Library).

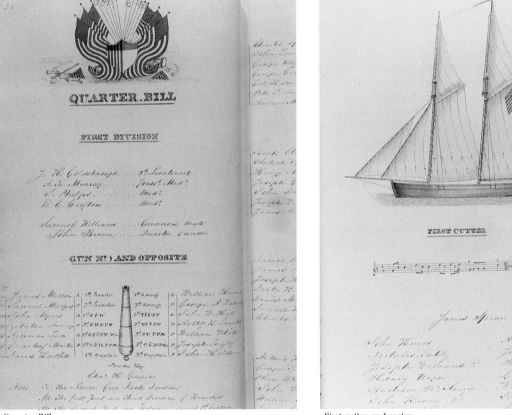

Quarter Bill

First cutter and roster

Superlative Examples of 1843 Sailor Art

289. USS Columbus. Unnamed Yeoman (attribution).

Watch, Quarter & Station Bill of the U.S. Ship of the Line Columbus, Bearing the Broad Pennant of Commander Chars. W. Morgan. *1843. 143 [56] p., illus., 35 cm.*

This richly illustrated watch, quarter, and station bill details positions for all shipboard evolutions from making sail to general quarters. It includes hand drawings of ships, ship guns, manning of the yardarms, sundry decorations, and drawings of St. Paul's Cathedral, Gibraltar, and Venice and music to accompany each ship call. Contents include "List of Officers," "List of Petty Officer," "Forcastle," "Fore Top," "Main," "Top Mizzen, Top," "Afterguard," "Waiste," "Apprentices," "Marines," "Band," "Quarter Bill," "Boarder's. Pikemen. Firemen. Wenchmen and Sail trimmers," "Mooring and Unmooring," "Reefing and Hoisting," "Tacking and Veering," "Making Sail from Single Anchor," and "Anchoring." Touched with color and falling technically between primitive and schooled in production, these drawings stand as superlative examples of sailor art. A series of twelve drawings depicts the cutters, gigs, lifeboats, and launches of *Columbus*. The unidentified artist has executed each drawing with remarkable coloration and linear detailing. In many cases he shows the oarsmen or crew handling the running rigging in position on board these support craft. Musical bars and notes followed by the names of the sailors assigned to the craft appear below the drawings. Six other noteworthy drawings detail sailors in position on the yardarms of the main and mizzenmasts. Attired in blue trousers and wearing broad-brimmed, black headgear, these sailors seem like a chorus line performing in the acrobat's domain high above the seas.

DANFS (2), 148, 150. **OCLC** (Navy Department Library).

Pioneer in Use of Thermometer as Navigational Tool

290. [Williams, Jonathan] (1750-1815).

Thermometrical Navigation. Being a Series of Experiments and Observations, Tending to Prove, That by Ascertaining the Relative Heat of the Sea-Water from Time to Time, the Passage of a Ship through the Gulph Stream, and from Deep Water into Soundings, May Be Discovered in Time to Avoid Danger, Although (Owing to Tempestuous Weather) It May Be Impossible to Heave the Lead or Observe the Heavenly Bodies . . . With Additions and Improvements. *Philadelphia: Printed and Sold by R. Aitken, No. 22, Market Street, 1799. [i]–xii, 98, [3] p., map (folding), 21 cm.*

This tract is a combination of Williams' own studies and those of Benjamin Franklin, Captain Thomas Truxtun, and several others. In 1792 Williams had issued *Memoir on the Use of the Thermometer in Navigation,* which "introduced a system of avoiding danger when in soundings by the recording of water temperatures. It attracted attention at home and abroad." Williams has dedicated this 1799 tract on navigation to Thomas Truxtun (1755–1822) as commander of the American frigate *Constellation* and as a pioneer in the concept he puts forward. He credits Truxtun for being instrumental in the use of this navigational technique, noting in dedicatory remarks: "Dear Sir, The experiments which induced me to believe that the thermometer might become a valuable nautical instrument to discover sound-ings having been first made on board a ship under your command. . . . The public voice, for obvious reasons, point you out as a character to whom American Improvements in Navigation ought to be dedicated; and I . . . embrace this opportunity of testifying the high sense I entertain of your patriotism, spirit and talents; as a firm friend to your country, a gallant officer, and skillful navigator . . . Jonathan Williams. Philadelphia, August 1, 1799." The [3] of the pagination includes extracts from an August 12, 1799 letter from Truxtun, noting in part, "Your publication will be of use to navigation, by rendering sea voyages secure, far beyond what even yourself will immediately calculate, for I have proved the utility of the thermometer very often since we sailed together." **Wroth** notes that in the works of Williams, Franklin, Truxtun, De Brahm, and Hoxton "it can be said with truth that there was already in existence the tradition of American interest in oceanography when in the nineteenth century Matthew Fontaine Maury became the virtual father of that science." The tract is accompanied by a folding map that charts the Gulf Stream along the eastern coast of the United States and its path into the Atlantic Ocean toward Europe.

Evans, #36722. **Howes** (not recorded). **Rink,** #3893. **Sabin,** #104300. **Wheat and Brun,** #725. **Wroth,** 31. **NUC** (University of Virginia Library). **OCLC** (19).

Title page

Naval Discipline in the 1840s
Views of a Sailor

291. Aegyptus, Tiphys (pseudonym).

The Navy's Friend: or, Reminiscences of the Navy; Containing Memoirs of a Cruise, in the U.S. Schooner Enterprise by Tiphys Aegyptus. *Baltimore: Printed for the author, 1843. vi, 45, [1] p., printed wrappers, 19 cm.*

The author, who had previously served on board USS *North Carolina*, joined *Enterprise* at New York during February of 1840. *Enterprise* under command of Lieutenant Fr. Ellery, then deployed to the squadron off the coast of Brazil. This sailor-author's combined naval service was 39 months, the majority of that on board *Enterprise*. His account of service is here given to disclose what he viewed as defects in treatment of personnel. He dedicates his account "To the Public—especially to the Committee of Naval Affairs, to persons interested in acquainting themselves with the Naval Discipline, and others, who are not aware of those heavy defects our Navy is yet burdened with."

Rinderknecht and Bruntjen, #43–65. **Sabin,** #52129. **Howes** (not recorded). **NUC** (Huntington Library, Library of Congress). **OCLC** (Library of Congress, United States Naval Academy Library, Navy Department Library, New York Public Library, Yale University Library).

Civil War Gunboat Sailor in
North Carolina Waters

292. Blanding, Stephen F.

Recollections of a Sailor Boy; or, the Cruise of the Gunboat Louisiana. By Stephen F. Blanding. *Providence: E.A. Johnson, 1886. vi, [7]–330 p., 20 cm.*

"Blanding enlisted in the Federal Navy at Boston in June, 1862. . . . He proceeded to Fortress Monroe and was attached to a squadron operating in Pamlico Sound inside the sand-pit fringe of North Carolina. Blanding had a few shore leaves which took him into the town of Washington, and on one occasion he proceeded on a minor expedition up the Tar [River] to Greenville. He found much Union sentiment among the North Carolinians along the coast, a circumstance which led some of them to enlist in the Federal forces . . . embellished with many imaginary conversations and other details probably not true, but as a general picture it has some value."—**Coulter**. Blanding's narrative covers the period from June 1862 into the latter half of 1865.

Coulter, #41. **Howes** (not recorded). **NUC** (16). **OCLC** (34).

Female Combat Veteran of War of 1812

293. Brewer, Lucy

The Female Marine, or Adventures of Miss Lucy Brewer, a Native of Plymouth County, Massachusetts. Who, After Being Disappointed in Love, Was Induced to Wander from Her Native Home; and, Either by Accident or Design, Took Up Her Abode, for Three Years, at an Infamous House in West Boston: at Length Being Disgusted with Her Manner of Life, She, in the Habit of a Male, Entered as a Marine On Board the United States' Frigate Constitution; Was in the Battles with the Guerriere, Java, Cyane and Levant, and after Three Years Faithful Service in Her Country's Cause, Was Honourably Discharged without a Discovery of Her Sex Being Made. *Printed January 1, 1816. [4], [7]–72 p., 18.5 cm.*

"Narrative of dubious veracity in which the seduced hero- ine, after a life of shame, serves for three years on board the 'Constitution.'"—**Howes.** Some 121 printings were issued between 1815 and 1818. For discussion of this work see Daniel A. Cohen's *The Female Marine and Related Works: Narratives of Crossdressing and Urban Vice in America's Early Republic.*

Howes, W279. **Sabin,** #7758. **Shaw and Shoemaker,** #39743. **NUC** (this edition not recorded). **OCLC** (Navy Department Library).

Navy Chaplain's View of Boy Recruits

294. Clark, Henry Howard (b. 1845).

Boy Life in the United States Navy by H.H. Clark, U.S.N. *Boston: D. Lothrop and Company, [1885]. [2], 3–313, [1] p., 19 cm.*

The author served as a chaplain in the United States Navy.

Young, 22–23. **NUC** (Boston Public Library, Cleveland Pub- lic Library, Library of Congress, Navy Department Library, New York Public Library). **OCLC** (8).

War of 1812 Prisoner-of-War Account

295. [Cobb, Josiah] (b. 1796).

A Green Hand's First Cruise; Roughed Out from the Log-Book of Memory, of Twenty-five Years Standing, Together with a Residence of Five Months in Dartmoor. By a Younker. *Balti- more: Cushing & Brother, 1841. 2 vols., [7], [13]–278; [3], [5]–329 p., 19 cm.*

Dartmoor was situated in Devonshire, England. Maintained for incarceration of American naval prisoners of war, the first Americans arrived on April 3, 1813. By April 1815, 5,542 Americans were resident in the prison, 252 dying there. "Discipline was strict and rations scanty, but hospital arrangements were excellent."—**DAH.**

DAH (Concise), 277. **Fredriksen,** #520. **Howes,** C511. **Sabin,** #28575. **NUC** (8). **OCLC** (8).

Impressed Sailor Narrative

296. Davis, Joshua (b. 1760).

A Narrative of Joshua Davis, an American Citizen, Who Was Pressed and Served On Board Six Ships of the British Navy . . . The Whole Being an Interesting and Faithful Narrative of the Discipline, Various Practices and Treatment of Pressed Seamen in the British Navy, and Containing Information That Never Was Before Presented to the American People. *Boston: Printed by B. True, no. 78, State street, 1811. 72 p., 19 cm.*

"My Friends, doubtless you are ever anxious to know the fate of your fathers, husbands, brothers, uncles, cousins, or sweethearts, when they have left you in order to get a living on the briny ocean, which is now ruled by the ships of his Britanick Majesty—I can tell you in a few minutes. Many of them are on board those hellish floating torments. . . . When they write a letter, they must get a friend (as they suppose him) to take it on shore. That pretended friend, for the sake of keeping the writer in the same predicament as himself (for misery loves company) and for the sake of getting in the favour of the officers, give the letters to them for their perusal. The commanding officer inquires for the person who wrote it. . . . If the officer happens to be a Washington, he will tell the man never to do the like again; but if he should prove a Nero, the man is ordered to be put in irons, until a time is set by the court of inquiry for the writer's destiny, and all this merely for attempting to let his friends know his unhappy situation.—There are nine Neros in the British navy, to one Washington."—**To My Readers and Others.**

Howes, D125. **Sabin,** #18860. **Shaw and Shoemaker,** #22665. **NUC** (8). **OCLC** (17).

Veteran of Tripoli Service
Seven Years' Forced Service in British Navy

297. Durand, James R. (b. 1790).

Life and Adventures of James R. Durand, during a Period of Fifteen Years, from 1801 to 1816: in Which Time He Was Impressed On Board the British Fleet, and Held in Detestable Bondage for More Than Seven Years, Including an Account of a Voyage to the Mediterranean, Written by Himself. *Rochester, N.Y.: Printed for the author by E. Peck & Co., 1820. 129 p., 18 cm.*

Durand was born during 1790 at Milford, Connecticut. He began his life at sea in 1801. His initial sea experiences were with American merchantmen. On April 1, 1804, he joined the crew of USS *John Adams* that would soon depart for the Mediterranean to fight the Tripoli pirates. Pages 38–50 describe the Mediterranean and are immediately followed by his comments on the American fleet and Algiers. By 1808 Durand was back in the United States. Having been caned by a midshipman, and commenting on the fallacy of allowing 10–12-year-old midshipmen to strike sailors, he left the Navy and began an account of a European cruise on a merchantman. Beginning with August 21, 1809, he found himself impressed on board a British warship, and was under British control for more than seven years. The earliest appearance of this work was 1817.

Harbeck, 79. **Howes,** D591. **Sabin,** #21411. **Shoemaker,** #1058. **NUC** (17). **OCLC** (17).

USS *Ohio* on Mediterranean Station 1839–1841

298. Gould, [Roland Freeman] (b. 1817).

The Life of Gould, an Ex-Man-of-War's-Man, with Incidents on Sea and Shore, Including the Three Years' Cruise on the Line of Battle Ship Ohio, on the Mediterranean Station, under the Veteran Commodore Hull. *Clarement, N.H.: Printed by the Claremont manufacturing co., 1867. 2, [vii]–xi, [1], [13]–239, [1] p. including plates and portrait, 18 cm.*

Gould entered naval service during June 1838. He was assigned to USS *Ohio* on October 13, 1838, and his vessel subsequently deployed to the Mediterranean. His three-year account is primarily oriented at personal experiences, shipboard and squadron life, and travel, as opposed to reform of the naval system. His running account covers Atlantic passage, rumors of war, quarantine, death of Commodore Paterson, theatre on board *Ohio*, the French fleet, shipboard dance, Turkish steam frigate, quarrel between two midshipmen, Commodore Hull's address to the crew, mutinous and discontented feelings of crew members, abuses of seamen, use of alcohol by a midshipman, whaling, and much description of places visited.

Portrait of Roland Gould, engraved by H. L. Penfield

Howes (not recorded). **Sabin,** #28124. **NUC** (9). **OCLC** (27).

Participating Sailor's Account of the Two Major Battles of Quasi-War with France

299. Hoxse, John (b. 1774).

The Yankee Tar. An Authentic Narrative of the Voyages and Hardships of John Hoxse, and the Cruises of the U.S. Frigate Constellation, and Her Engagements with the French Frigates Le Insurgente and Le Vengeance, in the Latter of Which the Author Loses His Right Arm. Written by Himself. With an Extract from the Writings of Rev. John Flavel. *Northampton, [Mass.]: J. Metcalf, 1840. 200 p. including frontispiece, 17 cm.*

On February 9, 1799, USS *Constellation*, commanded by Captain Thomas Truxtun, engaged and defeated the French frigate *L'Insurgente*. This was the first victory over a French man-of-war during the Quasi-war with France. Subsequently, on February 1, 1800, Truxtun engaged and "shattered in night battle the 40-gun *Vengeance*."—**DAH.** Pages 76–78 carry a list of officers and men, wounded and missing, in the February 1 action. Following page 153, the content is an extraction, which is religious in nature, from the writings of John Flavel.

DAH (Concise), 646–47. **Howes,** H744. **Rinderknecht and Bruntjen,** #40–3301. **Sabin,** #33394. **Sweetman,** 18. **NUC** (Boston Public Library, Clements Library, Library of Congress, Navy Department Library, New York Public Library). **OCLC** (66).

Contrast of Sailor Life on British and American Warships

300. Leech, Samuel (1798-1848).

Thirty Years from Home, or a Voice from the Main Deck; Being the Experience of Samuel Leech, Who Was Six Years in the British and American Navies: Was Captured in the British Frigate Macedonian: Afterwards Entered the American Navy, and Was Taken in the United States Brig Syren, by the British Ship Medway. Embellished with Engravings. *Boston: Tappan & Dennet, 1843. [i]–xvi, [17]–305, [1] p., illus., 16 cm.*

"My first impressions of the American service were very favorable. The treatment on the 'Syren' was more lenient and favorable than in the 'Macedonian.' The captain and officers were kind, while there was total exemption from that petty tyranny exercised by the upstart midshipmen in the British service. As a necessary effect, our crew were as comfortable and as happy as men ever are in a man of war." Leech was taken prisoner on July 12, 1814, when HMS *Medway* took USS *Syren*. He gives good account of his imprisonment. He subsequently served on board USS *Boxer*.

Harbeck, 20. **Howes,** L224. **Neeser,** #7758. **Rinderknecht and Bruntjen,** #43–2966. **Sabin,** #39812. **NUC** (13). **OCLC** (46).

Macedonian receiving visitors

Midshipman Life

301. Lynch, William Francis (1801-1865).

Naval Life; or, Observations Afloat and On Shore. The Midshipman. By W.F. Lynch. *New York: Charles Scribner, 1851. vii, [9]–308 p., 19 cm.*

Serving in the United States Navy in which he achieved the rank of captain by 1856, Lynch resigned in 1861 to join the Confederate States Navy. His 'Naval Life' is "partly autobiographical . . . [a] curious medley of tales, descriptions, and sea experiences."—**DAB.**

DAB (6), 524–25. **Howes** (not recorded). **Sabin,** #42818. **Webster,** 250. **NUC** (11). **OCLC** (41).

Intellectual Food
"Joyous" Opening Day of the Sailor's Library
Source for Herman Melville

302. [Mercier, Henry James].

Life in a Man-of-War, or Scenes in "Old Ironsides" during Her Cruise in the Pacific. By a Fore-Top-Man. *Philadelphia: L.R. Bailey, printer, 1841. 267 p., 24 cm.*

"This lively, well-written narrative presents a detailed view of life before the mast, both the daily details and the unusual details, including the effects of running out of whiskey (cologne was substituted!)."—**Lefkowicz.** "One of the scenes depicted in *Life in a Man-of-War* had to do with the joyous opening day of a purchased library of 300 or 400 volumes aboard 'Old Ironsides' in 1839. The books in the library had already been numbered and their titles noted in a catalog 'which was forcibly dragged' from one eager sailor to another in their efforts to make selections. Henry J. Mercier, the author, attributed to the crew the notion that they 'felt pleased to think that they had now in their possession a stock of intellectual food to beguile the heavy tediousness of the cruise, or to refresh their thirst for mental acquirements'. . . . What Melville wrote about the world of the man-of-war, 'Neversink,' in *White-Jacket* was not necessarily what he experienced when he served aboard the frigate *United States* in 1844. Of importance here is to note that Melville's description of the frigate's library is unreliable as historical fact."—**Skallerup.**

Lefkowicz (*Catalog Twenty-One*), #212. **Rinderknecht and Bruntjen,** #41–3486. **Sabin,** #41012. **Skallerup,** 86, 92. **Howes** (not recorded). **NUC** (Detroit Public Library, Library of Congress, Navy Department Library, University of Indiana). **OCLC** (14).

First Man from Intrepid to Board Philadelphia

303. Morris, Charles (1784-1856).

The Autobiography of Commodore Charles Morris, U.S.N., with Portrait and Explanatory Notes. *Boston: A. Williams & Co., 1880. 111 p., portrait, 25 cm.*

Morris "served in the Tripolitan campaign as a midshipman . . . first man from the *Intrepid* to board the 'Philadelphia.' "—**Skallerup.** He was "followed closely by Decatur."—**Webster.** "Unique. It is the only narrative published by a naval officer of the older period, giving in his own words the story of his own life. It begins with Morris' entry into the service in 1799, and ends in 1840."—**Larned.**

Harbeck, 92. **Howes,** M822. **Larned,** #1744. **Skallerup,** 125. **Webster,** 290. **NUC** (9). **OCLC** (Navy Department Library, Boston University Library, Harvard University Library, New York Public Library, United States Naval Academy Library).

Boy's Account of Voyage
Around the World

304. Nordhoff, Charles (1830-1901).

Man-of-War Life: A Boy's Experience in the United States Navy, during a Voyage around the World, in a Ship of the Line by Chas. Nordhoff. *New York: Dodd, Mead & Co., 1855. 286 p., illus., 17 cm.*

Contents include "Why I went to Sea and how . . . Inspecting the Boys . . . How the Commander cured a Lad of Chewing Tobacco . . . Breaking in the Green Hands . . . A Word concerning Thieving on Board Ship . . . Fourth of July at Sea . . . The First Flogging on Board . . . Wormy Bread . . . The Crew ask for 'Liberty,' and are refused . . . Lassoing a Sailor . . . Paid off."

Sabin, #55461. **Howes** (not recorded). **NUC** (Free Library of Philadelphia, Harvard University Library, University of California at Berkeley, University of Iowa, Xavier University in Cincinnati). **OCLC** (13).

African American Sailor's
Narrative

305. Paynter, John Henry (1862-1947).

Joining the Navy; or, Abroad with Uncle Sam, by Jno. H. Paynter. *Hartford, Conn.: American Publishing Company, 1895. 298 p. front., plates, ports. 20.5 cm.*

"A cabin boy in the U.S. navy describes his global adventures in 1894."—**Brignano**. Reprinted during 1911 by the Press of the Sudwarth Company of Washington, D.C., the foreword of that printing is by W.E.B. DuBois. Paynter also served for 39 years with the Internal Revenue Bureau of the U.S. Treasury Department. He produced a book on that experience as well as a novel and some poetry.

Brignano, #588. **Matthews,** 160. **Moebs** (*Black Soldiers*), #460. **Work,** 477. **NUC** (Auburn University, Boston Public Library, Duke University, Library of Congress, Northwestern University, University of Oregon at Eugene, Yale University). **OCLC** (36).

USS *Narragansett* in
Samoa

306. Rieman, George B.

Papalangee; or, Uncle Sam in Samoa. A Narrative of the Cruise of the U.S. Steamer "Narragansett" among the Samoan or Navigator Islands, Polynesia. . . By Geo. B. Rieman, Com'd Clerk. *[Oakland, Calif.: Butler & Stilwell, printers, 1874]. 43 p. 23 cm.*

Rieman narrates "Approaching Samoa," "Arrival at Pango Pango," "You My Flinn You," "Interviewing Pango Pango," "Samoa as it Was," "Diplomacy, Going for the Pirate," "Apia Upolo," "About the War," and "Uncle Sam Forms a Treaty."

Howes (not recorded). **NUC** (Library of Congress, Navy Department Library). **OCLC** (Dartmouth College Library, Johns Hopkins University Library, Navy Department Library, New York Public Library, Ohio Historical Society Library, University of California at Berkeley, Bancroft Library).

Naval Duties and Discipline

307. Roe, Francis Asbury (1823-1901)

Naval Duties and Discipline, with the Policy and Principles of Naval Organization, by F.A. Roe. *New York: D. Van Nostrand, 1865. 2 p., [iii]–vi, [7]–223 [12] p. 19 cm.*

Lieutenant Commander Roe, commended by the Secretary of the Navy for his performance in battle against CSS *Albemarle* in 1864, completed this volume of naval duties and discipline while commanding officer of USS *Michigan* on the Great Lakes in 1865. "During the engrossing labors of a previous command . . . I was importuned by the executive officer and others to write internal rules and regulations . . . it seemed positively necessary to have some regulations of details of duty, whereby the young volunteer officers might be guided as well as instructed."—**Preface.** According to the author, the "object of discipline is to protect men from wrong and to execute the law. I never knew an unhappy ship that was an efficient one, and I never knew a ship that obtained a good condition of discipline that was unhappy. The two conditions are inseparable."

Sabin, #72573. **NUC** (Boston Public Library, Library of Congress, Navy Department Library, State Historical Society of Wisconsin, Madison, University of Virginia). **OCLC** (18).

War of 1812 Sailing Master in USS *Constitution*

308. Smith, Moses.

Naval Scenes in the Last War: or, Three Years On Board the Frigate Constitution and the Adams; Including the Capture of the Guerriere Being the True Narrative of Moses Smith, a Survivor of the "Old Ironsides" Crew. *Boston: Gleason's Publishing Hall, 1846. 50 p., plate, 23 cm.*

Smith served as a sailing master from 1811 to 1814. Joining USS *Constitution* in March 1811, he "makes useful observations of naval life on board . . . witnessed the famous chase by a British squadron . . . vividly relates the capture of 'HMS Guerriere.'"—**Fredriksen.** Following service in *Constitution*, Smith was in USS *Adams* during several West African cruises. He was with *Adams* when a British squadron trapped and destroyed the ship off the coast of Maine.

Fredriksen, #462. **Howes,** S645. **Rinderknecht and Bruntjen,** #46–6543. **Sabin,** #83641. **NUC** (Brown University, Harvard University Library, Navy Department Library, Ohio State University, Texas Tech University). **OCLC** (9).

First Cruise of USS *Ohio*
With Commodore Isaac Hull in the Mediterranean

309. Torrey, F.P.

Journal of the Cruise of the United States Ship Ohio, Commodore Isaac Hull, Commander, in the Mediterranean, in the Years 1839, '40, '41, by F.P. Torrey. *Boston: Printed by S.N. Dickinson, 1841. 120 p., 15 cm.*

Torrey's account begins with departure from the Charlestown Navy Yard in Boston on October 16, 1838. The passage followed a route of Boston, New York, Gibraltar, Mahon, Lisbon, Mahon, Marseilles, Leghorn, Naples, Malta, Athens, Volo Bay, Mahon, Gibraltar, Madeira, Santa Cruz, Mahon, Espezia, Genoa, Toulon, Palermo, Espezia, Mahon, Trieste, Volo Bay, Smyrna, Mahon, Malaga, Toulon, Mahon, Malaga, and Boston. Interspersed in his account are details on deaths on board, comment on officers, discussions of courts-martial, and an occassional poem. Other commentary includes apprentice boys, Marine company, Washington's birthday, rumor of war over conflict between Maine and New Brunswick, reception of King Otho and his queen, repairing and painting ship and setting up rigging, shipboard theatre, and death of Commodore Chauncey. He ends his account with high praise for the leadership of Commodore Isaac Hull and criticism of Commodore Reed of *Columbia*, charging Reed with "cruel and arbitrary conduct," which resulted in several hundred of *Columbia's* crew demonstrating in Boston following discharge.

Rinderknecht and Bruntjen, #41–5174. **Howes** (not recorded). **Sabin** (not recorded). **NUC** (10). **OCLC** (17).

Poet of USS *Colorado*
Saluting Birth of Washington and
Describing Sailor Sports

310. Willis, George R.

Lines for the Day, Feb. 22nd, 1871. *[U.S. Frigate "Colorado," Hong Kong, China]. Broadside surrounded by ornamental border, 21 cm.*

The poet, identified only by the initials "G.R.W.," is cited in the **NUC** under the pseudonym Tom Stopper-Knot and credited with an 1877 book of poems from USS *Tennessee* of which book only the New York Public Library copy is recorded. G.R.W. served on board USS *Colorado*. Four of his poems, including the one in the main entry above, were printed in broadside format and are today found in a Navy Department Library album with the spinal entitlement *Admiral John Rodger's* [sic] *Scrap Book*. The broadside poem above is in seven stanzas, each of four lines. The poem tells of a Febrary 22 celebration by vessels of Britain, France, and the United States with Lafayette and Washington being the celebratory subject of the last two nations. The last stanza speaks of the three nations meeting in "manly sports." Possibly, the "manly sports" alluded to were boat races. The foregoing statement is made based on two other broadside poems by G.R.W. in this album. "One is entitled 'The Story of the Boat Race in Singapore Roads,' August 20th, 1870." The other is entitled "The Race Between the Cutter-Barge *Daring* U.S. Flag Ship *Colorado*, and the USS *Monocacy's* Racing Cutter 'Flora.' " It is dated January 1, 1871, from Nagasaki, Japan.

NUC (not recorded). **OCLC** (Navy Department Library).

Schoolmaster of Frigate *Constellation*, 1829–1831

311. Wines, Enoch Cobb (1806-1879).

Two Years and a Half in the Navy; or, Journal of a Cruise in the Mediterranean and Levant, On Board the U.S. Frigate Constellation, in the years 1829, 1830, and 1831, by E.C. Wines. *Philadelphia: Carey & Lea, 1832. 2 vols., xi, [1], 247; x, [1], 244, [32-adv] p., 19 cm.*

"In 1829 [Wines] became schoolmaster of midshipmen on the United States frigate *Constellation*."—**DAB.** "[G]ives a good account of the details of life on an American frigate."—**Lefkowicz.**

Bruntjen and Bruntjen, #17119. **DAB** (10), 385. **Howes** (not recorded). **Lefkowicz** (*Catalog Twenty-One*), #326. **Sabin,** #104775. **Young,** 142–43. **NUC** (14). **OCLC** (45).

Editor of a Shipboard Newspaper

312. Young, Louis Stanley.

The Cruise of the U.S. Flagship "Olympia" from 1895 t 1899: From San Francisco to Manila Bay by L.S. Young. *189 [3]–138 p., illus., 3 p. of plates, 26 cm.*

Pages (3)–130 constitute a reissue of seven issues of th shipboard printed newspaper, the *Bounding Billow*, Vol. No. 1–7. Issue No. 4 carries a black-bordered front pag memorializing the explosion of USS *Maine* in Havana ha bor. Issue No. 5 has a patriotic and colored front page an the entire issue is given to the Battle of Manila Bay. Issu No. 6 has a similar front page and is devoted to the fall Manila. The newspapers are illustrated with photographs ships, ports of call, and seamen at work and play. Als found in the newspapers is poetry by L.S. Young. The fir part of the book is a narrative of *Olympia's* voyage fro San Francisco to Manila Bay.

NUC (8). **OCLC** (12).

Shell and Fuse for Dahlgren Shell Guns

313. Alger, Francis (1807–1863).

A Petition to the National Government, Embodying Facts and Statements in Furtherance of the Claim of the Late Cyrus Alger for Remuneration for the Adoption and Use, by the United-States Army and Navy, of Certain Inventions of His Relating to Fuzes and Shells, As Herein Set Forth; with Corroborative Official Documents, Testifying to Their Introduction into the United-States Service, and Their Indispensable Value by Francis Alger. *Washington: Franck Taylor, 1862. 69 p., [10] leaves of plates, illus., 23 cm.*

Cyrus Alger (1781–1856) invented an "improved shell and fuze, which have been in general use in the navy and army of the United States, but more especially they have been used in the Dahlgren shell guns of the navy." Alger's "plant turned out the first perfect bronze cannon ever made for the United States Government and for the State of Massachusetts. Ordnance, in fact, after the War of 1812, was with him a primary interest, and his superior methods of casting iron brought to his foundry so many government contracts that for many years he was chiefly employed in gun making. He made improvements in the composition of fuses for bombshells and cast the mortar gun, 'Columbiad,' the largest gun cast in America up to 1850."—**DAB**

DAB (1), 177–78. **Sabin** (not recorded). **NUC** (Boston Public Library, Harvard University Library, Huntington Library, Library Company of Philadelphia, Library of Congress). **OCLC** (Navy Department Library).

Pioneering American Naval Architect
Concept Eliminating Metal Fastenings
Below Waterline

314. Annesley, William.

A New System of Naval Architecture, by William Annesley. *London: Printed by W. Nicol., and sold by G. and W. Nicol [etc.], 1822. [iii]–viii, 68 p., illus, plates (folding), 27 cm.*

The 1823 American printing provides introductory notes that place this work in perspective: "Mr. Annesley's improvement in ship and boat building originated in the State of New-York, a few years ago. He carried it into operation in England subsequently to his patent, and printed the explanation of it, with plates, in London, in 1822. After building above fifty vessels he returned home to secure the patent right of his improvements. . . . In describing his invention he says the principle excludes frame, timbers, beams, knees, and the necessity of metal fastenings below water. At Albany, in the year 1813, a small vessel of 10 tons was first built, which sailed excellently." The **NUC** also locates an 1818 printing under the title *A Description of William Annesley's New System*, 48 p., frontispiece (folding) of which three copies are located in the American Antiquarian Society, the Library of Congress, and the New York Public Library.

NUC (Library Company of Philadelphia, Library of Congress, New York Public Library, Yale University Library). **OCLC** (8).

Father of the Steel Navy

315. Anonymous.

Facts in Relation to the Official Career of B.F. Isherwood Chief of the Bureau of Steam Engineering of the Navy Department. *Philadelphia: 1866. 57 p., 23 cm.*

Benjamin Franklin Isherwood (1822–1915) was "often considered the mid-nineteenth century's leading marine engineer [and]...was actively involved in designing what would become the foundation of the steel navy."—**Cogar.**

Cogar (2), 145–46. **OCLC** (Harvard University Library, Navy Department Library).

1869 Concepts of Submarine Warfare

316. Barnes, John S. (1836-1911).

Submarine Warfare, Offensive and Defensive, Including Discussion of the Offensive Torpedo System, Its Effects upon Iron-clad Ship Systems, and Influence upon Future Naval Wars . . . With Illustrations. *New York: Van Nostrand, 1869. 233 p., illus., 24 cm.*

Barnes has as the frontispiece to his book a handsome tinted lithograph entitled *Destruction of the U.S. Steam Sloop of War Housatonic.* This event took place on February 17, 1864, when CSS *H.L. Hunley,* a Confederate submarine, successfully sank *Housatonic* by means of a spar torpedo. *Housatonic* was part of the Union naval force blockading Charleston, South Carolina. Barnes includes discussion of Bushnell's submarine boat, General Washington on torpedoes, Fulton's plunging boat, torpedoes in 1812, Colt's electric torpedoes, first appearance of rebel torpedoes, clockwork torpedoes, Admiral Dahlgren's opinion of torpedo boats, U.S. plunging torpedo boat, methods employed to remove torpedoes, and Ericsson's torpedo.

Howes (not recorded). **Young,** 8–9. **NUC** (23). **OCLC** (41).

Remedy for the Backbone of Naval Construction

317. Barron, James (1768-1851).

A Brief Essay on the Causes of Dry-Rot in Public and Private Ships and Its Remedy. By James Barron. *Norfolk: Printed by Shields and Ashburn, 1829. 16 p., diagrams, 21 cm.*

"The condition in which many of our public and private ships have been found, from the effects of Dry-Rot, has, for the last thirty years, engaged much of my particular attention, to the important desideratum for remedying the evil, and preserving this branch of our national defence and commercial marine." This publication suggests another aspect of Commodore James Barron (1768–1851), a naval officer of considerable experience and service that included court-martial for loss of *Chesapeake* to *Leopard* and the mortal wounding of Stephen Decatur in a duel.

Shoemaker and Cooper, #37712. **Sabin** (not recorded). **Young,** 8–9. **NUC** (American Philosophical Society, Boston Public Library, Franklin Institute, Harvard University Library, New York Public Library, Yale University). **OCLC** (8).

Significant Iconography of Steam Warships

318. Bennett, Frank Marion (1857-1924).

The Steam Navy of the United States: A History of the Growth of the Steam Vessel of War in the U.S. Navy, and of the Naval Engineer Corps by Frank M. Bennett. *Pittsburgh, Pa.: Press of W.T. Nicholson, 1896. xv, 953 p., facsimiles, illus., plates (part folding), portraits, 24 cm.*

Extremely detailed treatment of the steam navy from Fulton's *Demologos*, first steam war vessel, to the steam war ships of the 1890s. Illustrated with 120 views, many of which are photographs of vessels no longer in existence.

Howes (not recorded). **NUC** (23). **OCLC** (52).

Semi-Submarine Twin Screw Gunboat

319. [Berdan Manufacturing Company].

The Berdan Iron-clad Destroyer, Milans. *Law Printer, 519 7th Street, N.W., Washington, D.C.: [January 16th, 1892]. [1], 2–8 p., plate (folding), front printed wrapper, 22.5 cm.*

Illustrated with a large folding plate of the vessel, this tract carries congressional authorization for purchase, specifications, description of mode of attack, ship's gun, etc. Congress had authorized purchase of one of these vessels. "This boat may be described as a twin screw armored semi-submarine gunboat; capable of steaming at full speed up to the side of an iron-clad and firing a large loaded shell with a time fuse into her below her belt of armor plating, at short range, without any injury to the boat from collision, from projectiles, or from torpedoes."

NUC (Library of Congress). **OCLC** (Navy Department Library).

Dahlgren on Shell Guns

320. [Dahlgren, John Adolphus] (1809-1870).

Shells and Shell-Guns by J.A. Dahlgren. *Philadelphia: King & Baird, printers, 1856. 16, 436 p., [8] leaves of plates, 24 cm.*

"This work was considered by many students of ordnance as the best ever written on the subject."—**DAB.**

DAB (3), 29–31. **Sabin,** #18277 (under). **NUC** (8). **OCLC** (20).

By-Product of the Mexican War
Dahlgren's 1852 System of Boat Armament

321. Dahlgren, J[John] A[Adolphus] (1809-1870).

System of Boat Armament in the United States Navy: Reported to Commodore Charles Morris, Chief of Bureau of Ordnance and Hydrography. By J.A. Dahlgren. *Philadelphia: Printed by A. Hart, 1852. 122 p., 11 plates (some colored), tables, 20 cm.*

"The boat armament now introduced into the equipment of the U.S. Navy may be considered as one of the results of the hostilities with Mexico."—**Preliminary Remarks.**

DAB (3), 29–31. **Sabin**, #18276. **NUC** (8). **OCLC** (14).

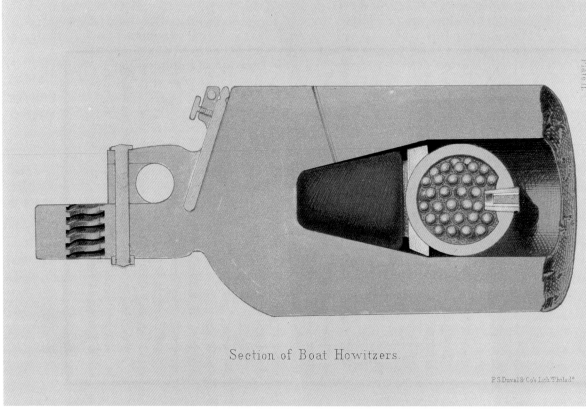

Plate II.

Section of Boat Howitzers.

P.S. Duval & Co's Lith. Phila.

Boat armament, 1856 edition.

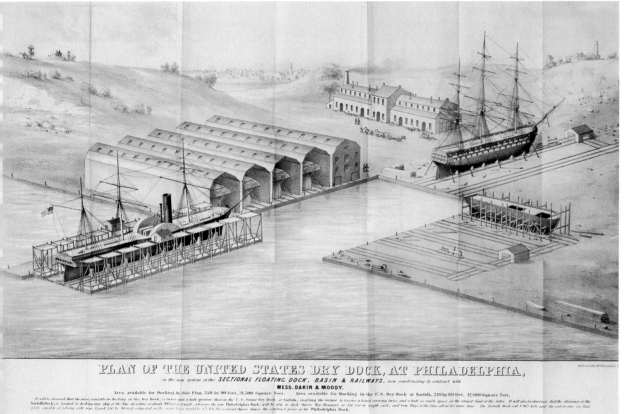

*Plan of the U.S. dry dock at
Philadelphia, lithograph*

1849 Contrasting of the Transition from Sail to Steam

322. Dakin & Moody Company.

Sketch of the Plans, Present Condition and Proposed Results of the United States Dry Docks at the Navy Yards of Philadelphia, Kittery, and Pensacola; upon the New System of Floating Docks, Basin & Railways; Now Constructing under Contracts with Messrs. Dakin & Moody, and Gilbert Secor, Made by the Navy Department, under a Law of Congress, Passed August 3rd. 1848. *New York: Printed by P. Miller & Son, 1849. 24 p., [3] folded leaves of plates, 25 cm.*

This tract is illustrated with a superb lithograph measuring 47.5 cm by 67 cm of the floating dry dock at Philadelphia. The lithograph emphasizes the progress in naval architecture by depicting two warships, one a three-masted frigate and the other a three-masted sidewheeler. A hull is shown under construction in open air and four constructed hulls are depicted under cover.

Sabin, #81532. **NUC** (Library of Congress, Pennsylvania Historical Society). **OCLC** (Cleveland Public Library, Harvard University Library, Navy Department Library, United States Naval Academy Library, University of Miami Library, University of Michigan Library, University of Rochester Library).

Leading Engineer in Transition to the "Steel Navy"

323. An Engineer.

Report of the Board of Naval Engineers, Ordered by the Secretary of the Navy, to Experiment with the Martin Vertical Water Tube Boiler and the English Horizontal Fire Tube Boiler On Board the U.S. Steam Frigate "San Jacinto," Navy Yard New-York, June 24th 1859. *[New York?: 1859]. 8 p., 23 cm.*

"A criticism of B.F. Isherwood as chief of the Bureau of steam engineering."—**NUC.** Benjamin Franklin Isherwood (1822–1915) was "often considered the mid-nineteenth century's leading marine engineer... was actively involved in designing what would become the foundation of the steel navy."—**Cogar.**

Cogar (2), 145–46. **NUC** (Library Company of Philadelphia, Library of Congress). **OCLC** (Navy Department Library).

Gatling Gun's Fleet Employment

324. Franklin, William B[uel] (1823-1903).

The Gatling Gun, for Service Ashore and Afloat: With a History of the Invention, Description of the Gun, Official Reports of Recent Trials Written and Compiled by William B. Franklin. *Hartford: Case, Lockwood and Brainard Co., 1874. 30 p., 13 plates, tables, 30 cm.*

The excellent illustrations include "Navy Carriage for Gatling Gun," "Navy Gun Carriage Converted into a Limber," and "Light Gatling Gun Mounted on Gunwale of a Ship." Franklin served at the rank of major general in the United States Army. Detailed technically and operationally, this tract was issued by the Gatling Gun Company in Hartford, Connecticut.

Webster, 130. **NUC** (8). **OCLC** (Connecticut State Library, Mariner's Museum, Navy Department Library, Smithsonian, United States Naval Academy, United States Military Academy Library).

Armored Frigate "New Ironsides"
The First Successful Seagoing Ironclad Steamer

325. Franklin Institute Journal.

The U.S.S. Armored Frigate New Ironsides. *[1865?]. 11 p. 23 cm.*

"This vessel, famous in naval history as our first successful sea-going iron-clad steamer, as well as for the service she performed in the great rebellion, was destroyed by fire, in the League Island channel, near this city, on the 16th of December last (1862)." First printed from the *Journal of the Franklin Institute*, this tract covers armor, battery, machinery, and record of firing.

OCLC (Navy Department Library).

Anchored and Harpooning Torpedoes

326. Fulton, [Robert] (1765-1815).

Concluding Address of Mr. Fulton's Lecture on the Mechanism, Practice and Effects of Torpedoes: Delivered at Washington, February 17, 1810. Printed at the Desire of the Audience. *[Washington: 1810]. [2], [3]–10 p., original blank leaf, 22.5 cm.*

The bottom of the title page carries the following note: "In this lecture Mr. Fulton exhibited the anchored and harpooning Torpedoes; the harpooning gun and the harpoon all of the real size as prepared for action. His demonstration excited the most lively interest, and seemed to carry to the minds of his audience a universal conviction of the practicability and success of this mode of attacking and destroying ships of war."

Shaw and Shoemaker, #20176. **Webster,** 132–33. **DAB** (4), 68–72. **Sabin** (not recorded). **NUC** (American Philosophical Society, Boston Public Library, Library of Congress). **OCLC** (Cambridge University Library, Library of Congress, Navy Department Library, Tulane University Library).

1810 Classic in Torpedo Warfare

327. Fulton, Robert (1765-1815).

Torpedo War, and Submarine Explosions, by Robert Fulton. *New York: W. Elliott, 1810. 57, [3] p., illus., 5 plates, tables, 22 x 28 cm.*

"In 1810, Robert Fulton's motive in corresponding with Secretary Paul Hamilton . . . was not to sell books, but to get the United States government to test further his idea of underwater explosions in naval warfare. To do this, he used a book to explain his inventions and was successful in convincing Congress to appropriate $5,000 for experimental tests. Several copies of his little *Torpedo War, and Submarine Explosions* were sent to six senior naval officers by the secretary on May 4, 1810, with the request that they read it with the object of informing the inventor, through Commodore John Rodgers at New York, of the possible ways his system could be circumvented. Apparently they studied the book well, for Commodore Rodgers created a formidable defense for the 16-gun brig *Argus* and defeated the main experiment in New York that October."—**Skallerup.**

DAB (4), 68–72. **Howes,** F417. **Sabin,** #26199. **Shaw and Shoemaker,** #20177. **Skallerup,** 122. **Webster,** 132–33. **NUC** (15). **OCLC** (23).

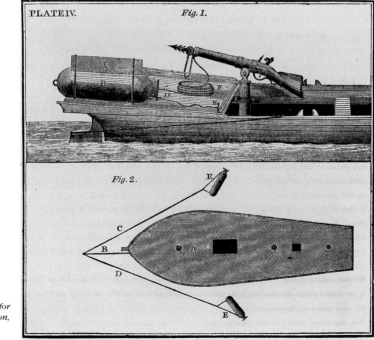

Fulton's inventions for underwater explosion, woodcut

"Original Blueprints of First U.S. Naval Submarine"

328. Holland, John P. (1841-1914).

Twelve Actual Blueprints, and One Original Engineer's Drawing on Linen, of the Submarine "Plunger," Torpedo Tube and Power Details, etc., and of Two Submerging Torpedo Boats. *1892–1897. 13 technical drawings, blueprints, 48 x 722–92 x 177 cm.*

The rare book firm of John Howell in San Francisco notes that "these blueprints . . . are in some cases the actual copies submitted to the U.S. Navy for approval. . . . The earliest blueprint, drawn to a scale of ¾ inch to 1 foot, is the design of the 80 foot *Plunger,* 1893, offered in competition for the first submarine authorized by Congress. This design was selected over many entries, and construction authorized. This is followed by a 'rough draught' of improvements on the design, 1894. The next plan is a further refinement of the last, 1895, and in greater detail. It is marked and signed in the print as approved by the Chief Naval Constructor; on the back are stamps and signatures showing the Navy's receipt of plans, their return to Holland, Holland's receipt, etc. Though launched in 1897, the *Plunger* was never commissioned by the Navy, as Holland had learned so much in its development that he arranged to refund the entire cost of construction, and built the famous *Holland* which was commissioned in 1901, and in use until 1910. The *Plunger* was, however, the first successful submarine, and all modern submarines are constructed after Holland's system of a diving rather than a sinking vessel. . . . There are also two over-all designs for 150 foot and 180 foot submerging torpedo boats, designed to operate with the deck four feet under water when in action."

OCLC (Navy Department Library).

First American Submarine with Internal Combustion Engine

329. Lake Submarine Company.

The "Argonaut": Her Evolution and History What She Was Built For and What She Accomplished. *New York, N.Y.: The Lake Submarine Co., [1900]. 32 p., illus. 24 cm.*

Demonstrated by Simon Lake on December 15, 1897, *Argonaut* was the first United States submarine powered by an internal combustion engine. The demonstration took place near Baltimore on the Patapsco River. This tract from the Lake Submarine Company was issued to "give prospective investors in the companies which are about to be organized to engage in the various fields of commercial work for which vessels of the 'Argonaut' type are adapted a thorough knowledge of the principles involved, and of the possibilities of vessels of her type in various branches of work."—**Preface.** The tract includes some fine photographic illustrations. The copy of the tract located by the **NUC** (see below) is described as of identical title to that in the main entry above but having just 16 pages and printed "[New York, 190?]." The Preface notes date of issue of the tract as July 1900.

DAH (Concise), 998. **USNI Almanac,** 205. **NUC** (New York Public Library). **OCLC** (Clearwater Public Library, Navy Department Library, United States Naval Academy).

First and Rarest American Shipbuilding Manual

330. M'Kay, Lauchlan (1811-1895).

The Practical Ship-Builder: Containing the Best Mechanical and Philosophical Principles for the Construction of Different Classes of Vessels, and the Practical Adaptation of Their Several Parts . . . Plainly and Comprehensively Arranged for the Instruction of the Inexperienced . . . By L. M'Kay . . . *New York: Pub. by Collins, Keese and Co., and sold by the principal booksellers in the seaports of the United States, 1839. x, (1), 12–107 p., 7 folding engraved plates, 24 x 28 cm.*

"The first American book on shipbuilding and the rarest."—**Paine.** Lauchlan McKay was brother of Donald McKay (1810–1880) who became for the clipper ship, "the foremost builder, completing such famous clippers as Flying Cloud and Lightning."—**Carruth.** The rarity of this work is attested to by there being just a single appearance of it at auction since 1975. During 1993 a damp-stained copy in worn binding brought at auction $4,000. During 1940 a reprint of 250 numbered copies was published, carrying a biographical sketch of Lauchlan M'Kay, the last name spelled as "McKay."

Carruth, 189. **Chapelle** (*The Search for Speed under Sail, 1700–1855*), 7. **Howes** (not recorded). **Paine** (*Catalog 14*) #46. **Rinderknecht,** #56977 locates five copies: Cleveland Public Library, Massachusetts Institute of Technology, New York Public Library, Smithsonian Institution, University of Colorado at Boulder. **Sabin** (not recorded). **NUC** (Boston Public Library, Harvard University Library, John Carter Brown Library, Navy Department Library, Stanford University). **OCLC** (9).

1870 Remington Navy Rifle

331. National Armory.

Description and Rules for the Management of the Remington Navy Rifle, Model 1870. *Springfield, Mass.: National Armory, 1870. [3], 4–13 p., illus., front printed wrapper, 22 cm.*

Provides sectional views and illustrations of the rifle components and a section on "Directions for Use" is also included.

NUC (not recorded). **OCLC** (Navy Department Library, Sharlot Hall Museum Library, United States Military Academy, United States Naval Academy).

1865 Submarine
Report of Navy Engineer to
Secretary Gideon Welles

332. Pacific Pearl Company.

The Pacific Pearl Company, Incorporated under the Laws of the State of New York: Capital Stock, $3,000,000 . . . *Jersey City: Printed by John H. Lyon, 1866. 29 p., illus, 23 cm.*

"A prospectus."—**NUC.** The company was formed to gather pearls and pearl-shells on the Pacific coast, the gathering to be accomplished by a submarine that is handsomely illustrated by the frontispiece lithograph. The illustration shows the submarine to be of a design quite plausible. The Navy was sufficiently impressed to cause inspection of the vessel under construction by Julius H. Kroehl in New York City. A report (pages 17–25) by William W.W. Wood, general inspector of steam machinery for the Navy, includes a scientific discussion of air within a submarine. Wood's report on the submarine is dated February 2, 1865, and recommends post-launch tests. On June 11, 1866, Wood wrote to Julius H. Kroehl congratulating him "most sincerely on the success of your sub-marine boat. You deserve all the success claimed for this valuable and remarkable production of engineering skill, founded on true scientific principles." The **NUC** records just two other Pacific Pearl Company publications: an 1863 report and an 1865, president's report. Of the first, only one copy at the New York Public Library is located. Of the second, two copies are located at Harvard University Library and Huntington Library. The first has a frontispiece that is presumably the same as that in the tract discussed here. The 1865 president's report deals with "the purpose and work of the company."—**NUC.**

Sabin (not recorded). **NUC** (Huntington Library, Library of Congress, University of Rochester). **OCLC** (Library of Congress, Navy Department Library).

Ridgway's 1862 Vertical
Revolving Battery

333. [Ridgway, John].

Statistical History of John Ridgway's Vertical Revolving Battery: With Drawings: Recommended for Trial by the Board of Naval Examiners, June 13, 1862, and for Adoption As "Due to the Public Interest," by the Naval Department, Permanent Commission, May 11, 1864. *Boston: Prentiss & Deland, 1865. 30 p., 3 illus., 22 cm.*

"The first rough model of the battery was shown to the Department, at Washington, in April, 1862 . . . twice officially recommended to the Government, it being, the first time, one of only two inventions recommended out of about two hundred; and the second time, it being the only one recommended out of a still larger number."

Sabin, #90809. **NUC** (American Antiquarian Society, Boston Public Library, Harvard University Library, Huntington Library, New York Historical Society, Pennsylvania Historical Society). **OCLC** (Library of Congress, Navy Department Library, University of Chicago Library).

Armored Vessels in 1864

334. Simpson, Edward (1824–1888).

Paper on Armored Vessels Addressed to the Secretary of the Navy. By Commander E. Simpson, U.S.N. *[New York?: 1866].* 8 *p., 24 cm.*

This paper originally was published in the June 1864 issue of the *Army and Navy Journal.* Simpson covers "Classes of Armored Vessels," "The Sea-Going Class," "The Floating Battery Class," "The Harbor Defence Class," and "Rams." "From September 1858 to May 1862 he [Simpson] had charge of ordnance instruction at the Naval Academy, being made first head of that department in 1860. His *Treatise on Ordnance and Naval Gunnery* (1859) was long an academy textbook. . . . His high service reputation is evidenced by his selection as president of the United States Naval Institute, 1886–1888."—**DAB.**

DAB (9), 178. **Sabin** (not recorded). **NUC** (not recorded). **OCLC** (Independence Seaport Museum, Navy Department Library).

1886 Electric Torpedo
Applicability to Naval Warfare

335. [Sims-Edison Electric Torpedo Company].

Sketch of the Sims-Edison Electric Torpedo: Historical, Descriptive, and Illustrative of Its Efficiency for Harbor and Coast Defense, and Its Applicability to Naval Warfare: With Official Charts and Descriptions of Tests, Trials and Runs, Made by the Board of Engineers of the U.S. Army, the Sims-Edison Electric Torpedo Company. *New York: [1886].* [5], *6–27 p., chart (folding), plate, 22.5 cm.*

"The Sims-Edison Electric Torpedo from its shape and its facility of movement under water in every desired direction, popularly known as the Fish-torpedo, is a submarine boat with a cylindrical hull of copper and conical ends, either 28 feet long by 18 inches in diameter for one mile service, or 28 feet long by 21 inches in diameter, for two-mile service, made in four parts or sections united by means of lock-joints, and supplied with a screw propeller and rudder."

NUC (Case Western Reserve University, Duke University). **OCLC** (Case Western Reserve University Library, Duke University Library, Navy Department Library, University of Virginia Library).

Controversy over Design of Ericsson's Ironclad *Passaic*

336. Anonymous.

Engineer Stimers' Report of the Last Trip of the "Passaic": Unparalled Attempt to Throw Discredit upon Superiors: Language Unbecoming an Officer: His Dismissal from the Service Demanded: The Public Probably Deceived As to the "Result" of the Experiment of Firing Inside the Turret. *New York: 1862. 15 p., 21 cm.*

Passaic, an ironclad designed by Ericsson, was the subject of controversy and subsequent trials. The controversy revolved about the "porthole [being] too small to allow the muzzle of the great gun to pass out, and the parties interested won't enlarge it, but insist on hooding the muzzle." Stimer, an engineer reporting on the trials of the *Passaic's* ordnance, is accused in this tract of falsely crediting the design with success, when, in fact, during the trials "three shots were fired, the muzzle hood was torn to pieces, and the vessel came back to await the construction of something new." The anonymous author of this tract signs himself as "One of the People." He accuses Stimer of attempting to slander some of the best naval minds of the period. Stimer's report on the *Passaic* trials constitutes pages 11–15. Integral to this controversy was a desire to see rapid operational deployment of Monitor design ironclads.

Sabin (not recorded). **NUC** (Library of Congress, University of Virginia). **OCLC** (Boston Athenaeum Library, Independence Seaport Museum Library, Lehigh University Library, Navy Department Library, University of Chicago, University of Rochester, University of Virginia Library).

Superb 1853 Color Plates of Naval Steamers
Presentation Copy to President Millard Fillmore

337. Stuart, Charles Beebe (1814-1881).

The Naval and Mail Steamers of the United States. By Charles B. Stuart . . . Illustrated with Thirty-six Fine Engravings. *New York: C.B. Norton; [etc., etc.], 1853. 216 p., 35 plates (part double), 34 x 27 cm.*

"The nature of my professional engagements, and the great advancement made during the first half of the present century in Ocean Steam Navigation, have suggested to me the propriety of compiling for future reference, the origin, rise, and progress of our National Steam Marine. . . . Pre-eminent as our country has become in great achievements in every department of civil and mechanical engineering, none have been more marked and successful than those connected with our Naval and Mail steamers."—**Preface.** This copy is in presentation gilt and morocco binding and bears the following inscription on the front end paper: "Millard Fillmore from the author March 2. 1853." The frontispiece is a stunning lithograph in color of the U.S. naval steamer *Powhatan*. There are many plates devoted to propulsion equipment and vessel profiles as well as three superb tint lithographs, one each of the steam vessels *Fulton*, *Illinois*, and *Mississippi*.

Bennett (not recorded). **DAB** (9), 163. **Howes,** S1094. **Sabin,** #93147. **NUC** (10). **OCLC** (24).

U.S. naval steamer Fulton, *engraving, drawn by S. McElroy*

American Developed System of Frameless Hull Construction

338. Sullivan, John Langdon (1777-1865).

A Commentary on the New System of Naval Architecture of William Annesley, Architect. By John L. Sullivan. *Troy, N.Y.: Printed by William S. Parker, 1823. 59, [1], iv, 7 p., 10 folding plates, 22 cm.*

"Mr. Annesley's improvement in ship and boat building originated in the State of New-York, a few years ago. He carried it into operation in England subsequently to his patent, and printed the explanation of it, with plates, in London, in 1822. After building above fifty vessels he returned home to secure the patent right of his improvements and implements—and it became necessary to reprint the description, with directions for building, for use in this country, which is the purpose of this illustration. In describing his invention he says the principle excludes frame, timbers, beams, knees, and the necessity of metal fastenings below water. At Albany, in the year 1813, a small vessel of 10 tons was first built, which sailed excellently." The ten foldout plates are high-quality delineations of Annesley's hull construction methods and other techniques.

Howes (not recorded). **Sabin** (not recorded). **Shoemaker,** #14238. **NUC** (Franklin Institute, Library of Congress, New York Public Library). **OCLC** (Library of Congress, Navy Department Library, New York Public Library, New York State Library, Texas A&M University Library, Upper Hudson Library System).

Farragut's Report on Navy Gun Tests in 1852

339. United States. Bureau of Ordnance and Hydrography.

Experiments to Ascertain the Strength and Endurance of Navy Guns. *Washington: A.O.P. Nicholson, 1854. 29 p., illus., tables, front printed wrapper, 23 cm.*

Carries the August 31, 1853 report by Commander David G. Farragut on the September 3, 1852 tests of Navy guns at Fort Monroe, Virginia. Tests include guns of 8-inch and 10-inch caliber and 32 and 64 pounders.

NUC (Huntington Library, New York Public Library, New York State Library). **OCLC** (Harvard University Library, Independence Seaport Museum Library, National Archives at College Park, Navy Department Library, United States Naval Academy, University of South Carolina, Virginia Military Institute Library).

"One of the Great Unwritten Facts of History"

340. USS Wampanoag. Captain and Engineers.

The Wampanoag Reports: A Few Remarks on the Reports of the Captain and Engineers of the U.S.S. Wampanoag upon Her Late Run along the Coast with a Fresh Breeze Aft of the Beam. *New York: MacDonald & Swank, Printers, 1868. 8 p., 23 cm.*

USS *Wampanoag* was one of eight vessels of a class conceived of by Benjamin Franklin Isherwood who had served as the engineer in chief of the Navy during the Civil War. "In 1868 there was launched, as a finishing touch to our immense Civil War naval building program, a vessel of such remarkable speed and endurance as to fail of credence among maritime nations. This vessel and her 7 sister-ships were designed to carry 15 guns and attain a speed of 15 knots. Such was their forbidding aspect from a maritime standpoint that, according to Marvin, the historian of our American Merchant Marine: 'It is one of the great unwritten facts of history that it was the warlike potentialities of the Wampanoag and her sisters, rather than an abstract love of peace, that persuaded the British Government to submit the Alabama claims for arbitration' Yet in spite of their great naval potentialities, as attested by a careful study of the Anglo-American situation at the time, just one year after attaining their greatest success in the trial trips, this noble vessel and her sisters were condemned by a naval board in 1869 to destructive conversion to improve their sailing qualities."—**Gurley.**

Gurley, 1732. **NUC** (Library of Congress). **OCLC** (Library of Congress, Navy Department Library).

Sources

Adams, F.B., and Thomas W. Streeter. *One Hundred Influential American Books Before 1900.* New York: The Grolier Club, 1947. 139 p.

Allibone, Samuel Austin. *A Critical Dictionary of English Literature and British and American Authors, Living and Deceased, from the Earliest Account to the Latter Half of the Nineteenth Century: Containing Over Forty-Six Thousand Articles (Authors), with Forty Indexes of Subjects.* 3 vols. Philadelphia: J.B. Lippincott Company, 1882.

Appleton and Company. *Appleton's Cyclopaedia of American Biography.* 6 vols. New York: D. Appleton and Company, 1887–1889.

Beers, Henry Putney. *The Confederacy: A Guide to the Archives of the Government of the Confederate States of America.* Washington, D.C.: National Archives and Records Administration, 1986. 536 p.

Bennett, Whitman. *A Practical Guide to American Nineteenth-Century Color Plate Books.* New York: Bennett Book Studios, 1949. 132 p.

Boatner, Mark Mayo, III. *The Civil War Dictionary.* New York: David McKay Company, Inc., 1959. 974 p.

Brignano, Russell C. *Black Americans in Autobiography: An Annotated Bibliography of Autobiographies and Autobiographical Books Written Since the Civil War.* Revised and expanded edition. Durham, N.C.: Duke University Press, 1984. 193 p.

Campbell, John F. *History and Bibliography of the New American Practical Navigator and the American Coast Pilot.* Salem, Mass.: Peabody Museum, 1964. 134 p.

Carruth, Gorton. *The Encyclopedia of American Facts & Dates.* 8th edition. New York: Harper & Row, Publishers, 1987. 1006 p.

Chapelle, Howard Irving. *The Search for Speed Under Sail, 1700–1855.* London: G. Allen & Unwin, 1968. 453 p.

A Checklist of American Imprints. Metuchen, N.J., and New York: Scarecrow Press, Inc. 1964–1997. Vols. 1826–1829 compiled by R.H. **Shoemaker,** assisted by Gayle **Cooper.** Vol. 1820–1829 title index compiled by M. Francis Cooper. Vol. 1830 compiled by Gayle Cooper. Vols. 1831– compiled by Scott and Carol **Bruntjen.** Vols. 1840–1846 compiled by Carol **Rinderknecht** and Scott **Bruntjen.**

Clements, John. *Chronology of the United States.* New York: McGraw-Hill Book Company, 1975. 247 p.

Cogar, William B. *Dictionary of Admirals in the U.S. Navy: Volume 1, 1862–1900.* Annapolis: Naval Institute Press, 1989. 217 p.

Coletta, Paolo E. *American Secretaries of the Navy.* 2 vols. Annapolis: Naval Institute Press, 1980.

———. *A Bibliography of American Naval History.* Annapolis: Naval Institute Press, 1981. 453 p.

Concise Dictionary of American Biography. Edited by Joseph G.E. Hopkins. New York: Charles Scribner's Sons, 1964. 1273 p.

Concise Dictionary of American History. Edited by Wayne Andrews. New York: Charles Scribner's Sons, 1963. 1156 p.

Cooney, David M. *A Chronology of the U.S. Navy: 1775–1965.* New York: Franklin Watts, Inc., 1965. 471 p.

Coulter, E. Merton. *Travels in the Confederate States: A Bibliography.* Norman: University of Oklahoma Press, 1948. 289 p.

Crandall, Marjorie Lyle. *Confederate Imprints: A Check List Based Principally on the Collection· of the Boston Athenaeum.* 2 vols. Boston: Boston Athenaeum, 1955.

Dictionary of American Biography. 20 vols. Edited by Allen Johnson and Dumas Malone. New York: C. Scribner's Sons, 1964.

Dictionary of American History. 8 vols. Edited by Louise Bilebof Ketz and James Truslow Adams. New York: Scribner, 1976–1978.

Dictionary of American Naval Fighting Ships. 9 vols. Edited by James L. Mooney et al. Washington, D.C.: Naval History Division; Naval Historical Center, Dept. of the Navy, 1959–1991.

Dumond, Dwight Lowell. *A Bibliography of Antislavery in America.* Westport, Conn.: Greenwood Press, 1961. 119 p.

Edel, W.W. "The Golden Age of the Navy Chaplaincy, 1830–1855." *United States Naval Institute Proceedings* 256 (June 1924): 875–85.

Evans, Charles. *American Bibliography: A Chronological Dictionary of All Books, Pamphlets and Periodical Publications Printed in the United States of America from the Genesis of Printing in 1639 Down To and Including the Year 1820.* With bibliographical and biographical notes. 14 vols. Privately printed for the author. Chicago: The Blakely Press, 1903–1959.

Ferguson, Eugene S. *Bibliography of the History of Technology.* Cambridge, Mass.: Society for the History of Technology, 1968. 347 p.

Field, Thomas W. *An Essay Towards an Indian Bibliography.* Detroit: Gale Research Company, 1967. 430 p.

Fredriksen, John C. *War of 1812 Eyewitness Accounts: An Annotated Bibliography.* Westport, Conn.: Greenwood Press, 1997. 311 p.

Geary, James W. "Blacks in Northern Blue: A Select Annotated Bibliography of Afro-Americans in the Union Army and Navy During the Civil War." *Bulletin of Bibliography* (September 1988): 183–93.

Gleaves, Albert. "The United States Naval Home, Philadelphia." *United States Naval Institute Proceedings* 338 (April 1931): 473–76.

Groce, George C., and David H. Wallace. *The New-York Historical Society's Dictionary of Artists in America, 1564-1860.* New Haven and London: Yale University Press, 1975. 759 p.

A Guide to the History of Florida. Edited by Paul S. George. Westport, Conn.: Greenwood Press, 1989. 300 p.

Gurley, Lieutenant Ralph R. "The Wampanoag." *United States Naval Institute Proceedings* 418 (December 1937): 1732–1736.

Harbeck, Charles T. *A Contribution to the Bibliography of the History of the United States Navy.* New York: Burt Franklin, 1970. 247 p.

Harwell, Richard Barksdale. *The Confederate Hundred: A Bibliophilic Selecton of Confederate Books.* Urbana, Ill.: Beta Phi Mu, 1964. 58 p.

———. *In Tall Cotton: The 200 Most Important Confederate Books for the Reader, Researcher and Collector.* Austin: Jenkins Publishing Company & Frontier America Corporation, 1978. 81 p.

Historical Times Illustrated Encyclopedia of the Civil War. Edited by Patricia L. Faust. New York: Harper & Row, Publishers, 1986. 850 p.

Howes, Wright. *U.S.iana, 1650–1950: A Selective Bibliography in Which Are Described 11,620 Uncommon and Significant Books Relating to the Continental Portion of the United States.* Revised and enlarged edition. New York: Bowker for Newberry Library, 1962. 652 p.

Kane, Joseph Nathan. *Famous First Facts: A Record of First Happenings, Discoveries and Inventions in the United States.* Third Edition. New York: The H.W. Wilson Company, 1964. 1165 p.

Langer, William Leonard. *An Encyclopedia of World History: Ancient, Medieval and Modern, Chronologically Arranged.* London: Harrap, 1987. 1609 p.

Langley, Harold D. *Social Reform in the United States Navy, 1798–1862.* Urbana: University of Illinois Press, 1967. 309 p.

Larned, J.N., ed., *The Literature of American History: A Bibliographic Guide.* Boston: Published for the American Library Association by Houghton Mifflin, 1902. 596 p.

Laws and Joint Resolutions of the Last Confederate Congress (November 7, 1864–March 18, 1865) Together With the Secret Acts of Previous Congresses. Edited by Charles W. Ramsdell. Durham, N.C.: Duke University Press, 1941. 183 p.

Lefkowicz, Edward J., Inc. 500 Angell Street, Providence, Rhode Island 02906 is an antiquarian bookseller specializing in naval and marine materials catalogs.

Linton, Calvin D. *The Bicentennial Almanac.* Nashville, Tenn., New York: Thomas Nelson Inc., 1975. 448 p.

Logan, Rayford W., and Michael R. Winston. *Dictionary of American Negro Biography.* New York: Norton, 1982. 680 p.

Long, E.B. *The Civil War Day by Day: An Almanac, 1861–1965.* Garden City, N.Y.: Doubleday & Company, Inc., 1971. 1135 p.

Maclay, Edgar Stanton. *A History of the United States Navy, from 1775 to 1894.* 2 vols. New York: D. Appleton, 1897.

Matthews, Geraldine O., et al. *Black American Writers, 1773–1949: A Bibliography and Union List.* Boston: G.K. Hall, 1975. 221 p.

McGrath, Daniel F. *American Colorplate Books, 1800–1900.* Ann Arbor, Mich.: University of Michigan, 1966. 231 leaves.

Merli, Frank J. *Great Britain and the Confederate Navy, 1861–1865.* Bloomington: Indiana University Press, 1970. 342 p.

Moebs, Thomas Truxtun. *Black Soldiers–Black Sailors–Black Ink: Research Guide on African Americans in U.S. Military History, 1526–1900.* 4 vols in 1. Chesapeake Bay and Paris: Moebs Publishing Company, 1994. 1654 p.

———. *Confederate States Navy Research Guide: Confederate Naval Imprints Described and Annotated, Chronology of Naval Operation and Administration, Marine Corps and Naval Officer Biographies, Description and Service of Vessels, Subject Bibliography.* Williamsburg, Va.: Moebs Publishing Company, 1991. 578 p.

Mullins, Michael, and Rowena Reed. *The Union Bookshelf: A Selected Civil War Bibliography.* Wendell, N.C.: Broadfoot's Bookmark, 1982. 81 p.

Narrative and Critical History of America. Edited by Justin Winsor. 8 vols. Boston: Houghton Mifflin, 1884–1889.

National Union Catalog (NUC). 754 vols. London: Mansell, 1968–1981. One of the most important references for the researcher, this 754-volume set of atlas size volumes is alphabetically arranged. It reproduces the card catalogs of the Library of Congress and many other libraries for all cataloged materials in their possession printed before 1956.

It provides a wealth of knowledge to include collations (multi-volume sets not included), bibliographical and historical notes, and editions for books, pamphlets, broadsides, sheet music, circulars, etc. from the beginning of printing through 1955. Important for indicating a title's elusiveness, the *NUC* provides locations of known copies based on a survey of thousands of libraries in the United States and Canada. Using this work, researchers can begin to construct entire author bibliographies.

Neeser, Robert W. *Statistical and Chronological History of the United States Navy, 1775–1907.* 2 vols. New York: Macmillan, 1909.

Nevins, Allan, James I. Robertson, Jr., and Bell I. Wiley. *Civil War Books: A Critical Bibliography.* 2 vols. Baton Rouge: Louisiana State University Press, 1970. 326 p.

OCLC Online Computer Library Center, Inc. 6565 Frantz Road, Dublin, Ohio 43017–3395. OCLC is a nonprofit, membership, library computer service and research organization.

Oswald, John Clyde. *Printing in the Americas.* 2 vols. Port Washington, N.Y.: Kennikat Press, Inc., 1965. 565 p.

Parker, William Harwar. *Recollections of a Naval Officer, 1841–1865.* New York: Charles Scribner's Sons, 1883. 372 p.

Parrish, T. Michael, and Robert M. Willingham, Jr. *Confederate Imprints: A Bibliography of Southern Publications from Secession to Surrender.* Austin: Jenkins Publishing Co., 1987. 1133 p.

Ponko, Vincent, Jr. *Ships, Seas, and Scientists: U.S. Naval Exploration and Discovery in the Nineteenth Century.* Annapolis: Naval Institute Press, 1974. 283 p.

Richardson, Edgar P. *Painting in America: From 1502 to the Present.* New York: Thomas Y. Crowell Co., 1965. 456 p.

Rink, Evald. *Technical Americana: A Checklist of Technical Publications Printed Before 1831.* Millwood, N.Y.: Kraus International Publications, 1981. 776 p.

Robison, Rear Admiral S.S. "Commodore Thomas Truxtun, U.S. Navy." *United States Naval Institute Proceedings* 350 (April 1932): 541–54.

Rosenbach, A.S.W. *The Sea: Books and Manuscripts on the Art of Navigation, Geography, Naval History, Shipbuilding, Voyages, Shipwrecks, Mathematics, Including Atlases, Maps and Charts.* Philadelphia and New York: Rosenbach Company, 1938. 224 p.

Sabin, Joseph. *A Dictionary of Books Relating to America, from Its Discovery* to *the Present Time.* 29 vols. New York: Joseph Sabin, 84 Nassau Street, 1868–1936.

Scharf, John Thomas. *History of the Confederate States Navy From Its Organization to the Surrender of the Last Vessel: Its Stupendous Struggle With the Great Navy of the United States; the Engagements Fought in the Rivers and Harbors of the South, and Upon the High Seas; Blockade-Running, First Use of Iron-Clads and Torpedoes, and Privateer History.* New York: Rogers & Sherwood, 1887. 824 p.

Semmes, Raphael. *Memoirs of Service Afloat, During the War Between the States.* Baltimore: Kelly, Piet & Co., 1869. 883 p.

Shaw, Ralph R., and Richard H. Shoemaker. *American Bibliography: A Preliminary Checklist for 1801–1819.* 22 vols. New York and Metuchen, N.J.: The Scarecrow Press, Inc., 1958–1964.

Shipton, Clifford K., and James E. Mooney. *National Index of American Imprints Through 1800: The Short-Title Evans.* 2 vols. Mass.: American Antiquarian Society and Barre Publishers, 1969.

Sifakis, Stewart. *Who Was Who in the Civil War.* 2 vols. New York: Facts on File, 1988.

Skallerup, Harry R. *Books Afloat and Ashore: A History of Books, Libraries and Reading among Seamen during the Age of Sail.* Conn.: Archon Books, 1974. 277 p.

Smelser, Marshall. *The Congress Founds the Navy, 1787–1798.* [Notre Dame, Ind.]: University of Notre Dame Press, 1959. 229 p.

Smith, Myron J. *American Civil War Navies: A Bibliography.* Metuchen, N.J.: Scarecrow Press, 1972. 347 p.

_____. *American Naval Bibliography.* 4 vols. Metuchen, N.J.: Scarecrow Press, 1972–1974.

Sowerby, E. Millicent. *Catalogue of the Library of Thomas Jefferson: Compiled with Annotations by E. Millicent Sowerby.* 5 vols. Charlottesville: University Press of Virginia, 1983.

Spencer, Warren F. *The Confederate Navy in Europe.* University, Ala.: The University of Alabama Press, 1983. 268 p.

Sweetman, Jack. *American Naval History: An Illustrated Chronology of the U.S. Navy and Marine Corps, 1775–Present.* 2d edition. Annapolis: Naval Institute Press, 1991. 376 p.

Tutorow, Norman E. *The Mexican-American War: An Annotated Bibliography.* Westport, Conn.: Greenwood Press, 1981. 427 p.

United States. Naval History Division. *Civil War Naval Chronology, 1861–1865.* 6 vols. in 1. Washington, D.C.: GPO, 1971.

United States Naval Institute. *Almanac of Naval Facts.* Annapolis: United States Naval Institute, 1964. 305 p.

Unsworth, Michael. *Military Periodicals: United States and Selected International Journals and Newspapers.* New York: Greenwood Press, 1990. 404 p.

Venzon, Anne Cipriano. *The Spanish-American War: An Annotated Bibliography.* New York: Garland, 1990. 255 p.

Wakelyn, Jon L. *Biographical Dictionary of the Confederacy.* Westport, Conn.: Greenwood Press, 1977. 601 p.

Warner, Ezra J. *Generals in Blue: Lives of the Union Commanders.* Baton Rouge and London: Louisiana State University Press, 1986. 680 p.

Webster's American Military Biographies. Springfield, Mass.: G.&C. Merriam Company, Publishers, 1978. 548 p.

Wegelin, Oscar. *Early American Plays, 1714–1830: Being a Compilation of the Titles of Plays by American Authors Published and Performed in America Previous to 1830.* New York: Burt Franklin, 1970. 113 p.

Wells, Tom H. *The Confederate Navy: A Study in Organization.* (ix) 182 p. Tuscaloosa: University of Alabama Press, 1971. 182 p.

Wheat, James Clements, and Christian F. Brun. *Maps and Charts Published in America Before 1800: A Bibliography.* New Haven and London: Yale University Press, 1969. 215 p.

Williams, Vernon Leon. *The U.S. Navy in the Philippine Insurrection and Subsequent Unrest, 1898–1906.* Ann Arbor: University Microfilms International, 1985. 341 p.

Wise, Stephen R. *Lifeline of the Confederacy: Blockade Running during the Civil War.* Columbia: University of South Carolina Press, 1988. 403 p.

Work, Monroe N. *A Bibliography of the Negro in Africa and America.* New York: H.W. Wilson Company, 1928. 698 p.

Wroth, Lawrence C. *Some American Contributions to the Art of Navigation, 1519–1802.* Providence: Associates of the John Carter Brown Library, 1947. 41 p.

Young, Lucien. *Catalogue of Works by American Naval Authors.* Washington, D.C.: GPO, 1888. 149 p.

Index

Numerals refer to entries, not page numbers; bolded numerals indicate author or issuing authority; italics are used for publication titles and ship names.

ISBN 0-16-050565-8

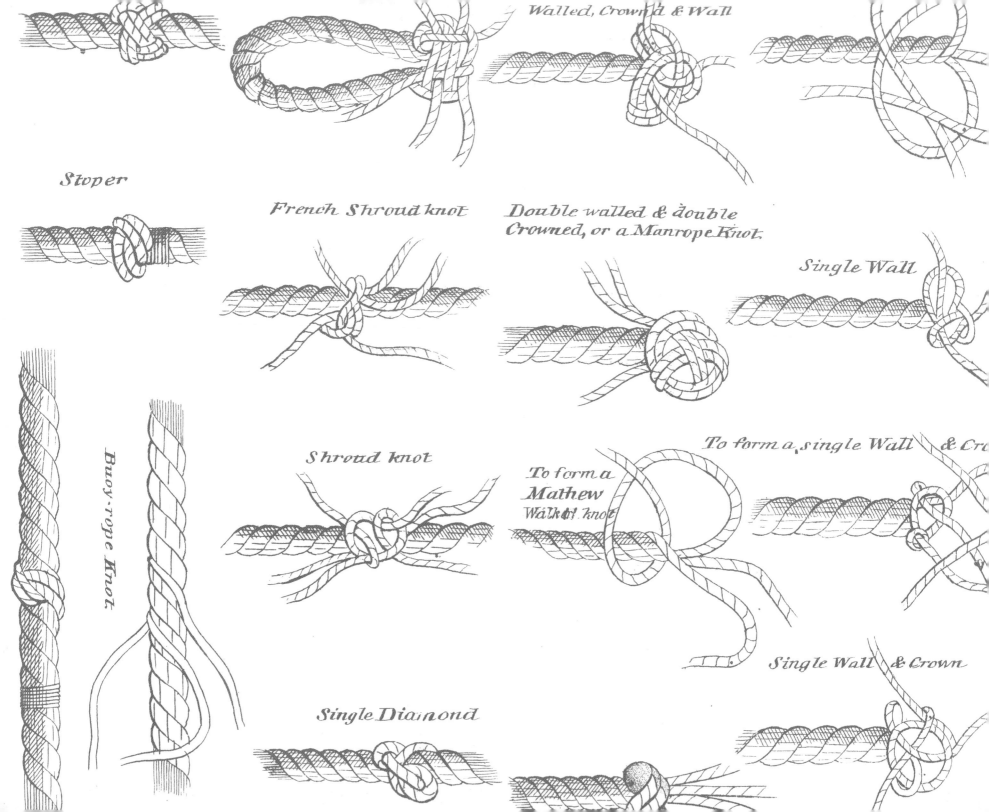

Walled, Crown'd & Wall

Stoper

French Shroud knot

Double walled & double
Crowned, or a Manrope Knot.

Single Wall

Buoy-rope Knot

Shroud knot

To form a
Mathew
Walker knot.

To form a single Wall & Cr

Single Wall & Crown

Single Diamond